OUR ROOTS
RUN DEEP
AS IRONWEED

Our Roots Run Deep as Ironweed

Appalachian Women and the Fight for Environmental Justice

SHANNON ELIZABETH BELL

UNIVERSITY OF ILLINOIS PRESS

Urbana, Chicago, and Springfield

∞ This book is printed on acid-free paper.

Library of Congress Cataloging-in-Publication Data
Bell, Shannon Elizabeth.
Our roots run deep as ironweed : Appalachian women
and the fight for environmental justice / Shannon Elizabeth Bell.
pages   cm
Includes bibliographical references and index.
ISBN 978-0-252-03795-5 (cloth : alk. paper)
ISBN 978-0-252-07946-7 (pbk. : alk. paper)
ISBN 978-0-252-09521-4 (ebook)
1. Women—Appalachian Region—Political activity.
2. Women and the environment—Appalachian Region.
3. Human beings—Effect of environment on—Appalachian Region.
4. Environmentalism—Appalachian Region.
I. Title.
HQ1236.B365   2013
305.40974—dc23   2013017243

For Cedar.
Now I truly understand.

CONTENTS

Acknowledgments   ix

List of Figures   xi

Introduction   1

1. "How Can They Expect Me as a Mother to Look
   Over That?": Maria Gunnoe's Fight for Her Children's
   Health and Safety   11

2. "We Became Two Determined Women": Pauline Canterberry
   and Mary Miller Become the Sylvester Dustbusters   27

3. "Let Us Live in Our Mountains": Joan Linville's Fight
   for Her Homeland   44

4. "You Gotta Go and Do Everything You Can—
   Fight for Your Kids": Donetta Blankenship Speaks
   Out against Underground Slurry Injections   60

5. "It's Just a Part of Who I Am": Maria Lambert
   and the Movement for Clean Water in Prenter   70

6. "I'm Not an Activist against Coal; I'm an Activist
   for the Preservation of My State": Teri Blanton
   and the Fight for Justice in Kentucky   84

7. "I'm Not Going to Be Run Out, I'm Not Going
    to Be Run Over, I'm Not Going Out without a Fight":
    Patty Sebok's Battle against Monster Coal Trucks   94

8. "Our Roots Run So Deep, You Can't Distinguish Us from
    the Earth We Live On": Debbie Jarrell and the Campaign
    to Move Marsh Fork Elementary School   112

9. "It's Not Just What I Choose to Do, It's Also, I Think,
    What I *Have* to Do": Lorelei Scarboro's Drive to Save
    Coal River Mountain   120

10. "Money Cannot Recreate What Nature Gives You":
     Donna Branham's Struggle against Mountaintop Removal   135

11. "I Want My Great-Great-Grandchildren to Be Able
     to Live on This Earth!" The Legacy of the Courageous
     Julia "Judy" Bonds   148

12. Conclusion   168

     Notes   191

     References   195

     Index   203

ACKNOWLEDGMENTS

I cannot begin to express how deeply grateful I am to the twelve strong, brave, and determined women whose stories fill this book. Donetta Blankenship, Teri Blanton, Donna Branham, Pauline Canterberry, Maria Gunnoe, Debbie Jarrell, Maria Lambert, Joan Linville, Mary Miller, Patty Sebok, and Lorelei Scarboro, you are amazing individuals. Judy Bonds, words do not adequately convey how much you are missed and what an inspiration you have been, and continue to be, in my life and in the lives of so many others. I have learned so much from all of you and am eternally thankful that I have had the chance to meet you, hear your stories, and share your stories with others.

Thank you also to Lisa Henderson Snodgrass, Andy Mahler, Vernon Haltom, Maria Gunnoe, and Bill Price for allowing me to include the beautiful tributes you spoke and sang at Judy Bonds's memorial service in January 2011.

My dear friends Vivian Stockman and Tricia Feeney with the Ohio Valley Environmental Coalition deserve special recognition and thanks for connecting me with many of the women in this book. Thanks also to Sarah Haltom, Vernon Haltom, and Matt Noerpel from Coal River Mountain Watch, who also helped me to make connections in the community. I would also like to acknowledge Melissa Ellsworth and Manali Sibthorpe, who were wonderful companions during a number of my interviews.

The Center for the Study of Women in Society (CSWS) at the University of Oregon believed in this project when it was just an idea in a new graduate student's mind. Many thanks to CSWS for providing me with a Graduate Student Research Support grant during the summer of 2007 to conduct the bulk of the interviews for this research. Thank you also to the following agencies and grant programs that funded the Photovoice component of this research: the University of Oregon Department of Sociology Wasby-Johnson Award; the American Sociological Association's Sydney S. Spivack Program in Applied Social Research and Social Policy Community Action Research Initiative Grant, the Greater Kanawha Valley Foundation, the Appalachian Regional Commission, CSWS, and the Ohio Valley Environmental Coalition.

I am indebted to my colleagues and mentors who read and commented on drafts and chapters of this manuscript during its various stages: Yvonne Braun, Joan Acker, Sherry Cable, Betsy Taylor, Sandra Ballard, Richard York, Dwight Billings, and Sandra Morgen. Thank you also to *Gender & Society* for allowing me to reproduce parts of Yvonne Braun's and my 2010 article, "Coal, Identity, and the Gendering of Environmental Justice Activism in Central Appalachia" in this book.

I am so grateful to Laurie Matheson at University of Illinois Press for her enthusiasm for this project and for believing in the importance of this book from the beginning.

Thank you also to my parents Susan and Tom Bell, who have unconditionally supported me and who have been my constant cheerleaders, no matter how far from home my projects and dreams have taken me.

Finally, I want to express my deep gratitude and appreciation for my wonderful partner Sean Bemis and the endless ways he continues to support me and our family. Thank you for your love and for always knowing how to make me smile.

Note to Readers

Throughout the text I use the term "women activists" rather than "female activists" to describe the individuals in the book. While I recognize that it is more grammatically sound to use "female" (an adjective) than it is to use "women" (a noun) to modify "activists," doing so would not be analytically correct. In this book I am examining the ways in which these activists' social location in the gender hierarchy affects their activism—not how their biological sex affects it.

LIST OF FIGURES

Figure 1:   "Strong Women of Appalachia." Photostory
             by Joan Linville   10
Figure 2:   Maria Gunnoe   11
Figure 3:   Pauline Canterberry and Mary Miller,
             the "Sylvester Dustbusters"   27
Figure 4:   Joan Linville   44
Figure 5:   "Landslide." Photostory by Joan Linville   47
Figure 6:   "Hauling Our Mountains Away." Photostory
             by Joan Linville   51
Figure 7:   "Underground Mine Fire." Photostory by Joan Linville   53
Figure 8:   "Dangerous Coal Trucks." Photostory by Joan Linville   55
Figure 9:   "Eyesores for the Community." Photostory
             by Joan and Janie Linville   56
Figure 10:   "Heaven Knows What Is Happening." Photostory
             by Joan and Janie Linville   59
Figure 11:   Donetta Blankenship   60
Figure 12:   Maria Lambert   70
Figure 13:   "The Changing of the Water Filter." Photostory
             by Maria Lambert   73
Figure 14:   "One Home, Mom, Dad, and Four Children."
             Photostory by Maria Lambert   75
Figure 15:   "PSD Water Showing." Photostory by Maria Lambert   77
Figure 16:   "Water Testing." Photostory by Maria Lambert   82
Figure 17:   Teri Blanton   84

Figure 18:   Patty Sebok   94
Figure 19:   "Nature's Beauty." Photostory by Patty Sebok   108
Figure 20:   "Loss of Access." Photostory by Patty Sebok   109
Figure 21:   "Coal Fork." Photostory by Patty Sebok   110
Figure 22:   "Pink Sunset at the Mouth of Prenter Hollow."
              Photostory by Patty Sebok   111
Figure 23:   Debbie Jarrell   112
Figure 24:   Lorelei Scarboro   120
Figure 25:   Donna Branham   135
Figure 26:   Julia "Judy" Bonds   148

INTRODUCTION

It's not just what I choose to do, it's also, I think, what I *have*
to do. I've always been a very fierce protector of my kids, and
I'm still doing that. I'm still protecting what I have left. . . .
Not only [my house and land], but the mountain behind it
and the environment and the wildlife and the vegetation. . . .
The majority of the Appalachian women that I know were born
fighting and protecting.

—LORELEI SCARBORO, 2008

People say that ironweed is the symbol for Appalachian women.
You know that tall purple flower that's all over the mountains
at the end of summer? Have you ever tried to pull it out of the
ground? It's called ironweed because its roots won't budge.
That's like Appalachian women—their roots are deep and strong
in these mountains, and they will fight to stay put.

—JUDY BONDS, 2006

Black coal dust rains down on a town, destroying property values as well
as residents' lungs. A house—with a family inside—is nearly washed away
by a flash flood caused by the presence of a mountaintop-removal mine. A
breach in an underground coal waste injection site pollutes the well water
of an entire community, and years pass before the toxic contamination is
discovered. These disastrous events are among the countless environmental
injustices that threaten the health and safety of thousands of Central Appalachian residents. Considered by many to serve as a "sacrifice zone" for cheap
energy (Fox 1999; Scott 2010; Bell [forthcoming]), the Central Appalachian
region[1] has suffered great ecological, economic, and social ruin from increasingly destructive methods of coal extraction and processing.[2]

The tremendous environmental burdens the people of Central Appalachia
have been forced to bear is part of a global pattern of inequality. Not all

people share the weight of the world's environmental hazards and pollutants equally; those with the least political and economic power—people of color, low-income communities, and residents of the global South—bear a disproportionate share of the waste, pollution, and environmental destruction created by society (Bullard 1990; Bullard et al. 2007; Masterson-Allen and Brown 1990; Čapek 1993; Pellow 2004; Pellow 2007; Faber 2008; Faber 2009). Coal is cheap, but only because the costs of energy production are externalized onto the natural environment and society in the form of pollution, destruction of the land, and limited economic opportunities.

The injustices in Central Appalachia have not gone without resistance, however; over the past decade, this region has become the epicenter of a grassroots struggle for human rights and environmental justice,[3] a struggle that has largely been initiated, led, and sustained by working-class women. This book is about some of those powerful, dedicated, tenacious individuals.

Preserving Women's Place in the History of the Central Appalachian Environmental Justice Movement

While there are notable local men who have dedicated themselves to the environmental justice movement in Central Appalachia (such as Chuck Nelson, Ed Wiley, Bo Webb, and the late Larry Gibson), it is women who overwhelmingly make up the leadership and membership of local, grassroots citizen involvement (Bell 2010; Bell and Braun 2010). Maria Gunnoe, Patty Sebok, Maria Lambert, Teri Blanton, Pauline Canterberry, Mary Miller, Joan Linville, Donetta Blankenship, Lorelei Scarboro, Donna Branham, Debbie Jarrell, and the late Judy Bonds[4] are just a few of the local women in Central Appalachia who have stood up and demanded that their children, their communities, their land, and their culture be protected from the costs of irresponsible mining practices.

The high proportion of women activists in this movement is not atypical among environmental justice groups across the United States. Many scholars have found that while women as a whole have lower rates of participation than men in the mainstream environmental movement (Brown and Ferguson 1995; Mohai 1992), women "are heavily represented in both the leadership and the membership" of environmental justice organizations, representing upwards of 70 percent of the activists in local and state organizations that are fighting such hazards as chemical plants, toxic waste dumps, and nuclear facilities (Brown and Ferguson 1995, 148–50; Kaplan 1997; Naples 1998; Cable 1992).

Despite the substantial literature on women's central role in environmental justice struggles throughout the United States, women's leadership and activism in the Central Appalachian movement has not been adequately acknowledged or fully examined.[5] One of the purposes of this book is to ensure that women's place in the history of this environmental justice movement is not forgotten as the landscape of protest against irresponsible mining practices continues to evolve and change.

While a decade ago the fight against mountaintop-removal coal mining was being waged largely on the local level, in recent years, the battle has been taken to the national—even international—arena. Since 2005, the number of films, documentaries, books, and feature-length articles about the impacts of mountaintop-removal coal mining has exploded. Thanks to the smart media work of grassroots organizations such as the Ohio Valley Environmental Coalition, Coal River Mountain Watch, Appalachian Voices, and Kentuckians For The Commonwealth, people in places as far away as Oregon, California, Germany, and Switzerland have heard of mountaintop-removal mining and its devastating effects on Central Appalachia.

A number of the individuals who have learned of these residents' campaign for environmental justice have chosen to come to the Central Appalachian mountains to see the destruction for themselves, many deciding to take on the struggles of local residents as their own. Since the summer of 2005, a movement called "Mountain Justice" has drawn hundreds of college students, Earth First! members, and others from across the nation to help organize protests, direct-action efforts, and educational outreach projects in Appalachian communities directly affected by mountaintop-removal mining. Mountain Justice participants have taken the local residents' stories back to their home communities, helping to broaden the base of support for environmental justice movement organizations working in Central Appalachia.[6]

The increasing attention that this movement has received has also come at a cost, however. The coal industry has not passively accepted these challenges. Launching retaliatory campaigns and "astroturf" organizations, such as the Friends of Coal, FACES of Coal, and Citizens for Coal, the industry has devoted massive amounts of money and resources in order to convince local citizens that being a good West Virginian, or Kentuckian, or Appalachian, means being loyal to the coal industry (Bell and York 2010). Ultimately, these groups' main strategy is to "other" the individuals participating in the environmental justice movement, labeling them as "out-of-state extremists," "radical environmentalists," and "tree-huggers." By drawing attention to the "outsider" support the environmental justice movement is receiving and the well-known, non-Appalachian figures who have expressed their solidarity with the movement (such as Bobby Kennedy Jr., actress Daryl Hannah, and climate scientist James Hansen), the coal industry works to cultivate an ideology of "us" versus "them," attempting to erase the local residents from the movement (Bell 2010).

At the core of the Central Appalachian environmental justice movement, however, are *local* citizens. And many of the most active—and vocal—participants at the local level are women. Just as Sandra L. Ballard and Patricia L. Hudson readily acknowledge that the inspiration for their (2003) edited anthology, *Listen Here: Women Writing in Appalachia*, originates from both practical and political motives, I too acknowledge that my own purposes in writing this book are simultaneously driven by scholarly questions and political concerns. Thus, while one of my objectives with this book is to make a contribution to the literature on women's environmental justice activism, I seek also to emphasize the central role that local women have played, and continue to play, in the Central Appalachian environmental justice movement.

Methodology and Overview of the Book

This book focuses on the lives and struggles of twelve women environmental justice activists in Central Appalachia, each of whom tells her own story, in her own words. Through their narratives and "photostories," the twelve women activists in this book reveal the varied circumstances that have brought them to the environmental justice movement. Each of these women experienced one or more personal encounters with coal-industry–related destruction or hazards, such as devastating floods; well-water contamination; perilous roadways from overweight, speeding coal trucks; coal dust air pollution; dangerous conditions resulting from a coal slurry impoundment and/or a mountaintop-removal mine close to one's house; or the threat of destruction due to a permit for a mountaintop-removal mine.

As they describe in their narratives, after experiencing one or more of these precipitating events, these women were led into the movement by various pathways. Some were contacted by organizers working with environmental justice organizations and were invited to share their experiences; others were asked by neighbors or family to participate in a meeting or protest event; some saw a sign posted about a community meeting concerning coal-related problems and decided to attend; and others actively sought out a group that could help them with their plight. Some of the women found an instant home with one or more of the environmental justice organizations, but for others, their involvement was a slow evolution into activism.

I conducted in-depth interviews[7] with these twelve amazing individuals from 2006 to 2009 while carrying out extensive fieldwork in southern West Virginia. Each interview was audio-recorded, transcribed in full, and then coded thematically. After using the original transcripts to conduct my analysis, I then edited the twelve interviews to create the narratives that make up the middle chapters of this book. Each activist's story is presented in a separate chapter, except for the narrative of Pauline Canterberry and Mary Miller—the "Sylvester Dustbusters"—who asked to be interviewed together and who present themselves as a team.

In an effort to contribute to the feminist project of democratizing the research process, I have chosen to foreground my interviewees' voices. While I do provide an examination of the shared themes, motivations, challenges, and transformations evident in the narratives, I wait until the conclusion to present my analysis. Throughout the bulk of the book—the middle eleven chapters—the women I interviewed speak for themselves. The purpose of my editing has been to arrange the pieces of each woman's story, as revealed to me through multiple hours of interviewing, into a self-contained narrative with a single voice—that of the activist. The only sentences I have written in these eleven chapters are set in a smaller font to clearly delineate them as my words. I limit my own voice to providing contextualizing details and transitions for the different sections of each woman's narrative. As much as possible, I have retained the women's speechways, word choices, and communication styles. If, for clarity's sake, I have felt that I needed to change a word or phrase within a particular narrative, I have signaled that it is a change by bracketing the word or phrase. Due to space limitations, there were some portions of the interviews I was not able to include, but I attempted to limit what I cut to discussions that were repetitive or tangential to the main narrative that the women were telling.

While the purpose of my editing was to free the activists' voices from the confines of the structured interview format and to increase the chapters' readability, I do acknowledge the possibility that my editorial decisions could have inadvertently changed the significance or meanings of some portions of the narratives. As Betsy Taylor and others have argued, narrative structure is not neutral and can convey important subtleties in meaning (see, for instance, Taylor 1992 and Hufford 2004). In order to correct for this possibility and to further democratize the writing process, I have shared the edited versions of these chapters with the women activists and invited their corrections, clarifications, and comments. I incorporated the modifications of all of those who requested them. The only activist with whom I was unable to do this "narrative check" was Judy Bonds, whose tragic passing occurred before I had completed her chapter.

Three of the women activists included in this book—Maria Lambert, Joan Linville, and Patty Sebok—were also part of an eight-month "Photovoice" project that I initiated in September 2008 with fifty-four women living in five coal-mining communities in southern West Virginia (Bell 2010; Bell 2011). The women involved in this project received cameras and were asked to take pictures to "tell the story" of their communities, including the positive and negative aspects of life. I met with the five community groups once every three weeks over the course of the eight-month project to facilitate discussions around their photographs. The women transformed their photographs into "photostories" by adding narratives to the images that they felt were most important. We held community exhibits and presentations of the photostories, created a website (www.WVPhotovoice.org), and produced a self-published book.[8] A number of the women used their photostories to communicate major problems to their legislators and others with political power. Many of the photostories that Maria Lambert, Joan Linville, and Patty Sebok created reveal the various ways that the coal industry has negatively affected their lives and communities. Some of these photostories are included within these three women's narratives in order to provide additional insight into their lived experiences and personal observations.

Before turning to the twelve women's stories, however, I believe it important first to place their activism within the history of women's social protest. Below I briefly discuss the rich legacy of women's activism in Central Appalachia and the literature on politicized motherhood.

Women's Activism in Central Appalachia and Beyond

Women's leadership in the contemporary Central Appalachian environmental justice movement is part of a long history of women's community activism and social protest in the region. While they have long been falsely stereotyped in the mainstream media as passive and ignorant, Appalachian women have, in actuality, been some of the fiercest and most active advocates for many social justice causes, such as healthcare rights, environmental protection, black-lung benefits, welfare, unionization, and employment rights (Norris and Cyprès 1996; Cable 1992, 1993; Seitz 1995, 1998; Maggard 1987, 1990, 1999; Hall 1986; Scott 1995; Giesen 1995; Weiss 1993). Appalachian women have resisted unjust circumstances in myriad ways, from the subtle "dissenting practices" that Anglin (2002) found in her ethnographic study of a mica plant in western North Carolina, to the community organizing efforts of working-class women who demanded the right to work in the coal mines (Weiss 1993), to the intense physicality of Harlan County coal miners' wives, who whipped strikebreakers with switches when they attempted to cross the picket line during the 1973 Brookside Coal Strike (Maggard 1987).

The effectiveness of women's leadership in social protest has also been recognized and mobilized by organizations run primarily by men, such as the United Mine Workers of America (UMWA), which enlisted the help of women during the Pittston Coal Strike of 1989–1990. In addition to populating the picket line, the women of the Pittston strike organized marches, pressured local businesses to publicly support the union, and protested in front of company headquarters and the homes of Pittston's management and lawyers (Seitz 1998). Appalachian women have, time and again, proved themselves to be a major force to be reckoned with.

Politicizing Motherhood

Women activists' gendered identities often serve as both a legitimizing force and a resource for their action. Seitz (1995) found that the Appalachian women activists in her study "domesticated their public work and politicized its connection to their private lives" by calling on their socially sanctioned roles as wives and mothers (35). Much of the literature on working-class women's protest has found that the well-being of family and community are often inextricably linked—even indistinguishable—in many women activists' minds.

This tie between family and community is not limited to the Appalachian region but instead appears to represent a broader pattern found among many working-class women activists. For instance, in her research on urban African American and Latina women community workers, Nancy Naples (1992, 1998) found that her research participants engaged in what she terms "activist mothering," which encompasses an understanding of mothering practices that reaches beyond a woman's caring for her biological or legal children to include fighting "against the debilitating and demoralizing effects of oppression" in the wider community (Naples 1992: 457). Similarly, Patricia Hill Collins (1990) reveals the ways that Black women's roles as mothers in their own families also extend into their position in the larger community as "othermothers." Kaplan (1997) draws on a similar concept she calls "female consciousness" to describe how certain women emphasize their identities as mothers and wives to legitimize the confrontational actions they take to protect their families' access to food, shelter, and a healthy environment.

A significant body of social science research has found an especially close tie between motherhood identities and women's motivations and justifications for environmental justice activism.[9] For instance, in their study of the environmental justice movement that emerged as a result of the Three Mile Island nuclear disaster, Culley and Angelique (2003) found that "motherhood as an identity and catalyst for action outweighed any ways in which gender was perceived as a barrier" to activism in the movement (454). Similarly, Krauss's (1993) study of the discourse of white working class, African American, and Native American environmental justice activists reveals that across these different groups, women activists' identities as mothers serves as a "resource for their resistance" (247).

In addition to functioning as a motivation or resource for environmental justice movement involvement, many women activists also draw on the motherhood identity as a rationalization for their activist activities, as Brown and Ferguson (1995) found of women toxic-waste activists in the United States and Braun (2008) found in her study of a woman activist in southern Africa who is fighting for the rights of her community in the wake of a World Bank dam project. The importance of this motherhood identity to environmental justice activism is also recognized by Peeples and Deluca (2006), who argue that the "rhetoric of Environmental Justice" transforms the conceptualization of motherhood to include participating in activities outside the home that may appear contrary to traditional notions of what constitutes mothering behavior.

The inclination of many women to describe their activism as stemming from their responsibilities as mothers, rather than from political concerns, may be the result of societal pressures that women face to place their family caretaking role above all else (Epstein 1995). As Epstein argues, framing their activism as originating in their concern for their children confers "moral legitimacy" to women's activism in a way that other justifications—such as concern for their own health or their interest in community work—do not (9).

Broader than Motherhood: The Protector Identity and Women's Activism in Central Appalachia

In our 2010 article, "Coal, Identity, and the Gendering of Environmental Justice Activism in Central Appalachia," Yvonne A. Braun and I add to the body of research on women's activism through an examination of the ways in which environmental justice movement participation in the coal-mining communities of Central Appalachia is gendered. Data for our article are drawn from interviews I conducted with twenty local residents (twelve women[10] and eight men) who are fighting irresponsible coal-mining practices. Through our analysis of these interviews, we examine the question of why there are so few local men involved in environmental justice activism relative to local women.

While the primary focus of Braun's and my article is an examination of the barriers to local men's involvement in the Central Appalachian environmental justice movement, there are also important findings related to local women's motivations and justifications for activism that we explore only briefly. This book picks up where our article leaves off. While nearly two-thirds of the women in our sample articulate that they are motivated to action by a desire to protect the health and safety of their children or grandchildren, in many cases this is not the only reason they cite. Most also describe feeling an obligation to defend their communities, the mountains, and/or the Appalachian way of life from the coal industry. Furthermore, while they are the minority, there are even a few in our sample for whom motherhood (or grandmotherhood) does not appear to be a dominant impetus for activism.

In this book I contend that it is something greater than a "motherhood identity" that motivates and legitimates the activism of many Central Appalachian women; rather, it is more precisely a broader "protector identity" that drives their fight against irresponsible mining practices. This protector identity both encompasses and extends the motherhood identity such that many women perceive the moral authority for their activism emanating not only from a calling to protect their children and grandchildren from irresponsible mining practices, but also from an obligation to protect their communities, their heritage, their family homeplace, and the physical landscape that surrounds them. Through my analysis, I seek to explore and understand more deeply the ways in which women activists mobilize this broader "protector identity" as a resource for the environmental justice movement and for their activist activities.

Bringing to mind the famous 1965 photograph of Ollie "Widow" Combs being carried off to jail after she sat in protest in front of a bulldozer poised to strip-mine her farm (see Carawan and Carawan 1996 [1975]), this latest wave of Appalachian women activists speaks of the mountain landscape as if it is an extension of their families, or even an extension of their very souls. The title of this book, *Our Roots Run Deep as Ironweed*, is a reference to these women activists' connection to—and determination to defend—the Appalachian land and culture. As Judy Bonds describes in her quote at the beginning of this chapter and Joan Linville articulates in the following photostory, the purple flowering plant with iron-like roots known as "ironweed" stands as a symbol for Appalachian women activists. They, like ironweed, are "rooted deep in the mountains, held to the land [they] love, willing to fight to save it."

"Strong Women of Appalachia"

JOAN V. LINVILLE

This is the flower Ironweed that grows in the mountains of Boone County. It not only shows the beauty of Boone County, but it represents the strength of the women of the Appalachian Mountains. Just like Appalachian women, Ironweed has strong roots that imbed it into the mountains, holding firm so it can't be uprooted without a fight. We Appalachian women are also rooted deep in the mountains, held to the land we love, willing to fight to save it.

"How Can They Expect Me as a Mother to Look Over That?"

Maria Gunnoe's Fight
for Her Children's Health and Safety

Maria Gunnoe in her beloved West Virginia mountains. Photo courtesy of Giles Ashford.

Maria Gunnoe is a lifelong resident of Bob White, West Virginia, and takes great pride in her Cherokee heritage. She is a community organizer with the Ohio Valley Environmental Coalition and recipient of numerous awards, including the University of Michigan Wallenberg Medal (2012), the Goldman Environmental Prize (2009), the Rainforest Action Network's David vs. Goliath Award (2007), the Joe Calloway Award for Civic Courage (2006), and the West Virginia Environmental Council's Environmental Courage Award (2005).

I interviewed Maria at her home in July 2007. Maria's narrative reveals that her entry into the environmental justice movement was largely motivated by her role as a mother, and her anger at that role being compromised. Maria's home was severely flooded on her daughter's birthday in June 2003 because of a mountaintop removal coal mine behind her house. Five acres of her land washed away that night, and the raging water nearly took her house as well.

"It was a night I will never forget": The flood of 2003

June the fifteenth of 2003 was my daughter's birthday—I'll start there. We had a birthday party, she got a bicycle for her birthday, had a real good day. The evening of her birthday, it started raining—about 4:00 in the evening. And it was a really heavy rain. But honestly, though, we get heavy rains here in the spring—we always have. It started raining about 4:00, and by 7:00, the water was literally running from one hill to the other right here behind me. A stream that you could raise your foot and step over turned into a raging river in three hours' time. I've lived here my whole life, and I've never seen anything like that. And I hope and pray to God that I never see anything like that again. The stream come up, and when it come up, it just kept coming up, and up, and up. It washed away about five acres of our property. I lost two access bridges, and one of my dogs was killed right up there. He was tied outside the creek and it took him, just tumbled him down the middle of all that flood. My daughter was over here at a friend's house when the flooding first started. And within twenty minutes after it started raining, I left out of here. It was raining hard—I [had to] go get my baby, you know. I wasn't gone maybe fifteen, twenty minutes, and we couldn't get back in.

I threw a rain slicker over her head and threw her over my shoulder and waded the water across. The water came up to my hips across that crossing. Once we got in here, there was no way out. We was surrounded by water. In forty-five minutes' time, life went from being just completely heavenly to just sheer hell. All night long, you could hear our structures—pieces and bits of our structures that was on up the holler—you could just hear them twisting and maiming in the water. It was a night that I will never forget. If

I live to be a hundred years old, I'll never forget that—because I mean it was hell—it literally was. You can imagine the sound of five acres of land washing by you. *Nothin'* like that had ever taken place here. I've played in this yard in water that come up to my knees as a kid, and it didn't do that.

After I got my daughter back in here, the water was eating away at my sidewalk—the end of my sidewalk was standing out in mid-air. My family was in this house. And, I didn't know what else to do. I literally thought we were gonna die in this house. We started up the mountain, and the mountain was sliding. So you can't, you can't put your kids on a sliding mountain. You know, at least inside the house, you're thinking, at least they're dry inside the house. There was no safe place to go. [Emergency] 911 could not get to me, I couldn't get to them. All I had to do at that point was to hit my knees right there in that sidewalk and pray to God that that water stopped. [Voice breaking] and thank God it did. Because if it wouldn't have, it would have taken the earth that my house was setting on—and me and my family in the process.

The Scars and Maria's Call to Action

The experience of this flood left scars on the Gunnoe family, and the psychological trauma it caused her children served as Maria's call to action:

There is tremendous fear when it rains. When the flooding of 2003, when it got bad, my daughter went through a, hey, I feel safe in calling it a post-traumatic stress disorder. She would set up at night—if it was raining or thundering, or any weather alerts or anything like that going on on the news, my daughter would not sleep. And I, I didn't notice this to begin with. I was so overwhelmed with everything going on that I never even thought, "What's this putting my kids through?" Until one morning—I had noticed that she had been falling back in school, things wasn't going right in school. That was my first sign. And, one of her teachers said, "She sleeps in class." She'd been a straight-A student ever since she started school, so that was never a problem. I found out one morning at 3:00 in the morning, it was thundering and lightning, and I go in, and I find her sitting on the edge of her bed with her shoes and her coat and her pants [on]. [Pauses, deep breath, voice cracks.] And I found out then . . . [pauses] . . . what it was putting my daughter through. [Crying.] And that is what *pissed me off.* How *dare* they steal that from my child! The security of being able to sleep in her own bed. The coal companies now own that. They now own my child's security in her own bed. [Pauses.] And how can they expect me as a mother to look over that? How is it, what if I done this to their kids? What if I created *terror* in their children's lives? And that is what it has done to my children.

It has dramatically, and I mean *dramatically* changed our lives. At this point, we can't use the water that comes into our house—it's not safe. There's a very strange odor to the water that comes into my house. It killed my fish that I had in my fish tank for over five years. So, with that right there, that's all the scientific studies I need. Excuse me, but I can't afford the tests that need to be done to find out exactly what's in my water, but I know it's not what it used to be. So I won't, we don't consume it. We buy all of the water and pack it in, across where two access bridges used to be.

We as a family have literally been robbed of our opportunity to be a family. The things that we have sacrificed, no one should have to give up. No one should have to give up their water. There are so many tentacles of—so many aspects of our life—it, it hasn't changed it, it has taken it away. The biggest thing that I aspired to do—all I wanted to do was to be a mother. That's all I wanted to do growing up. And the first years of their life, I was a very dedicated mother. And after all this had taken place, in order for me to be a mother, and in order for me to keep my children safe, and ensure my children's future as free American citizens, I've had—it's not an option—I've had to stand up and fight for our rights.

The Loss of a Way of Life

My father and my grandfather, and even some of the women in my family, worked in the mines growing up. So mining was, it was always common. But what really started taking place in the '70s right here [strip mining] started happening. My grandfather explained to me what it was and that that was a different type of mining that they was doing. And he despised it, because of the destruction it done. Throughout my lifetime I literally watched the horizons around me disappear. Without realizing the widespread destruction that was taking place—sitting down here in the valleys and watching it take place on the mountains is one thing, but when you get up there and you see how huge it is, that's something else. I never realized it was so bad. My first fly-over was with SouthWings [nonprofit aviation organization], and that right there is really what fired me up. When I got off the plane that day, I cried all the way across the tarmac, all the way home, and when I pulled in my driveway, I sat there and just literally felt a sense of fear that I could not, I could not overcome this sense of fear. After seeing this and then driving back into it, thinking, "My God, I live in the middle of it," and not knowing it until I done that fly-over. I mean, you feel the blasting and you see all the dust, all the trucks, but you don't really see the impact of it over time. I guess maybe the human mind doesn't have the capacity to accumulate all that without major research. It happens, and people don't even know that it's happening.

In 1996, my dad was offered a quarter of a million dollars for our place. Our place is not for sale—it's a homeplace, you can't buy and sell a homeplace, so of course my dad didn't sell. Last year, June of 2006, I had an assessor to come up here and reappraise this property. And it appraised for $15,300. My house appraised for $10,000. So the property is basically worthless. It's because of what they've done to it. I've got a neighbor behind me known as mountaintop removal coal mining. And it's, it's been hell. Since 2000, we've been flooded seven times. I've been flooded with no rain, which is something that people really do not believe. When they hear flood, no rain—"Oh, she's gotta be lyin'." No, it's the truth. The coal companies were working on the dam back here one day, and they were pumping water around the dam into the stream. The water came up about three feet—and there was no rain. I mean, it was blue skies. So we don't even need to have rain to be flooded; it's the manipulation of the headwaters of these streams is what's causing this. Each time that it's flooded I've looked at it—in 2001 I was flooded three times—each time, I look at it and I say, "Wow, I've never seen anything like that." And you know, each time it's got worse. And it's been, "Wow, I've never seen anything like that." When the 2003 flooding took place, it, it devastated me. I hope and pray to God I never see anything like that again.

There's days that I don't even want to get out of bed. Because I don't want to see that next layer of that mountain blasted off, you know, I just, I don't want to live it. There's days that I literally do not want to live it. I wouldn't trade my Sundays for nothing. Sundays are my quiet days. There's not drilling on the mountain behind me. There's no coal trains breezing by me. All the heavy equipment here on the highways, it's not present on Sundays. So Sunday, that's my day for gathering my thoughts.

I'm not real sure that moving away from it is gonna fix my problem. Moving away from it and into a community that has a coal-fired power plant or even two or three coal-fired power plants—how am I improving my life by leaving? I don't feel like I am, I'm just allowing them to run me out of my ancestral home. And with that, I'm allowing them to steal my children's culture and their heritage, and the upbringing that I had, which to me is a very unique upbringing.

Growing up, we always went into the mountains to gather. The men in my family and some of the women in my family were hunters, we gathered things:

mushrooms, berries. That's the reason our people settled this area initially, was because of the fact that the mountains were just full of foods that you can eat. My great grandmother was Cherokee, so she could definitely pick them out. To see that disappear, I mean, and in my lifetime, that's what's happened. Our ability as a people to take care of ourselves has disappeared along with the mountains. And quite honestly, there's people that I know personally that have grown old here taking care of themselves in these mountains. And now they're elder and they're no longer allowed into the mountain. So the herbs and the medicinal cures that they collected from these mountains that kept them healthy all these years, they're no longer allowed to go back into these mountains. That's like cutting off our life-source. How can they do that? It really angers you to know that they can blast thousands of acres of ginseng with no questions asked, and it'll never grow back. It'll never, never, ever, ever will it ever grow back on those sites. Not in ten thousand years. But our people are not even allowed to go into the mountains to dig it anymore. And it's, honestly, it's very telling of what's going on. The people don't matter. Let the corporations do whatever they want.

Just right here around me I've got elders that I've been around every day, all my life. When my grandfather passed on, they adopted me. You know, I'm now their granddaughter, and I'm thirty-nine years old. It's the sense of community here that makes it more home than anything else. The geographic location, I love it here. I think the mountains are beautiful. I can sit on my front porch and just look over a wide veranda of mountains that just absolutely is breathtaking. And that has always made me feel secure here in my home. As far as the people around me, I know everyone here. I can drive for fifty square miles any direction, and I guarantee you if I get thirsty or hungry there's a neighbor that I can knock on their door, "Hey. . . ." You know, or if I get a flat tire. That's the kind of community that we live in. The people here are different. You're not going to find people like this in other places. The people here will openly invite you into their homes, be good to you, offer you a warm place to sleep, offer you warm food to eat, water to drink. They will openly share their life with you. And you won't find people like this anywhere else in the United States. And honestly, I think society has bred this out of the humankind in the United States. It's just not in human nature to share anything anymore, you know. It's all in who can hoard the most the quickest. But here it's different. The people here are very kind, loving, giving people that have been taken advantage of for the past hundred and thirty years.

I sit right here at my home every day and I see U-Hauls headed up and down the road with people moving out. And I see it happening right here, right now. I try my best to stop it. I talk to people and say, "Please don't sell out [to the coal company]. If you sell out, not only are you selling out your homeplace, but you're also selling out your neighbors. You're selling out your community." Yeah, it's hell to stay, but if we can stay, then we can eventually put them out. The coal companies are attacking the citizens here and making life so hard on them that they have to leave.

Whitesville is an example of what happens when you depopulate communities. The people that lived in Whitesville, say fifty years ago, made that community what it was. Those people were the people that had been there for generation on top of generation on top of generation. And they've left. The people that was there, the families that grew up there, they've left. There're still a few of them dotted here and there, but most of them's left. And there you take the community out of the community. When you take the people out that has been there for generation on top of generation, when you take them out, the sense of community is gone. You take the kinship out of the community, so you don't have that close knit community like we have here. And that's one reason I'm fighting so hard to save it.

My family was here long before they started mining coal. And why should we have to leave? Who in the hell are they to think they can put us out? They make excuses, they call our area blighted. You know, they say, "Oh it's such a poor area." Well, start bringing something back! You know, everything that's ever left this county's left, and nothing's ever come back. Now everybody in the political régime in the state of West Virginia is looking at places like Boone County and going, "Oh, that place is so poor," like they don't know what's happened! They have sucked this place dry, and they want to set back and act like mountaintop removal and flat land isn't the reason that our area is so poor. That is such crap. Our place, before they started mining coal, the people here were wealthier than they are now. My third great-grandfather worked as a merchant, and he supplied these stores up and down through here. It was a dirt road at the time. On horse and buggy, he supplied these stores up and down through here with goods. He was a pretty wealthy man. He owned fourteen hundred acres, by the way, which was robbed from him up around Rock Creek, which is one of the biggest mining complexes in the county now. And my third great-grandmother fought the logging companies over that fourteen hundred acres. So, this has been going on for 130 years. It is a plan that has, it has been carefully planned every step of the way. For the past 130 years, they have planned on depopulating these areas, and they have slowly done it.

"There's nights that there is no sleep":
Backlash in the Community

Maria's choice to become an environmental justice activist has come at a cost: peace of mind. Threats, name-calling, and affronts to the safety of her family are all aspects of life that Maria deals with on a daily basis.

When I first started doing this, I worked at a local restaurant here. I took the job initially just to pay off my grandfather's funeral expenses. I had no intentions of keeping it as long as I did. But I had a lot of threats. A lot of it started taking place there. When they found out, some of the customers and the people I worked for, when they found out what I was doing, of course they had problems with it. And it started cutting into my job. The people that I worked for cut me back to working one day a week.

I have been accused of—and this is such a man's idea of things—I have been accused of sleeping around with local law enforcement. It's just completely, totally ridiculous. And I mean, that's one way of putting us [activists] in a bad light. When you run out of everything else to say, bring that up. It'll work every time. And that's what it is—they really can't find anything to say about us. We're parents, we're good parents at that. We take care of our children, we see to it our children has got the necessities in life, and we see to it that they are educated beyond what these rural schools are able to educate them. And really, it's always a gender attack. When I run into a strip miner and they have a problem with me, I'm always a "bitch" or a "whore," you know, something to that effect. I've been called a "loud-mouth woman."

I can sit here right now, unknowingly, there could be someone vandalizing some aspect of my life. Like my home. It's not much, but it's all I got and it's all I want. You know, me and my husband haven't been out to dinner together in probably two years because of the fact we can't leave our home. You're afraid to leave your home because, I mean, there's so many people here that has been fighting the coal industry and they got put out of the fight because their house was burnt to the ground. That's a very common thing here—houses burning. There's always somebody here; my home is never left alone. If I'm not here, my husband's here. And I've got Rottweilers—I've got big dogs. We've always had big dogs around here. When somebody is here that's not supposed to be here, they know what's going on. My dogs at night are untied and left to guard while we sleep. There's nights that there is no sleep. You never know. I could go over and get my truck right now and go to drive down the road and there could be something wrong with it, I may not make it out of the driveway. You know, because my truck is about five hundred yards [away], I can't even see my truck from where my house sits. So it's a target. It's big, it's red, and it's got lots of [anti-mountaintop removal] stickers on it, and that makes it a target. People spit on my truck all the time because I got stickers on my truck. So I end up with lots of tobacco juice on my truck.

I had a tire that was slashed completely across. I hit a pothole, and it literally blew the tire completely off the rim. Brand new tires, too. Me and my kids [were] expecting absolutely nothing to happen to the vehicle, and my tire blows off when we were in the middle of a curve. I drive a pickup truck, and it just went fishtailing all over the road when the tire blew off the rim. And then, in 2004—my truck was new so there was no reason for it to be running bad—and it was like it wouldn't take gas. I was like, "What in the world's going on with my truck?" So I took it to a mechanic, and I've only got one mechanic that works on my truck. I took it to the mechanic and he told me, he said, "Somebody has attempted to vandalize your truck [by putting sand in the gas tank]." He said, "And the way that your truck is designed is the only thing that kept it from blowing up your engine." As the gas came out of the tank it had a filter, and as it went into the fuel injectors it had a filter. So those filters caught all of the sand and stopped up before the sand made it into my engine. So, through taking the gas tank, dropping everything underneath it, taking it all out, flushing it out, replacing parts— it took probably about three or four months for me to get my truck back to running right. And through all this, my mechanic also notices that my brake line was collapsed to the point that, if enough pressure would build up behind it, I could hit my brake and my brake line would rupture and I would have no brake. There were strikes on the rear end of the vehicle, like with maybe some kind of tool, like a piece of metal. There were strikes on it where they had struck at it two or three times, and they missed and they missed, and then they finally hit it. And when they did, it was collapsed, I mean to the point that I really, I don't know how I had brakes. You know, and he wasn't looking for this when he found it. But thank God he found it, because if he hadn't found it, especially here in this terrain you have a lot of mountain roads, no guardrails, and if you lose your brakes, you're going over a mountain. You're going over a mountain or into a mountain.

And then after that, it's just been numerous things. There've been people seeing my kids getting out of my truck, and I'll pull away, be dropping them off somewhere, I'll pull away and then they start yelling things out at my kids, calling my kids tree-huggers, you know, and things like that. Everywhere I go, I get the finger, everywhere. I come back from New York here not too long ago, and as I come up the road, it was either they was waving at me or they were giving me the finger, every car that went by. It was one or the other. But, you know, that don't hurt me. It takes a whole lot more than that to get to me.

Just here recently, there was an incident on a parking lot down at Magic Mart, which is maybe ten, fifteen miles down below where I live at. It's the local department store. And myself and my daughter was setting there alongside of the road. We had went into Subway to get us lunch, and we pulled along into this little shady spot alongside of the road to eat. We was setting there, and all of a sudden there's a truck, a big truck, much bigger than mine, come real slow, real close to my truck. Over my shoulder I was like, "Well, what is that?" I turned and looked and there was this man setting in the truck, and he was reading my stickers on my truck. And all of a sudden I see arms a-flying and his head starts flailing around in the truck, and I'm going, "What in the world?" And I realized that the man obviously has a problem with my stickers. And he just starts, I mean he's just going off, literally. And he had his windows up, so I couldn't hear a word he was saying, but I could tell there was a problem inside the cab of that truck. And he circles the parking lot and he comes, first he throws his hands out to the side and he says, "Fuck you, bitch!" like that. He turns around, circles the parking lot, and comes back in behind me again, and I see him, he's got a paper and he's back there writing down my plate, my license plate number and all this information. I opened up my truck door and turned to the side, and I'm sitting there looking at him. You know, eating my sandwich and, while he's writing down his information. He sees that I'm turned sideways and now looking him in the face, watching what he's doing, and he pulls up alongside of the truck and he holds up a sign that says, "My family depends on coal." Well you'd have thought somebody set a fire in my truck seat, because I came out of it pissed off with a mouthful of sandwich! That was it, I had had it at that point. And I just, basically I told him, I said, "This ain't about you and your family. It's about me and mine." That pissed me off. He thought he was going to stand there and talk to me like that in front of my daughter. And I just basically told him, "No, this ain't about you, it ain't about your job, it's about me and my family and our health and our well-being." And he got very angry, he got very upset. And he took his cell phone, and he never did step out of the truck, he never once, he would not step out of that truck. He didn't want to discuss it, he just wanted me to hear what he had to say, but he didn't want to hear nothing I had to say. I took a pretty big offense to it. And yet there's always another one waiting. You know, always. Everywhere you go.

A lot of people believe that we are out to destroy coal mining. And that's a misunderstanding that people commonly have. If I was out to destroy coal mining, I'd be putting my own brothers out of work. So there's no truth to that. We're out to make them enforce the laws, is what we're out to do. These laws protect our safety and well-being in our communities. We have to.

"The Women Are More Fierce": Women's Leadership in Environmental Justice Activism

Women involved in environmental justice activism are challenging the traditional gender ideology of the region through their leadership and activism. When asked why she believes women are at the front lines of the movement for justice in Appalachian mountain communities, Maria articulated her belief that women's identities as mothers are central to their motivations for action.

The Appalachian women are the backbone behind the Appalachian family. And our Appalachian families are being put in danger. And—it's our natural— it's our natural instinct to step up to the plate and say, "Excuse me, but you're killing something I love." You know, and we will fight for it. That is our link to who we are. And it's a link to who our children are. And we can't allow it to be destroyed. As mothers of future generations of Appalachian boys and girls, we can't allow them to steal this from our children—it's too precious. And it can't be replaced.

It's real hard to intimidate a mother bear away from her cubs—almost impossible. But the first thing the father bear does is hit the road. You know what I'm saying? The men do not feel the sense of dedication that we do. Most mothers on the face of the earth would be willing to lay down their lives for their children. And I'm definitely one of those mothers. The men are just . . . the men are more easily intimidated by the workers and the people in the coal industry, too. I think that's a serious concern because of the fact that miners—the male, men, strip miners—are more likely to jump onto a man than they are a woman. The men here that work in the movement realize that they're more targets than what the women are. The women are stronger, and they're more likely to speak out when something they love is being destroyed or harmed.

The women are more fierce. They really are. The reason is they're more responsible and obligated to the future, mainly because of the fact that the future holds their children's health, their children's well-being. As a mother, you have to realize that a part of seeing to it that your child grows up in a safe environment is seeing to it that the environment is tended to and not done the way that it is now. People are connected to this environment. Their health is connected to this environment. When you see your kids' water—future water—being polluted so that you can keep your lights on, it just becomes a no-brainer. All of a sudden, lights aren't that important anymore—and I really think that women see that. Men don't see that. Men can be made to understand that, but I really don't think that it's in a man's instincts to see that. I really believe that it's the mother's instincts that makes you realize how detrimental what's going on is to our children's future. Men and women are as different as day and night, especially when it comes to this fight. Women are relentless.

Transformations through Activism

Both in her own life and in the lives of other women activists, Maria has found that being involved in the environmental justice movement can bring about growth and change in activists' personal lives and relationships.

Back years ago you couldn't have told me that this country was as corrupt as it is right now. Working as an activist from southern West Virginia fighting mountaintop-removal coal mining has taught me more about the corruption in the political system in the United States of America and other countries than I ever dreamed that I'd ever know. And it's changed things, it's changed me too, as far as the way that I've raised my children. My children are avid news readers. They read a lot of world news. My son, my daughter, both watch world news, and not Fox News. And my children can recognize the media's attempt to mislead the public. I mean, and most kids don't pick up on that, and my kids can see it a mile away. "That's one of Bush's plans right there," you know. Or, "Oh my God, look at that commercial. That's sick. How can they get by with that?" You know, it's really changed the way that I have thought about things, and it's also changed the way I've brought up my children. Dramatically. And it's changed me as a person, too.

Working in this kind of work, it teaches you so much about getting along with other people and being able to resolve what seems to be the most serious problems. It teaches you how to be able to sit down and talk about these things and come to resolutions that work for everybody. It teaches you a lot. We have trainings—we have nonviolent trainings, we have media trainings. We have conflict resolution trainings. I mean, just everything you could imagine. It really teaches you how to better handle things in life. And I believe that the trainings have, they've been applied to more than the coal aspect of life. In some cases, it has really restructured households. It's pretty amazing to watch some of it come together. When you see someone that's been beaten down, that's in fear of their home life, and you see them stand up and literally take on the world, it just absolutely makes you so proud to be a part of that transition. It's just amazing to be a part of it—to see them go from somebody that you could literally stand and talk down to, and they wouldn't say a word back to you, to being the first one to jump up in your face is just like, I mean, it makes you so proud. As an organizer, it really does. To see anybody in that situation just really, quite honestly, appalls me—I don't think anyone should be controlled by anyone else, whether it be a political power or a husband or a wife. There've been women that's worked as volunteers [in the movement] that has been in bad situations at home that's come out of it like warriors. [They have] literally taken themselves by the bootstraps and pulled themselves up out of the gutter and looked at their man and said, "We're not doing this anymore" and has taken her life in her own hands and changed things. I think [most of them have] pretty much been able to reshuffle how things work in the household. And that is a true success—one that don't land in divorce is of course a success. To see someone take that control back over their life is invigorating, to say the least. I really think that it creates a sense of power when you see that a minimal amount of work that you can do can bring about a huge change. It creates an internal power that makes you feel like you can literally take on the world, and no one can convince you that you can't take on the world. It creates an internal power that can't be stopped.

Preserving Appalachia for Future Generations

The coal-mining region of southern West Virginia is often looked down upon by people living in other regions of the state. Maria continually finds herself needing to defend her home to the many individuals who view this region as "blighted" and worthless. Maria and other local residents find a great deal of value in the lifestyle, landscape, heritage, and culture of the area. Many, like Maria, are enraged by the ways in which the lives and choices of residents living in southern West Virginia are devalued and disrespected.

We have just as much right to be who we are and where we are as anyone in America. We're more connected to our land than most people are. The thought of there never being another generation of hillbilly children makes my skin crawl. You've got Boone County, you've got Logan County, you've got McDowell County, and each one of them's different. Their dialect's different. And the more southern you go, the more the dialect is noticeable. Their language, it changes. And I just, I can't imagine there not being any more kids raised in the hollows of McDowell County, because, I mean, we're different. You know what I mean? They want to breed the hillbilly out of the West Virginians. They want this land. And if they have to make it look like the people here are not smart enough to realize that they have a "bad life"—by whose standards? "There's something wrong with them people. They don't realize how horrible their life is." You know, it's ridiculous. Who's to say—and I'm pretty sure that God's the only one that has this authority—who's to say who's living life right or wrong? If the people in McDowell County and the people in Boone County and Logan County and Mingo County, the southern part of West Virginia, if they continue to sell out and move out, they are selling out their children's heritage. The things that make us as adults the proud hillbillies that we are—and we are—I'm very proud to be a hillbilly. You can call me hillbilly anytime you want, just don't call me stupid. That's the way I feel about it. I've never met a stupid hillbilly. In order to be a hillbilly, you had to be smart because you had to survive. Just the thought of there not being any more people like us, well of course, that's what the political leaders want. They want people that can be led around by the nose. Well, we can't be led around by the nose, and that's the reason they want to do away with strong-willed people like us.

The culture and heritage is not to be ashamed of. Over the years, people in southern West Virginia, and other parts of Appalachia, have been shamed for the way that they lived because they chose to live with the well-drawn water, and they chose to live growing their gardens, and they chose to live on farms, you know, supplying their own food and taking care of themselves. For years, people were shamed for doing that. You know, "Well, that's just them poor inbred hillbillies that choose not to leave the holler." You know, and people were shamed for it. And now OVEC [Ohio Valley Environmental Coalition] is giving them the sense of pride back—the pride of what we are, and who we are, and where we come from. I think the biggest benefit that people get from OVEC, and the other groups, I think the biggest benefit is a sense of community. We're hillbillies, yes, but we're not stupid hillbillies. We're very smart. When the rest of the world crumbles, when the grid crumbles, they'll be coming to us: "Now how was it you growed your garden?" You know, "How was it you took care of your family?" Times will change. And I see, honestly, I see the people in the state of West Virginia being survivors under any circumstances because we've already been survivors under very hard and almost impossible circumstances.

I don't expect no reward or award or anything like that for the work I do. I expect for my children to have a better life than what I have. And that's what I want. I want my grandchildren to be able to run and play in the yard. And you know, I want my grandchildren to be able to play in the streams. I want life to turn around to where it can be simple again, and I sure can't accept my grandchildren and my great-grandchildren living in an environment where there's no air and there's no water, and there's no land.

I can't imagine that kind of life. But I really believe that that's the ultimate award—what will benefit the future generations. I don't think in my lifetime, I don't think that there'll be that much change. But I think what I do with my lifetime will bring about a renewable energy future for my children.

Appearing in numerous documentary films, speaking at press conferences and protests, and testifying before congressional hearings, Maria has continued to be an outspoken advocate for Appalachian communities. Her impassioned speeches have moved many to act on behalf of mountain communities; however, Maria's ability to inspire others has also been viewed as a threat by many coal-industry advocates. The events of June 1, 2012, demonstrate just how great a threat she is perceived to be. Maria was invited to testify on this day before the House Subcommittee on Energy and Mineral Resources about the impacts of mountaintop-removal coal mining. As part of her presentation, she included a slideshow of photographs revealing the costs of this type of coal extraction on Central Appalachian citizens. Among these photographs were images of floods caused by mountaintop-removal mining, orange acid mine drainage polluting West Virginia streams, coal-slurry-contaminated well water pouring from the faucets in people's homes, and a powerful image by professional photographer Katie Falkenberg of a young girl in a bathtub filled with rust-colored water, water that is polluted with toxins from neighboring coal-mining operations. Despite having the permission of the girls' parents and the photographer to show the image during her testimony, Maria Gunnoe was told to remove the photograph from her presentation at the direction of Representative Doug Lamborn (R-Colorado), the Chair of the Subcommittee, because he and others "felt it was 'inappropriate'" (Goodell 2012). Immediately after testifying, Maria was escorted to a private room by a special agent with the U.S. Capitol Police and was questioned for forty-five minutes about the photograph. She was informed that she had been reported to be in possession of "child pornography" and that the Capitol Police were obligated to investigate that accusation.

In the days that followed the hearing, news of what many asserted was clearly an attempt to smear Maria's character spread quickly through various national media outlets. In an interview that appeared in *Rolling Stone* on June 7, Maria recounts the experience, stating that accusing her of possessing child pornography "was an act of desperation, and it showed these congressmen's true colors. They would have done anything to stop that photo from being displayed during this hearing. . . . And it wasn't because the little girl didn't have a shirt on. It was because she was bathing in mine waste" (Goodell 2012).

As journalists and activists have pointed out, Representative Lamborn "has long kept close ties to coal" (McDonnell 2012), which is a powerful industry in his home state of Colorado. In fact, as McDonnell reveals, last year Lamborn gave a keynote address to the American Coal Council, during which he decried what he referred to as President Obama's "war on coal."

Despite this latest attempt to intimidate Maria, she—as always—vows she will not back down. When asked if the events of June 1 scared her, she responded,

"No, it's made me angry. I know I have to stand up and defend not only my name but my character. I work with many children throughout southern Appalachia, and I'm not going to let this be defined as anything but what it is—obscene. This whole thing is obscene. What's most obscene is the idea of a little girl bathing in poisoned water. But that's what's happening in southern Appalachia, and people need to know about it. And we need to stop it" (Goodell 2012).

CHAPTER 2

"WE BECAME TWO DETERMINED WOMEN"

Pauline Canterberry and Mary Miller Become the Sylvester Dustbusters

Mary Miller and Pauline Canterberry, the "Sylvester Dustbusters," at the entrance of Elk Run Coal Company. Photo courtesy of Giles Ashford.

After coal is mined, it must be chemically cleaned and crushed in order to prepare it for burning in coal-fired power plants. Communities neighboring such plants, such as the town of Sylvester in Boone County, West Virginia, contend with massive amounts of coal dust in the air, making life unbearable for some residents. Pauline Canterberry and Mary Miller, who are known as the "Sylvester Dustbusters," have been fighting coal dust in their community for nearly a decade. I conducted interviews with Pauline and Mary during the summers of 2006 and 2007.

PAULINE:

Sylvester was *the* place; everybody wanted to move here because there were no coal mines. This town was never a coal camp. In 1945, when I lived in Whitesville and went to Sherman High School in Seth, I traveled through what is now Sylvester every day to get to and from school. This spot of land through here was a golf course and a small aircraft landing strip. They lotted it out in 1949, and people began to build houses here. [Living in Sylvester] got you away from the coal-dust communities and everything. Once anybody moved here, they didn't leave. It was a wonderful place to live, it was a wonderful place to raise your family, and to me, it was just as close to Camelot as you could get.

MARY:

When a home would go up for sale, it would be sold within two or three days—that's how bad people wanted to move into Sylvester. I've lived here fifty-two years. This was such a beautiful little town.

PAULINE:

Sylvester was a wonderful place to live up until Massey Energy decided to put in a [coal] preparation plant. They already had a facility over there—an underground mines.[1] They cut the bluff off [which was between the mine and the town of Sylvester] and put the processing plant right on top of the ridge where they had cut off the hillside—right in the direct airflow of the town. When we found out the preparation plant was being put over here, there were fifty-four letters [from residents] of this town to the DEP[2] asking them not to [approve the permit for the facility]. Not only that, we had petitions with over 75 percent of the town's signatures on it asking them not to put the preparation plant in. [We] knew it would simply destroy the area—we knew what would happen.

This facility sits in the western side of Sylvester, and the wind blows from west to east 90 percent of the time, which means 90 percent of the time [the dust] is pouring over the town of Sylvester.

Just as soon as they got it finished and it started into operation, which was in April of 1998, it *instantly* began to cover the town in coal dust. Within one month we were completely covered. It was horrible. We could walk outside here on [sunny] days like today and the sun looked like you was looking through a kaleidoscope, there was so much coal dust in the air. You couldn't do nothing outside—you couldn't have cookouts outside, you [couldn't] hang your clothes outside when you wash[ed] them. It just *plastered* our homes. And not only that, then it began to seep through your windows and inside your home. Coal used to travel in lumps—even on your railroads. Now it is crushed into very fine powder, and it can seep in anywhere. Our homes were just polluted completely with it. And I mean, right now, in order to get all the coal dust out of our homes, we're going to have to take them apart and rebuild them because there's no way you can get it all out—there's just no way you can do it. It comes in under your windowsills, it's everywhere. Your attics are full of it, everything is full of it. Your filter from your air conditioners and your furnaces are full of it. You have to change them every two weeks or a month—constantly. They're full of coal dust. So that means we're breathing it constantly.

Gathering Evidence and Demanding to Be Heard

Residents of Sylvester attempted to have the coal-dust problem fixed by going through the regulatory channels. They soon realized it was going to be more difficult than simply telling state officials that there was a coal-dust problem.

PAULINE:
[Because] we have an Environmental Protection Agency in the state of West Virginia, I thought all I had to do was go tell them that, hey, I was being covered with coal dust, and they would correct it. But it didn't take me long to find out that didn't work. When we first approached DEP, we were ignored. For two years, we were completely and totally ignored. Everything we said just bounced off like water off a duck's back until finally, in the year 2000, after the plant had already been in operation from April of 1998 until April of 2000, we went to the Office of Surface Mining with our evidence, and we *demanded* to be heard. I guess the first trip we made in April of 2000, maybe there were fourteen or fifteen of us, but the rest of the people [in Sylvester] were behind us. Our evidence was pictures—videos, still pictures with time periods on them, dated film—the whole nine yards of what we were battling here, which was coal dust on top of coal dust on top of coal dust. I firmly believe that if you're going to fight a battle, you have your evidence and you have it in black and white [so] you've got something to fight with.

I spoke [at the hearing]. I was a nervous wreck—they thought I was going to have a stroke! I was shakin' from the top of my head to the bottom of my feet. I mean, I had never done anything like that—I'd never spoke out against anybody. I never had no reason to. I've never battled nothing like this. The farthest thing from my mind was ever being an activist of any kind.

We won that hearing, which was the first hearing that anybody has ever won against Massey Energy. And as their lawyer walked out in front of us he said, "Well, they sort of set us back on our butts today." The DEP told them that they had to stop the coal dust. [Massey] pleaded a good cause showing. Well, their good cause showing was to put up two measly screen wires—if you look over there closely now, you can see them, [they're] not even a fraction as big as what the plant is. That was supposed to stop the coal dust, [but] all it did was just put another layer of black dirt up there for the wind to blow through. And they [also] put in pine trees that will take 150 years to grow tall enough to catch any coal dust from that preparation plant. [Then] they were going to pave the roads because [they claimed] the dust was coming from the roads. This dust has never come from the roads—this dust was coming from a stoker plant that was burping up coal dust constantly, twenty-four hours a day.

They [also said] they would [spray] foam over the coal within the preparation plant and that was going to stop it. That didn't stop it. Then they put in a water system that—if they had used it—*would* have done some good. But the only time they used it was when the DEP was coming over for an inspection. Now, how they knew when they were coming, I don't know, but they did, because it was the only time [the watering system was] run. Why don't they go ahead and run [it]? Why are they fighting all this much? Well, come to find out, the more you wet coal, the less value it has—the encyclopedias told me that. So they're not going to wet that coal any more than they have to.

Fighting Back

It became clearer and clearer to the residents of Sylvester that the only way the coal-dust problem was going to be addressed was through residents' own persistence. Massey was not going to do more than the minimum required to contain the coal dust, and the DEP was not going to go out of its way to monitor Massey. Pauline and Mary stepped forward as the main watchdogs over the coal-preparation plant. They carefully monitored the coal-dust problem, continuing to gather evidence to document the extent of the pollution that the residents of their community were forced to endure.

PAULINE:

One of the DEP inspectors told us to start taking dust samples and storing them to show how much dust we were getting. So, Mary and I picked out ten spots [around town], and we told the people we were going to be doing dust samples [at their homes], for them to not bother them, just wait and let us come around so we could film [the dust] and document it and put [the dust samples] in a Ziploc bag. We did that every seven or eight days for two-and-a-half years. Rain, snow, sunshine, sleet, and hail—we did it. The DEP never did come back to pick them up. We thought this was just something to get us off their back—they do things to keep you occupied, [thinking] you'll stop.

We didn't trust [Massey or the DEP]. Anything you asked them, you never got an answer. You always got, "I don't know. I don't know. I don't know." They never did what you told them [to do], and so that's when we said, "We've got to protect ourselves."

In February of 2001 we called everybody together that was interested to come to a meeting [about the coal dust]. We had the building full that night. We said, "What are we going to do? We've got to come up with a solution—this cannot go on." Somebody brought up that we needed to get a lawyer. Well, [one man], he knew a fellow that worked for Bailey and Glasser, a law firm in Charleston. He said, "Would you like for me to call him and have him come up here and talk with us?" We said, "Yeah," because we needed to talk to somebody within the law to find out what our rights were. I mean, these people in this town, nobody had ever been to court—they had had no reason to go to court. We took 154 people over there that had never been in a court. That ought to tell you something right there.

[The lawyer] said yeah, he would be glad to come up here. So they come up here and talked with us—the building was full from the people that lived here in the town. Naturally, none of us had a lot of money or anything in order to hire a lawyer. The coal firms know this—they know you don't have the money to battle them, that they could do just what they want to. So [Bailey and Glasser] agreed to take [our case] for a [percentage] of any compensation that we might get.

> With the help of Bailey and Glasser, in February 2001, 154 residents of Sylvester (more than 75 percent of the town's population [Burns 2007]) filed a lawsuit against Massey Energy's Elk Run Coal. It would be another twenty-two months before the trial finally began in December 2002. In the meantime, Pauline and Mary continued to collect dust samples around the town.

PAULINE:

Mary and I continued to gather evidence, and, in fact, I think we gathered all the evidence that they had in that court over there. We became two *determined* women. I was fortunate in my case that I was retired—I had retired in '91. I had time to put in on it and took time from family and everything in order to do it. And Mary has got a very patient husband that tolerates us!

We had stakeouts everywhere. You'll notice my camera sits plugged in all the time on my table ready to go. I told Helene, the cook at [Sylvester Elementary School], I said, "If you see anything, I don't care if it's night or day, [call me]." The school was only about eight hundred feet from where they put the facility. Our school is closed now because of the coal dust.

On October the 29, 2001, [Helene] called up here, [but] my sister was visiting, [so I didn't answer the phone]. Then she called Mary, and she said, "I can't get a hold of Pauline," she says, "They're peppering us with coal dust." She told her that the dust was coming down and just big gobs of it. She said, "Get her right now and get down here with the camera." Mary couldn't get me on the phone, so she jumped in her car and run up here, and she just shoved in the door and she said, "Get your camera and come on." So I grabbed it and run, no questions asked, you know. We went down there, and we filmed the coal dust leaving the preparation plant. It was pouring up over there—it was coming over the schoolhouse, the children were on the playground playing underneath it. We filmed the coal dust falling on the teachers' cars, and I mean you could go out there and you could just wipe it up in piles on your car. The cook's car was sitting right at the back where the kitchen was, and she just stood there and wiped it up on the car. I have a film that shows this. We filmed [the dust] about halfway up Sherman Street, which is the middle street here in Sylvester. It was going right straight up the middle street. The lady's house right over here, she was on her porch. She's an avid cleaner, she cleans constantly, and she was standing there saying, "I just cleaned this two days ago! I just cleaned this two days ago!" And [her porch] was black—it was just black with it. We filmed that.

Then we left here and went on the hill. We filmed [the dust cloud] on the hill, leaving that facility over there, coming up and over the town of Sylvester. Not a sprinkler in sight nowhere, no water running. They had a sprinkler system over there, but it wasn't on. The dust [was] just pouring up through here. I mean, you couldn't even see the hillside on this side, it was so thick. Then I told Sue [who lived] on the hill, I said, "Sue, call Johnny [at Elk Run Coal] and tell him to turn them damn sprinklers on because he's peppering us with coal dust!"

We got in Mary's truck, and she drove on down in front of their complex over here. [I said], "I want to see what's on the other side of that stoker plant." If you'll notice, their office is on the lower side of the hill [on the opposite side of the plant from Sylvester]. So we filmed coming up [from that direction]. Over there was no coal dust. Nice and clear, just nice and clear. No dust [on that side of the plant]—it was all coming this way. By the time we got back to Mary's house, the sprinklers were running on the preparation plant. So we pulled in at Mary's house, we pull in right here, and I got out. You could watch the coal dust settle down in the film. By the time we stopped that car, that dust died right down. "See?" I said, "If they run the sprinklers, it helps." You could see the biggest difference in the world in the dust, if they would run the sprinklers, but they won't do it. But we know why they won't do it—the more wet [the coal] gets, the less value it has. We took that [film] to DEP and said, "This has got to stop." That was the film that got the dome.

Less than a month after Pauline and Mary filmed Sylvester being "peppered with coal dust," the DEP ordered Massey to remove, relocate, or cover the Elk Run Coal preparation plant's enormous stockpile of crushed coal, which was thought to be a major cause of the air pollution. The company was told that if it did not comply, the next action would be to shut down the entire operation (Burns 2007). In response, Massey proposed erecting an enormous nylon dome to cover the stockpile. The dome was completed during the summer of 2002. Although the dome has helped reduce the amount of coal dust blanketing the town, coal dust contamination still plagues local residents—it still settles on patios, air filters must still be changed every few weeks, and residents still cannot enjoy cookouts or outdoor gatherings.

The Trial

The trial against Elk Run Coal/Massey Energy began in December 2002. During the six-week trial, seventy Sylvester residents testified against the coal company. The evidence that Pauline and Mary gathered—in the form of video footage and weekly dust samples labeled with the date and location—was one of the most vital and convincing components of the town's case against Massey.

PAULINE:

They spent one whole day showing [our evidence]. Our lawyer had one of his men go through the whole thing, all the tapes that I had took and [all the dust samples] and everything. They had this dust expert from Pennsylvania [who] went over them and studied them, and then we had another dust expert out of Lexington, Kentucky.

The little stupid lawyer [Massey] had, boy he was a jury-worker. You could just watch him, you know, making up to the jury big-time. When the evidence was showed, he had nothing to fight us back. He asked Mary [when she was on the stand], he said, "When you were doing those samples, did you rub it easy or did you rub it hard?" Mary said, "How many ways is there to rub it?! There is a code in West Virginia that says they cannot let anything leave their premises and come onto ours that will destroy [our property]." Mary told the judge afterward, she said, "I know the laws."

In his closing statement, [Massey's lawyer] referred to the people in Sylvester as inbreds because we chose to live here, you know, among our people and our friends. He didn't say it in so many words, but he implied it in what he said. He was talking very low to the jury, thinking we wouldn't hear, and he referred to me and Mary as glory seekers. Oh yes. Then he said that the people in Sylvester was old and cantankerous and could no longer tolerate coal mining!

> On February 7, 2003, the town of Sylvester won the case. Massey was ordered to pay $473,000 in economic damages and to reduce the number of coal trucks traveling through the town from 35,000 per year to 7,000 per year (Burns 2007). In addition, Massey was forced to pay the residents' court fees, and the town of Sylvester was granted an injunction against the Elk Run Plant.

PAULINE:

We should have gotten more compensation—we got [compensatory] damages, but we didn't get punitive damages. [We got] about 4 percent of our loss. But they paid all court costs. They had to pay all court costs for our lawyers—we didn't have to pay any of that. The one thing we worked for through that court trial more than anything else was an injunction. The injunction was my main thing—I'm not after their money. We got the injunction, which was what we were after. That keeps them in court. Anytime they do something they're not supposed to do, every time they make a crooked move, we can take them to court again. [It's a] permanent opening to the courtroom, on a standing order.

After the Trial: The Fight Continues

> While the residents of Sylvester won their court case against Massey, the fight did not end there. They have had to continue monitoring the company's actions and plans for expansion.

PAULINE:

You have to be on your toes about everything they do, just like the permit for this new underground mine over here, where they were going to take the beltline through the mountain to the other side. Now surely they checked that, but they were going to put [the beltline] right into a cemetery up there. It's an old cemetery, but still it's a cemetery. They thought we forgot about it. The man that the town of Whitesville is named after is buried in that cemetery! Now they [have] changed the [plans], and they have fenced in the cemetery and put up a couple of stones. But you know, we shouldn't have to ask them to do all this stuff. We shouldn't have to watch them night and day.

MARY:

Their intentions was to put [an open] beltline across [Sylvester, and] they were only going to cover [the beltline where it crossed] the road, river, and railroad track. We said, "No. We get the dust from one end, and we're not going to get dust from this end. It has to be *completely* covered." We got that. We had a hearing on that, met with the DEP, and we told them the things that we wanted done. And another thing that they did, they were going to haul the coal out of the hollow up there, which they call Round Bottom. They were going to use trucks to haul the coal, so we told them, "OK, then you're going to haul the coal down through here, through the mines; we want the streets swept, the highway kept clean." We did get a sweeper out of the deal—they have to clean our streets once a week. They go through on Wednesdays and clean our streets. If they don't, we call the DEP, "Hey, they didn't clean our streets." We did get that accomplished.

Right now we're in a battle because of the homes that's been completely covered in coal dust from the coal trucks. We wrote down the names of all the houses the people wanted washed down, and we even put the address and the telephone number. So we called the DEP [official] that represents us here, and he came and picked it up. He took it down and gave it to the Elk Run Coal Company. That's been two weeks now, so I called the DEP Thursday, and I said, "Have you heard if they're going to wash down these homes or not?" He said, "No, they haven't contacted me. I told them to contact you or Pauline Canterberry." Well, I laughed. I said, "They're not going to call us, that's for sure." We're going to give them until next Thursday, then we'll contact our lawyer—because we can take them back to court [since] it's about the coal dust—and then it will be left up to the lawyer what they want to do.

PAULINE:

Most of my talking now I do to the DEP. It's just like I told Randy Huffman [a DEP official] the other day, "I know they're starting this [new mine] over here on this side of the mountain. I know the blasting is ready to be started." I said, "If they don't do what they're supposed to, there'll be a picket line from one end of this town to the other one, because I didn't ask for much." I said, "What I asked for, I expect to get."

You know, it's not easy to sit and watch your home being destroyed, something you have worked for all your life. I don't have a castle. Mary has a beautiful home here; you can see the work that they have put into it and everything, and she works herself to death trying to keep it clean and nice. [The coal dust] just took the value completely away from it. We found out through our lawsuit—because we all had our homes appraised—that our homes have lost 90 percent of their value.

In fact, Mary's large brick home, which in the 1990s appraised for $144,000, is now worth only $12,000, according to the appraisal that was conducted for the lawsuit. Pauline's home appraised for only $10,000.

PAULINE:

I was mad. I worked hard for my home. I worked under a lot of hard conditions for my home, and I didn't think anybody had the right to destroy it. But I think what pushed it most was the fact that my husband was a POW for 116 days in World War II. He was captured during the Battle of the Bulge. He went to Germany and fought against exactly what is happening to us here in this valley—somebody else coming in and taking over, ruin[ing] your life. I thought, "If he can suffer what he did, then I can start suffering some, too."

When [my husband] left the coal mines, he was diagnosed with black lung, which was what killed my husband. [He] passed away in '91. I had to fight for his black lung benefits. Nine and one-half years, I fought them. Now here I am, having to fight for my home that we bought, we paid for, I still pay the insurance on it. I have to pay taxes on it, but I can't protect it. It's injustice.

MARY:

We were seeing our homes being destroyed, and our mountains being destroyed, too. We couldn't sit back and let them completely destroy [us]. We need to get out and fight. We are not going to move off—we shouldn't be the one to be moving. They should be the one to obey the law. So we [said], "We got to get together, we got to do something—we got to try to save our homes." [Pauline's] husband was in the service, and my husband was in World War II and was wounded, with a Purple Heart, to serve our country. They were trying to save our country, and we're here now trying to save our home—which we should not have to be doing. You know, Pauline and I are both retired and we should be enjoying life. We shouldn't be living under these conditions.

I just think that's about the worst thing [that] could happen to somebody—when you see that you've worked all your life for this, and you're losing what you've loved and worked for. There's no inheritance. There's nothing, not even enough to bury us. Twelve thousand dollars wouldn't even build a garage, and like I said, it's certainly not going to bury us. If [we'd] ever have to go and borrow money, what have [we] got to put up for collateral? There's nothing there. Nothing.

We're not against mining; we know we need the coal. But there is a right way, and there is a wrong way—this should have never happened to us. They should have never put the stoker plant where they did to destroy us. Plus, then they put a [slurry] impoundment above us, right behind the house here. We live in fear of it, too. When we go to bed at night, we don't know if we're going to wake up or not. There is no alarm system [in case of a breach or collapse], and we're surrounded by three of the most dangerous impoundments. Within fourteen to fifteen minutes, the one right up the road at Marfork will be in Sylvester [if it collapses]. The one at the Marsh Fork School, that one would probably take, I'm just guessing, maybe from eighteen to twenty minutes to get us. If one of these break loose, there's going to be thousands of people gone—especially at night, because we have no escape route. I mean, if that starts coming down the road at us, we have [nowhere to go] but [up] the mountain. See, that is what makes [us] so mad, that our government is allowing this to happen to communities, to citizens, and taking away everything from us.

I asked the governor, when we were down there and took these [dust] samples, and I held them up and I said, "Would you want your family to live in this?" Well, he kind of hesitated a minute, and he just said, "Probably not." So where do you go? What do you do? I mean, when you can't get help there, you have to fight. And like I said before, I am not against coal miners, I'm not against mining. But there's a right way, [a] wrong way, and modern technology—citizens should be protected.

PAULINE:
You can see what the towns are like—the towns are dead, the towns are deserted. There's billions of dollars' worth of coal going out of here, and we have nothing. There's nothing left in return except disaster, destruction everywhere you turn. That's all that mountaintop-removal mining is leaving behind. Now I'm not going to say stop *mining*. I know a lot of the environmentalists, they [say], "Let's get rid of this coal completely." I can't say that—that's our livelihood in this valley. But they could go back to doing it like it used to be—the coal can be mined different. It can be mined responsibly with the people in mind.

"I Firmly Believe This Was Done Intentionally": Suspicions of Forced Depopulation

What has perhaps been the most enraging to Sylvester residents is that there were alternative building plans that could have been implemented to protect the town. Knowledge of these alternatives, coupled with the discovery of Massey's additional mineral holdings behind Sylvester, has led many residents to feel that the coal dust pollution was deliberate.

PAULINE:

I think that all this was done intentionally in order to drive us out of here. They want the town of Sylvester to close. Before that preparation plant was over there, there was a mountain bluff that came down that ridge, clear to the river. Their facility was back in that hollow—all of it. When they put the preparation plant in, they come down, they cut the ridge off, flattened it off, and that's where they put the preparation plant. We found out that preparation plant was supposed to have been three hundred feet farther back up that hollow. Because [if it had been] back up that hollow, when [the dust] come up, that mountain would have caught it. It would have landed on the mountain instead of coming in the airflow over the town. If they had done what they should've done, we wouldn't have had this problem here. That's the part that makes me really furious, that they really didn't have to do this. But the further I got into this, the further I studied it, [I saw that] what was done to us was done intentionally. Yes, I firmly believe that it was done intentionally. When I really got to reading and studying, I found out that the two mountains behind this area over here, Massey Energy has the mineral rights to them. So, they had to find a way to get over [Sylvester] and get that coal. This spot here is available to everything: to water, to railroad, to roadway. I mean it has all that they needed for what they wanted to do, and damn us over here. I think they thought we were a group of elderly people here and we wouldn't put up any fight, and they would just run over top of us and they would get their way. When they come in here, they didn't come in here to be a part of the community. They don't believe in that anymore.

We found out through the trial that for ten million dollars, they could have made this perfectly safe over here for us. The technology is available—this could have all been in silos, it could have been covered, it could have been belt-lined with enclosed beltlines, but they chose not to do it. One of their engineers said on the stand [in court], he said, "Well, if we did that, we wouldn't have drawed any bonus."

The way I feel about it, we've been discriminated against. We're being sacrificed here for energy for the rest of the world, for more money for people that already has more than they know what to do with, and it isn't right. To me, it's not the American way, it will never be the way of the America that I envision we're supposed to be here. It's horrible what they're letting happen, and it's just for greed. Why should we give up everything we own for somebody else to have cheap energy? For a world of people that's already pampered to death. It's the injustice of it. Honey, this is discrimination—and I don't use that word lightly, either.

Laughing through the Struggle: Becoming the "Sylvester Dustbusters"

Despite all of the injustices that they have experienced, Pauline and Mary have tried to keep a positive attitude and not let anger overrun their lives. They know that finding fun in the midst of the fight is the key to their ability to persevere. Evidence of this belief is clear in the story of how Mary and Pauline earned their name the "Sylvester Dustbusters."

MARY:

We have *had* to laugh through this—we have always tried to make fun out of this. We called ourselves "the little bag ladies" [in the beginning]. We had our Ziploc bags and our cloths to wipe the dust, and I was doing the wipes and she was [video]taping it. [One day] we went up to the mayor's house, and he had a screened-in patio there. We could see all this coal dust [stuck in the screens]. We thought that was so funny, so we took our glasses off and we rolled our face [in it]! The mayor come out, and he said, "I've got to have a picture of that!" In fact, he put our picture over here at the town hall with a "Most Wanted" [sign]—and the reward was a half a penny or something! Well anyway, we got our little [dust sample] bag, and we went over to the next little place we wiped. Usually they'd come out to meet us and talk with us, so [the owner's] son come to the door, and he looked at us. He never asked us in, he just stood there and looked at us—he probably thought [we were] nuts! Well, finally [his mother] came and she looked at us and she said, "You know your face is dirty?" We just laughed, we did our wipe, and on down the road we went. So we came down to the last little house that we [sampled] up here, we was doing our wipe, and the [woman] and her son come out. She looked at us and said, "Do you know your face is dirty?" We cracked up! Then her son looked and said, "Oh, Mom, you know who they are—they're the Dustbusters." So this is how we got our name as the Dustbusters! He named us, and we've gone by that ever since.

The "Sylvester Dustbusters" have dedicated the past decade of their lives to fighting the injustices of the coal industry. Because of their commitment—and their successes—they have also drawn the attention of those whose power they have threatened, such as Don Blankenship, who was the chair of Massey Energy's board of directors from 1992 to 2010 and the company's CEO from 2000 to 2010.

MARY:

[Don Blankenship] calls us "the two bitches." He asked our lawyer, "I would like to know what would please those two bitches." So the lawyer called us, and we made a list of everything, and we mailed [it to him]—it was a certified letter and return receipt. We're just asking for them to stop the dust. Would that be a problem to solve if you did it right? You know, there are sprinklers sitting here on this coal pile, which we always thought was supposed to be automatic, on a timer. They only turn [the sprinklers] on when they know the DEP's in the area. I think that ["the two bitches"] is probably the worst thing [Don Blankenship] could think to call us. I really think he thinks that would make us mad. It doesn't make me mad. You know, he wants to call me a bitch? That's OK. I'll continue to fight, and he can continue to call me [a bitch]. They probably think a woman's place is not to go out and speak out [but] to stay home and take care of things and not come out into the public with this. We don't care; we're going to keep on, as long as the good Lord lets us live. This is what we intend to do. And he can call me a bitch, he can call me whatever he wants to, but I will continue to fight for my home and to stop the coal dust and the mountaintop removal and valley fills. They don't care because they're going to move on, they're just going to walk off and leave it. *We're* the ones to suffer for what they leave.

PAULINE:

I know Don Blankenship calls me a bitch, but you know there's a difference [between] me and Don Blankenship. I know what I am, and Don Blankenship hasn't got the realization yet of what he's become. He won't face me. I've tried and tried to get that man to come face to face with me. I even went to the courthouse in Madison one time and tried to face him, and he walked away. I mean, come on! I'm an old woman! I worked hard for everything I've got. I worked forty-five years—I never took nothing from nobody, I never begged nothing from nobody else. I believe in doing for yourself, and I don't believe in nobody coming and taking it away from me.

MARY:

I think we've really got more accomplished than anybody else has. I think the fact that we're two old women has helped. Us two old women stepping out—I think we're probably two of the oldest women around in Raleigh County that is fighting this. This shows you that old people can continue to help fight, too. We don't just give up. I think that [the coal companies were] probably hoping us two old women would die and give up, but we hope the Lord will let us keep on fighting. We want them to know that we've got the fight in it, and that we're wanting to save our home and our mountains and our water. I mean, it's not only the coal dust. It's the whole surrounding of everything that really has affected us—these impoundments behind our home [have us] living in fear. *Somebody* has to get out and fight it.

You can't sit back and be a "good lady" anymore. You got to get out here and you have to continue to fight for what you should not have to be fighting for. They've got the money, and they know we don't have money. The only thing we've got is a big mouth. We don't have the money, but we can use our mouth. I feel it has accomplished a lot, just being able [to] open your mouth and speak out.

I think that women, they speak up more than the men do. I think we're the fighters. If you see these organizations, most are women out fighting to save our mountains or save our home or whatever. It seems like we have mostly worked with the women and talked with the women. I think women are stronger, as far as speaking up—we don't care, we just keep on fighting.

There is the fact that we do have the time we can spend doing this. A lot of the men, they work, and they don't have the time. The women more or less have a lot of time. I [also] think it's things that we see that maybe the men don't see, as far as like coal dust and breathing coal dust. They don't have to clean it, and they don't have to see this every day. We have to continue cleaning the coal dust and all—I don't think men notice that as much. You know, I think a lot of men see what they're doing to our mountains, [but] it's hard to get them to speak out. I'm just kind of going on my husband, as far as speaking out for the men. He's just not a type to speak out. We've got some [men who speak out], and they are good speakers. But there are some that are just kind of backward-like, and they just don't want to get involved. A lot of people are afraid, they're afraid to speak out. They have families working around the coal companies or their children working around the coal companies, and they don't want to speak out because of the jobs and all that. Where the women, you know, we really don't care. We're ready to fight.

PAULINE:

Some think [the environmental justice organizations] are wasting their time. I mean it's not that they're against them, they just think that, you know, money can do anything. They're not fighters, they just give up. Then, there are those that would help, but they've got family that works for Massey. It's just a conglomeration [of things]. One thing about the coal-mining people, they're faithful people, and they will not do anything to harm anybody else. They've always had to care for themselves, because the coal companies sure never did care anything for them. They just won't speak out, and that's what makes it doubly hard. That's the reason I say the only way we're going to really get this stopped—some of it anyway—is we're going to have to get all the people in all the communities that are opposed to the way they're being treated to come together. It's going to be hard to do because they're so scared. It's a problem.

Strength through the Support of Friends

PAULINE:

One thing that has happened to me and to Mary both through this, we've met some wonderful people. We've made some wonderful friends, [and] we still hear from them. It's been a great experience. And I mean not only here, but other places, too. Everywhere that we have been, because we have been on PowerPoint presentations, we've been everywhere. We've been to Duluth, Minnesota, we've been into Pennsylvania, we've been into Ohio, we've been into Texas, Virginia—and I mean we've made friends that are staying friends.

MARY:

Oh, we have. We've met a lot of friends, we really have. Everywhere we've gone, we've made such good friends, and they keep in contact with us—it makes you feel good. It's sad, a lot of them have cried when they see what is happening to us. They're very concerned about us.

[Ohio Valley Environmental Coalition has] been a lot of help to us [and so has] Coal River Mountain Watch. You know, everyone that we have met in OVEC and Coal River Mountain Watch and Appalachian Voices, they have been *wonderful* people. If we have a problem, we can call them and they would tell us who to contact or they would come and help us. We know that we've got the backing of these people, and that makes you feel really, really good. That makes you feel like you're really close to these people when you know that if we need them, they would be here. That means a lot, because two of us can't fight it—it has to take everybody to help fight it.

PAULINE:

I don't know what we'd have done without them. They've opened up avenues for us that we would have never gotten to without them.

MARY:

I think what really keeps you going is speaking out to the people. Their heart actually goes out to you, and that's something that just keeps you wanting to go. You know, people encouraging you to continue to fight it and all—that really helps. I think it really makes us feel good that the younger people are stepping in. This is what it's going to take—that keeps us going.

We climb the ladder and we fall back, but we don't stop. We're going to go back up that ladder, and we're going to continue to climb this ladder until we can get to the end of the tunnel. We've had a lot of downs, but I feel we're climbing now. And I think that's a big success right there, that you feel like that you are climbing—I really feel that this ladder is going on up.

PAULINE

We're hoping to get to the end of this tunnel somehow. We are going to beat them if the Lord lets us live long enough!

In 2011, Alpha Natural Resources bought Massey Energy for $8.5 billion (Ward 2011). In a conversation I had with Pauline in September 2012, she told me that the new coal company seems to be making an effort to be a better neighbor than Massey was. She reports that Alpha has been using the sprinkler system to keep the dust levels better controlled and that the company helped the town celebrate its sixtieth anniversary in August. The dome had recently collapsed (again), but Pauline told me that Alpha had assured the people of the town that it would replace the dome as soon as all of the parts had arrived.

CHAPTER 3

"Let Us Live in Our Mountains"

Joan Linville's Fight for Her Homeland

Joan Linville and her camera, which she uses to document problems the coal companies are causing in her community. Photo by the author.

Joan Linville was born in Kentucky in 1938. When she was eight months old, her family moved to Boone County, West Virginia, where she has lived most of her life. I interviewed Joan at her home in Van in July 2007. She was also a participant in the Photovoice project I organized from 2008 to 2009, and some of the photostories she created through that project appear in this chapter.

In her narrative, Joan simultaneously speaks of a deep love for her mountains and an intense anger over the losses she has experienced because of coal mining. The same horrifying flood event that nearly destroyed Maria Gunnoe's homeplace in 2003 also hit Joan's home. Joan and Maria, who is "Marie" to Joan, were brought together in a common purpose—to fight the injustices of the coal industry.

You know why I became an activist? It was because of the mountain coming in on my house, and losing my husband the way I did to coal mining. He was in the mines twenty years exactly, and he died at sixty-one with pancreatic cancer. The lawyer told me what killed my husband was the water here—[he] said, "I know it's what killed your husband." The first thing [the mines] destroyed was our water. They had to close our [water treatment] plant down. When I found out what killed my husband, I got madder by the day. How can you like anything that does so much destruction?

He got sick the second day of August [in 2000], and he was dead by the twelfth of November, it spread so fast. He'd never been sick or been in the hospital or anything, but when you get the cancer from these things, it goes fast. Since my husband died seven years ago, I've heard of four or five cases—there's men here dying at forty with pancreatic cancer now.

On June 16, 2003, the mountain behind me came in on my house. It had rained here on and off for days, and it started coming down so bad. We'd been watching the creek—and I was sitting here in my dining room looking out the window, and I was seeing this water just rise in the creek [in front of my house]. It went up three feet just in a short time. I was sitting there, and that water was coming out of the banks [of the creek]. It was coming in up here, and it was coming all the way over to my fence here. It was already underneath my car. My mother-in-law couldn't really walk that well. She's eighty-eight, and I was trying to get my brother-in-law to get her out. Finally, the mountains started coming in—trees and everything was coming down off of this [mountain behind my house], water just pouring off of it like Niagara Falls. It flooded all my garden, ruined everything in it with mine wastewater. All this is just nothing but mine slurry waste in here. My garden is the only thing that spared my house. If it had come in the back of my house instead of my garden, it would have knocked my house off the foundation.

Right behind me, right up here, they're doing mountaintop removal. I'm at the toe of this. Marie [Maria Gunnoe] is at the beginning of it, and I'm at the end of it. That's why the mountain's coming down—there's no trees up there to stop the rain from tearing it all down. [The landslide] brought trees and everything, the whole back of my mother-in-law's yard [who lives next door], the mud and stuff come in all the way up to her house. It went underneath her floors and hooved her floors up.

It was about 4:30, 5:00 in the afternoon, and when I seen that water coming I had to make a decision, and I had to make it then. I got the dogs, I picked up my purse, threw my medication in my purse, said "Come on dogs," and we got in that car. I didn't even have a coat, never thought about it. I waded out and got in my car, backed out, and I went up this way. And I thought, "If that bridge goes out with me on it"—you know, but I could be trapped in here because I didn't know how much more [of] the mountains was coming down. I did not want to be in this house if the mountains come down on me. So I got out and I hit that bridge [that crosses the creek], and I went across it just as fast as I could go. I got out and went down this road and got right down here before I got to this other railroad track, and the mountain started coming down and knocked the railroad tracks out. Power lines was all over the road and everything. I turned to cross the [next] bridge, went over towards the fire department. I was going to go to another friend's house up in Van, [but when] I got to McCoy's Market, they made us turn around because [the landslides] came off up there too. Couldn't get past. We were just blocked off everywhere. So I spent fifteen hours at the fire department, parked there. I spent the whole night in my car with my dogs. [The landslides and water] was all over the roads. We were completely blocked off from everybody. And do you think we had anything in the newspapers? Do you think we had anything in the media? Do you think anybody ever wrote a story about this? The only stories that's been told is the stories I've told when I've traveled and went places and told them what I went through.

The next morning when it got daylight, this lady that lives up here in the parsonage, she came, she seen me over at the fire department and she pulled up beside of me and she said, "Mrs. Linville, I think your house is OK. Your house looked like it hadn't been hit." The mountain come down and flattened her garage. It came down so hard, rocks and mud and all, that it just hit that building and flattened it just like it was a pancake.

The first thing I did, I heard everybody talking in the community, all this clean-up, the county come up here and looked at all this mess. And this guy, he was in a car, and he said, "Well, Ms. Linville, I'd like to help you—I know you're here by yourself. But if I help you, I'd have to help everybody else." I

"Landslide"

JOAN V. LINVILLE

My vegetable garden beside my house was destroyed a few years ago because of landslides from abandoned mine lands. I had to pay a couple thousand dollars to have all of the mud and debris removed from my land. Neither Pocahontas Land Company, which owned the abandoned mine lands, or the coal company that mined the land would help me pay for the removal of the mud. Leaving it was not an option because water is constantly running off the mountain behind my house, and all of the water would have went under the house. After the landslide, I also had to have a ditch dug and a wall built behind my home to protect it. I am now afraid to grow vegetables in my garden because the soil is so contaminated.

said, "Who pays your salary?" I says, "It's the taxpayers of this state. What's your job?" The county never did anything. They didn't give me anything. [The flood] got in my buildings out there and destroyed all kinds of stuff, but they didn't help me in no way, no how—the county, the state, nobody. You can look at my patio, those bricks used to not heave through—it's because the mountain's moving. It cost me two thousand dollars to have this little wall built here, to dig this out and have a pipe run all the way through my garden under the ground, all the way out here to that river. And when this water comes off of this mountain here, it can go through that pipe and out to the river. Otherwise, it will come out and go right under my house. So, we had to clean it up ourself.

I went to the post office the next morning, and I said, "I'd just like to know what's going on in this community, that all these things are coming in on us and we're getting flooded now. I've lived here all my life [and never seen something like this before]. If this continues, we're all going to get killed here." And Barbara [the person who was working] said, "Well, if you think this is bad, you ought to see Marie Gunnoe's place up there. She lost five acres of her land." I said, "Who's Marie Gunnoe? That name sounds familiar." I said, "I believe she went to school with my youngest daughter." She did, she graduated the year before my daughter did. I called her and told her who I was. She remembered my daughter, thought very highly of [her]. She said, "I'm going to come down and meet you," and I said, "Well, you come right on." She come down here and she got out of her truck and wanted to see my property and all that. She looked around. I said, "I'll be up to see yours, too." We stood out there and talked, and I looked at her and I said, "We've gotta find out what's going on here." She told me how many times she'd been flooded [in two years], how much of her land she'd lost up there. I said, "Well, where's it coming from?" She was telling me about [mountaintop-removal mining] on the back of the hill. I said, "If the people that lives here, if we don't do something, our politicians and the people who work here aren't doing anything. Why is all this happening? We need to start looking into this." She looked and me, and she said, "Well, I've been trying this and I've been trying that." And she started crying. She said, "I thought I was doing this by myself 'til I met you," and she was sitting there crying in the truck. I hugged her, and I said, "Stop crying." I said, "Get mad and let's get with it."

Me and her started right here trying to figure it out. We started getting water samples from some of these mines, and we tried to do some research to find out how we could get somebody to help us to find out what all was happening. I didn't have no idea there was six impoundments around us. I had no idea there was this many mining things anywhere! Before [the flood], I wasn't paying that much attention.

It wasn't long after that that we almost had another flood. I got up and I was having my coffee, and I looked out, and I seen a big tree coming down the river. I got my camera out, and I was up here in my nightgown, in my robe making pictures. Who comes down the road in her truck? Marie. She's out there. She said, "I believe we're on the same wave, Ms. Linville." I said, "Yeah, we sure are, aren't we?" [We] went on up the road here. We was making pictures everywhere—everywhere that water was coming off them mountains. I said, "We're going to find somebody that's going to put these pictures in the paper and we're going to start raising hell." We've been fighting it ever since.

We [heard] something about Coal River [Mountain Watch], so we marched over to Coal River, and Marie [volunteered] over there for a little while. And then OVEC [Ohio Valley Environmental Coalition] hired her full time. She was working as a waitress, and [OVEC] hired her full time. She works herself to death though, she really does. She does too much. I get onto her all the time, "You're trying to do too much." "Well," she said, "We ain't got enough time. We got to get it done." She puts in too much, I mean she is going to be old before her time.

Appalachian women are the backbone of the family in this state. They've got more guts than the men do. They really do. My father always told me, "You can do anything you want to do except trouble up a man. Women ain't made to whip men. They were made to outsmart." That's what he said. I think that the women, you know, women are nourishing people and they nourish their families. We don't just educate our children here—we teach them a way of life. We teach them to grow food, we teach them to make quilts, we teach them everything that was handed down to us. We teach them how to survive in the woods if they need to.

My grandmother used to doctor me—I never went to the doctor when I was a kid. If you got sick, if you had a boil or something, they made poultices and put them on your arms. You didn't go to the hospital unless you were dying, unconscious. You know, that's just the way it was—the women took care. We were the doctors. The husbands [would] come home, leave their paycheck on the table for the woman to manage. And really, I think the women in Appalachia end up smarter than the men—and they're stronger. [Women] have watched so many of their loved ones die so young over diseases and stuff here from these coal mines that the women have to be strong.

Effect on Quality of Life

The coal industry has deeply affected Joan's life in many ways. From forcing her family out of their home in order to make room for a coal mine to compromising her health and safety, Joan feels that her life has been a constant battle with the coal companies.

I've lived here most of my life. My father came here during the war because he was building bridges. He went to college in Kentucky and couldn't find any work during the war, so somebody told him they had coal mines here and they were hiring people, so he came here. Fell in love with the mountains and the people and he never did go back. So, he got settled and got a home before my mother came and brought me here when I was eight months old.

I've lived [in this house] since 1974, so I've been here thirty-two years. [Before living here], we lived about four miles up the road in a little town called Cazy, [but] they took my home for a mines. They decided that they were going to put a deep mines in there, and so they gave us all six weeks to get out. I didn't want to move. It was a company house, and they offered to sell us the house if we wanted to move it. My husband didn't want to buy it because he didn't want to go to the expense of [moving it].

We ended up right here [in Van] because his parents lived next door and my parents lived on up the road. He was born right here in this town. His grandfather was a very-well-thought-of person, and this town was named after his great-grandfather Van Linville. My husband worked so hard building [this] house. We couldn't afford to have somebody to build it, so me and him built it ourself. Our kids helped some, but we worked like dogs to build our home.

I lived here and did not know what was going on around me until 2003. [The coal companies] sneak in here like thieves in the night—they really do. They don't call any meetings, they don't ask the community if they want anything done. They just come in and take over your whole community without your permission. They don't come and say, "Hey everybody in the community, come, we're gonna vote—can we do this and can we do that?" No. You have no say. They should never, never be allowed to come in here and wreck people's lives like that. In any [other] state, this would be illegal. Anywhere except for West Virginia. The coal industry has always got their way [here]. I think we have the dirtiest politicians in the whole world, really, I think so.

The river out here in front of me used to be a little tiny creek, and now when it rains it's a raging river. They have mine wastewater from three different mines on up through here pumping into this creek. We have six [slurry] impoundments around us here—six! I didn't know we had *any*. And we have one so huge, about two miles up here, it's back in this hollow, you can't see it

"Hauling Our Mountains Away"

JOAN V. LINVILLE

At the end of the day, CSX is hauling our mountains away. This is the livelihood of southern West Virginia, but there must be a better way. This train was about two miles long—most likely it came from the hollow where I live. The destruction that is left behind after removing the coal from our mountains causes so much damage to our communities and our health. Is this progress?

from the road. They've had some close calls of it leaking. If it would burst, we'd all be dead here in no time. There's no getting out of it. They don't have any evacuation system or anything here. It's like you're playing Russian roulette.

It's a few cents cheaper to tear our mountains down [than to mine underground]. On the ton, it's only a few cents. And to me, that's ridiculous, to tear our mountains down and cause all this destruction to the communities and the people. [The coal companies] are hardly paying anything. Where is the money that is supposed to come into these communities to restore all this stuff? What are they doing with it? I've noticed that the trees, they don't bloom like they did, some of them are dying. The soil is not the same.

There's a mines, underground mines, right there in front of my house that I didn't even know [about]. A guy that does surveying was up here. He kept surveying, looking up towards that mountain. Knowing what was behind me, I thought, "Oh my God, is Massey going to move right in here [in front of my house], too?" I walked up there, introduced myself to him, and I said, "Can I ask what you're doing?" and he said, "Mrs. Linville, Peabody Coal has an underground mines here on that other side." And he said, "The mountain's on fire there." You can see the smoke coming out [of the mountain]—it's been doing it for years. We've got several underground mines here that's on fire. He said if they hit that [fire], the whole mountain will blow up. He said, "That's why I'm here surveying this." Can you believe it? I mean the whole mountain could explode into pieces. It's going to come right over here, probably all the way across that mountain and get me, too. If I hadn't asked, nobody would have known.

I used to be able to come out here [and sit on my patio], and you wouldn't hear that many cars go by. Now you can't sit on your patio for all the traffic, trains blowing, trucks hauling coal out of here, or [else] they're bringing in equipment in to tear the mountains up. It's made my blood pressure so much worse. I didn't even have high blood pressure until my husband died. I've [always] had trouble with my blood pressure being sort of low. [After] this mountain started coming down on me and everything, one day I was standing out there with an engineer and my head was killing me. I thought, "I've got to go to the doctor, this is happening every day, I'm getting a headache." I went up there and [the doctor] said, "Let me take your blood pressure." She said that's what [was causing the headaches]. She made me come every day, and she took my blood pressure. She said, "What kind of stress are you under?" She said it was stress that caused me to have high blood pressure. This place will kill you, that's all there is to it. When you work as many years as I have, you want to enjoy your retirement years. You don't want to sit here

"Underground Mine Fires"

JOAN V. LINVILLE

The old underground mines in front of my house—"Y&O," also called Old Detroit Mines—has burned 24–7 for fifty years or more. West Virginia could have thousands of jobs cleaning up the destruction the coal industry has caused. I believe this is why I stay sick all the time with lung problems. The doctors have told me that I have nodules on my lungs. I have learned that exposure to coal dust causes lung nodules.

and be aggravated to death. I shouldn't be fighting mountaintop removal to try to save that mountain in front of my house.

I [once] was talking with a man [whose] son-in-law was a big CEO for Arch Coal, and I said, "I've got so I just hate coal mining." He said, "You're not supposed to hate nobody." I said, "I didn't say I hated people, I just said I hated coal mining. I hate coal mining because of what it's done to my family and what it's done to me." I said, "If you and your son-in-law would come and live in my house for awhile and have to put up with what I have to put up with [you would see]." I said, "We've got holes in these roads up here that's been here all winter. They wake me up sometimes hitting those holes at 6:00 in the morning—I think they're putting off a blast up here on the hill it's so bad. It scares me, you know, wakes me up." I said, "And just one old truck, one after the other, and I don't live right on the road. Then we got all the dirt from the road grime, and it is so much worse than what it was ten years ago. Then they got blasting behind you, you've got smoke in front of you." I said, "It's just something all day long to irritate you. And then you've got all these impoundments around you with all those chemicals that they put in [them]. [On] these hot days, those chemicals rise up and it goes in the air here. And all the blasting, it comes over these hills and lands on our houses and our cars and stuff." Let them come here and live for just about a month and see if they could cope with it.

"I love these mountains—this is my home"

Despite all of the trauma Joan has experienced because of the coal companies, she expresses her fierce desire to stay in her mountains.

A professor [once told me] that we were a sacrifice for other people to live comfortable in the way they're used to living. You know, I was very timid when I first started all this, but then I got mad. They're taking our rights away from us! They are taking our rights. They will come in here and take our homeland. They will, whether you want to sell it or not, they'll take it. I love these mountains—this is my home. I don't need to leave—they need to leave. I was here before them. You know, get the hell out of here and leave us alone, we love this place. God made these mountains and we're tired of men destroying them. This is our home, it belongs to us. Let us live in our mountains. We have roots here. I like it here better than any place I've ever been. This is my homeland; I've got my roots here.

I'm sixty-seven years old. If I wanted to be somewhere else, I could have been gone a long time ago. We had been a lot of places: Texas, Florida—my

"Dangerous Coal Trucks"

JOAN V. LINVILLE

This coal truck is hogging the road and is over the yellow line. Coal trucks are dangerous for our community, especially along the many narrow, winding stretches of road along Route 85 and Route 26. Not too long ago, two women from this area who were best friends were killed on these roads within two weeks of each other. It is so much cheaper to haul coal by trains instead of trucks, and it's much safer for the citizens living here.

"Eyesores for the Community"

JOAN V. LINVILLE

Bethlehem Coal Tipple, which is between Van and Bandytown, was closed about five and a half years ago. The coal companies leave all of their dirty mess behind for the community to have to cope with as eyesores.

brother used to live in Florida, we'd go down there. We couldn't wait to get back home. You go to New York City or you go somewhere, when you get back here, whew! My God, you feel like somebody's took a rock off of you. I can remember [my husband] being out of work once and we went to Columbia, South Carolina, to go into business with another man down there. They rented us a place on Lake Murray. It had everything in it, even the coffee pots, silverware, and everything—all we had to do was take some clothes. Took my youngest daughter out of school, put her in school down there. One day she came in—it was in June, school was almost out—and I was cooking supper. She said, "Momma, I want to talk to you," and I said, "What is it, Honey?" She said, "I only have about another week," she said, "I'm going home." She was nine years old. And I said, "What do you mean you're going home?" She said, "I don't like it here." And I said, "Honey, you can't do that." She said, "I don't know why not. I can live right there in our old house by myself. Mamaw and Pop's home's right next door." I said, "I can't let you do that. It's against the law." She said, "Well I'm not staying here. I don't like this place." I said, "Well, we'll just have to have a talk when Dad comes in." We ate supper and I told him, I said, "We need to talk to you." He said, "What's going on?" I said, "Rhonda's wanting to go home." I said, "She don't like it here. She's homesick. She's wanting to go home and stay in that house by herself." I looked at him and I said, "I don't like this place either. I'm going home too." He looked at her, and he looked at me and he said, "Well, if you all are leaving, I'm not staying." He said, "Just give me time to clean this up," he said, "and we'll go home."

When school was out, we got in the car and [came] home. We come up through Virginia, and the higher them mountains got, the better they looked to me. I said, "When I get home, don't you ever ask me to leave again, because I ain't going." I said, "Because you'll find something. Things'll work out. We'll make do. We'll find a way when we get there. Money's not everything." So we came back home, and he never did ask me to go anywhere else again. I've been here ever since.

We like living here. That's why we're here, and we're mad as hell that these people are coming here doing what they're doing to us. It's inhumane. You know, if I went over to the governor's house with a big bulldozer behind his house and shoved all that stuff down on him like they're trying to do to us, I'm sure he'd be madder than hell. You know what I mean? These people do not care about us. They say some people have to be sacrificed for the wealth of others, so others can live conveniently. To hell with those people. Just because they might have a little more money than me don't mean—I've worked and paid for this house. This piece of land is mine, mine.

I [volunteered] for OVEC, and I belong to Sierra Club, and I belong to Coal River, too. They're all organizations that work for the better[ment] of this state. I like the work they're doing, I like everybody there, and I go and help them all I can. We do everything we can. We have meetings here and everything, trying to get these people to come out. Some of them are afraid of the coal companies. [Coal company workers] followed me and Marie when we used to go places when we first started doing this. They know our automobiles. They think that we're going to take their jobs by trying to stop this. And of course, I'm sure that the company knows that [their workers] harass us all the time. And they've even formed [pro-coal] organizations in Madison around that area. They're getting just like a cult, really they are. They say if we don't like it, why don't we leave? I'm sorry, but I was here first!

The corporations and the CEOs are destroying this state. That's why there's no other industry here, is because of coal. Coal keeps them out. You just feel helpless and you feel hopeless living in a place like this because everybody keeps saying, "Well, you can't win. I don't know why you're wasting your time because coal, they've always done what they wanted to here." I said, "Yeah, that's because you people sit here and let them do it." The churches here will not take sides, which I think is wrong, because the Bible says you're not to destroy God's creation. That's why I feel that it goes against God's will by doing this. Because see, if God wanted these mountains tore up, He would tear them up himself.

"Heaven Knows What is Happening"

JOAN V. LINVILLE AND JANIE LINVILLE

Most people living in the communities right below mountaintop removal cannot see how widespread the devastation is unless they are able to ride a four-wheeler up in the mountains. This picture is a reminder that while people may not always know what is happening to their mountains, God sees it all. I bet He is mad when He looks down on this mountaintop removal site.

CHAPTER 4

"You Gotta Go and Do Everything You Can—*Fight* for Your Kids"

Donetta Blankenship Speaks Out against Underground Slurry Injections

Donetta Blankenship holding jars of coal slurry–contaminated well water from her house. Photo by the author.

Donetta Blankenship lives in Rawl, West Virginia, where residents' well water became contaminated with coal slurry from an underground coal waste injection site. Before coal is sent to market for processing, it must be cleaned in order to reduce sulfur and noncombustible materials present in the coal. The waste product generated in the washing process is called "slurry" or "sludge" and contains chemicals, water, and small particles of coal, which contain a number of toxic metals. Billions of gallons of this coal-chemical sludge have been produced throughout Central Appalachia. This coal waste is either stored in huge impoundments on the surface of flattened mountaintops or injected into abandoned underground coal mines. In an area where most residents rely on well water, the consequences of a breach in an underground slurry injection site are profound; residents whose water has been contaminated with coal slurry have been found to have high rates of liver cancer, kidney cancer, and brain cancer, as well as gallbladder disease, skin disorders, and even organ failure (Orem 2006; Wells 2006).

At the time of our interview (July 2007), residents of Rawl had just recently been connected to a municipal water line, and for the first time in many years, clean water was flowing through their faucets. However, the health impacts of the contaminated water still haunt many people in the community, like Donetta, who came close to liver failure at age thirty-eight because of high levels of toxins in her water.

"Why are they allowed to do this?" Slurry Injections and Community Illness

When I moved up here six years ago to Rawl from Sydney, Kentucky, just as soon as I got up here, I saw how the water was—the smell of it, the looks of it—what a little bit will do to you. I was automatically in for getting city water, so [in 2005] I started going to all the meetings [about the water problem]. Even though I knew [the water] was bad, I didn't know it was that bad. Everybody takes it for granted when they have good water—including me. They don't know what it's like—I didn't know what it was like until I moved up here and I ended up almost dying from it. You can see right here what kind of water we had.

Donetta picks up a mason jar filled with brownish-black tap water that she collected from her kitchen faucet a year earlier.

In 2004, [the nearby coal company's mining operations] made our well collapse. So we ended up having to drill another well. When we first drilled it, it was ok without the filtering system. But then after a few months, it started gettin' about like this. So then we had to put a filtering system on.

Donetta and other residents of Rawl installed water filters to remove what they believed to be simply dirt in their well water. However, unbeknownst to these residents, what was turning their water brown and black was actually coal slurry that had leached from an underground coal slurry injection site.

I started getting sick at the end of February 2005. I thought I was pregnant the way I kept on getting sick. I stayed nauseous, I stayed tired. My urine was changing colors. I started having problems with my eyes. I would see the outside of the circle would be like grey—bluish grey, the inside would be orange. I kinda wondered about me being pregnant because even my period was getting irregular—it wasn't right.

The first week of April, I started noticing I could look at my skin, and it looked a little yellow. But then I thought maybe it was just me getting out in the sun too much 'cause I was out selling [second-hand items] by the road. So I thought maybe it was the sun doing it to me. And, my husband, he kinda noticed it, even getting in my eyes. You know, the white parts of my eyes was lookin' yellow. Then on that Tuesday morning, my kids, I got them up for school, and my daughter looked at me, she said, "Mommy," she said, "What's wrong with you? You look yella." And she got Josh, my son, to look at me, and he agreed with her. And I told him, I said, "Honey, when you look yella," I said, "that means you're about to die." Me not knowing, you know, that I was about ready to. I told him that when people turns yella, that means they're about to die. I wouldn't have never said anything like that to him if I thought that I was, you know?

I didn't tell my husband what they said or anything, I just went on doing my normal thing. And then Amy, my daughter, she said [to my husband], "Look at Mommy, doesn't she look yella to you?" And, he said, "Yes she does. I've been telling her that for days"—which he had. And they kept on telling me that they thought something was wrong. So, I decided to call my pharmacy and ask them. I asked [the pharmacist] about it, and he said, "Well, Sissy, it's too late now, but first thing in the morning, I want you to go have your liver checked." He said, "Something might be wrong with your liver." I promised him I would—he made me promise. I thought, "Well, I'll take my stepdaughter to the doctor, and after I take her, then I'll go." 'Course I look out for everybody else first [short laugh]. I told [my husband], and he said, "No, you ain't waiting 'til tomorrow." He said, "Go out and ask Mom if she don't think you look yella." So, I did, and she said, "Well, yeah, now that you mention it, you do look yella." And I laughed; I said, "You're all color blind!" Again, I just thought it was where I'd been out in the sun.

I ended up having to go to the hospital. At one o'clock in the morning they put me in the hospital. My enzymes—liver enzymes—was up in the—it was close to 10,000.

A normal liver enzyme count is below 50.

It scared me. Next day, the liver specialist come in—and unfortunately my daughter Amy had to hear it—he told me that my liver was failing, that I was dying. You can't believe how I started feeling. I really started getting scared. They took tests, they even took hepatitis tests. [Voice breaks.] He was even asking me about drinking, you know. I told him no, because I never did drink.

When I called [my husband] and told him, he said, "I bet'cha I know what it is," he said, "It has to be this water." We had been involved with getting city water and had heard about some stuff that [contaminated water] will do.

One of the community activists, he called the lawyer and told him. And then the lawyer got in touch with me, and then Abe [an organizer] with OVEC [Ohio Valley Environmental Coalition], he contacted me. They stuck right in there with me. I was sent to [University of Kentucky Hospital] in Lexington for a [liver] biopsy. The biopsy come back fine, and the doctor put me on some medication, and I finally got out after a couple weeks. But it took awhile for me to build up my strength and everything. It was really scary. My daughter, she took spells. She took nightmares and everything—afraid that I was gonna die. My son, he don't say much, but I could tell with him coming and checking on me all the time that, you know, he was scared too.

> Donetta was not the only one in her family who became ill because of the contaminated well water. Her son Josh started to develop "bumps all over his back" that did not go away. Because of his skin condition, Donetta would take her children to her parents' house in West Williamson to bathe. Her son's skin condition did not go away, however. Donetta's children also experienced difficulty with breathing, headaches, and stomach problems.

"Coal Has a Price": Donetta Finds Her Voice

> After she recovered from her hospitalization, Donetta was invited by B. I. Sammons, a community member activist from Rawl, and Abe Mwara, an organizer from OVEC, to become more involved in speaking publicly about the way her life and the lives of her family members were being affected by coal-slurry contamination. Donetta was very shy and unsure of herself, however, and she initially resisted becoming publicly vocal about the water issue. With repeated encouragement, Donetta finally agreed to be interviewed by Tricia Feeney, a young intern with OVEC who later became an organizer with the group. Tricia was conducting an informal needs assessment in Mingo County to learn more about the health problems facing residents there. Being interviewed by Tricia helped Donetta realize that she

did have an important story to tell, and soon after their meeting, she started to become a vocal advocate for the health of her family and community.

Donetta's first experience speaking publicly about the water contamination problems came soon after her interview with Tricia, when she agreed to participate in a meeting that Abe Mwara organized with a small group of sympathetic state legislators to discuss the water issues Mingo County residents were facing. Donetta traveled with the group to the state capitol in Charleston to tell her story. According to Tricia, Donetta's story made one of the legislators cry. After this initial meeting, Donetta became heavily involved with OVEC's political work during the 2006 legislative session. She and a small group of others from her community would leave Mingo County every Tuesday morning at 5:00 to arrive at the capitol in time to talk with legislators about the water contamination problems in their communities.

Later that same year, Donetta became part of a group of Central Appalachian residents who served as representatives to the 2006 Civil Society Caucus of the United Nations' Commission on Sustainable Development, which was formed at the U.N. Global Earth Summit. Donetta and other local residents traveled to New York City to testify about energy policies and how the coal industry was negatively affecting their health and safety. This was the first time Donetta had ever been to New York City. For Tricia, witnessing Donetta speak before the United Nations was one of the "defining moments" of her career as an organizer. Tricia recalls that as the meeting was coming to a close and the group from Central Appalachia had not had an opportunity to speak, Donetta stood up and interrupted the meeting. Holding a jar of brown-black sludge water in one hand and a picture of her family in the other, Donetta told the caucus about the contaminated water flowing through the pipes in her home. Unwilling to allow her community's story to go unheard, Donetta announced that "coal has a price" and that she wanted everyone there to see who was paying that price for cheap energy.

During that same summer, Donetta became involved in the lawsuit that the residents of Rawl filed against Massey Energy, the coal company responsible for the water contamination in their community. Donetta agreed to testify about the problems the water was causing her family. During her deposition, the defense lawyer attempted to undermine her testimony by asking her how it was possible that the water in Rawl could be responsible for her son Josh's skin rash if he was not bathing at the house (recall, Donetta had started taking her children to her mother's house in West Williamson to bathe). With her newfound confidence, Donetta stood her ground and explained how the water was still affecting her children, even though they were no longer drinking or bathing in it.

He said, "If your son doesn't take a bath or shower [at the house], then why do you think the water is causing his bumps?" The way I look at it, [Josh] was still wearing the clothes that I had to wash in [the water]. When he sweats, it's gonna cause the bumps because he's wearing the dirty clothes. Right now he don't have no bumps on his back because I've been washing our clothes in this city water.

Skin rashes were not the only problems that her family members experienced, however.

[My kids] had terrible breathing problems after we moved here. Now [that we have city water], they don't have breathing problems—you know, what's that saying? The vapors ain't in our house, we're not having to [breathe] it. [My stepdaughter], she was complaining with headaches all the time. Well, the hydrogen sulfide that they was using—the gases—that was one of the smells that was in here. Now she ain't complaining as many times with the headaches.

We've got stomach problems, and there for awhile, my fourteen-year-old even had stomach problems. [My husband's] oldest daughter Lisa—she's twenty-one now—when she was nineteen, she had her gallbladder taken out. My mother-in-law has pancreatitis. These common illnesses and problems that we have around here, you know, there's been a lot of cancer.

What we don't understand is, why are they allowed to do this? The coal mines inject the sludge underground into our wells—it is like speeding up our death. You know, I may have had liver disease later on [when I was older], but because of the water, I got it at thirty-eight. You know? My husband, he's been on blood pressure medicine for years and he's just forty-three. Because of the water and the things that are in the water, it's speeding it up, it's hurrying up and killing everybody here.

The day school started—August 28 of last year [2006], I had my deposition with the lawsuit, with Massey's lawyer. I could tell then that I was getting the same way as I did in 2005—I was getting sick again. The thing about it is, I wasn't cooking with [the water], I wasn't making coffee, we wasn't drinking it. But you know, people puts these patches on their skin to help [them] lose weight, quit smoking, and all that—if that's going through your skin, [then the water is, too]. You take a shower, it goes through your skin. You breathe it. You wear clothes and sweat, it goes through your skin. You know what I'm saying? So I was still getting [exposed to] it.

I ended up going back into the hospital again the second time in September [2006]. And when they tested me, again they done the same tests. They done a liver biopsy—nothin.' They tested me for hepatitis B and C—all that was clear. One thing they did do different—they checked copper. My body was loaded with copper. Copper! And I looked at them and told them like a little joke—but really it wasn't, you know—I told them, "Well," I said, "How does people get too much copper in their bodies?" I said, "I didn't go around eating pennies!" [Laughs.]

Copper is a metal that is present in coal (and coal slurry).

"I Guess in a Way I Might Be an Activist"

Like many other Central Appalachian residents who have spoken out for the rights of their communities, Donetta expressed some discomfort with the label "activist." She sees her "activism" as simply being about caring for her family and her community.

I guess in a way I might be an activist, you know, with what I'm doing. That lawyer—Kevin—mentioned about me more or less being an activist. But I look at it just like I seriously do care about people. I may not even know them, but I care about people—I care about homes for people. Everybody has a right to live healthy. I'm going to go out and support and help my—I guess you call it—friends and neighbors and communities, because they need clean water, they need good health. I'm going to fight against what these people are doing so that [my friends and neighbors] can have homes and better health. As far as homes, I put that in there too because, with that sludge pond impoundment—or whatever they call it—back there, for awhile my son couldn't even sleep because his room is right back there, right where that creek is at. If that sludge pond breaks, it's gonna come and wipe us out. Where are we gonna go? The whole place here is gonna be gone. You know? So it's not just our health, but now it's our homes, too. We do have city water now, but that [sludge pond] could break anytime. I just feel like I need to go and help other people that is in situations like this. It needs to get better for them.

When I asked Donetta why she thought there were more local women involved in the environmental justice movement than men, she, like many of the other women in this book, also mentioned motherhood as being an important reason for her own choice to speak out.

I know as far as me—I don't know about [others], but I know [for] myself, I'm a mother. I just basically want to see what's best, and simple things for my kids. I'm not sure how to answer, but it just seems like when it comes to things like that, we women are a little stronger. [Laughs.]

"I've Met So Many Friends"

Donetta expressed that one of the greatest benefits she has experienced since becoming involved in the environmental justice movement is the sense of community she now feels and the wonderful friends she has made. She found it very difficult at times to convey how much these friendships have meant to her.

I really didn't realize that there was so many—so many caring people out there. And what makes it even greater—I'm forty years old. I'm not young, you know? To see so many young people out there wanting to make something better—[caring about] babies and kids that are younger than them—you know, it just *overwhelms* me. It's just so great to see that. I think about that so much.

I've met so many friends, and everybody's been great to me. Again, I really didn't think there was so many caring people out there. Everybody's so supportive and encouraging [me] on, and, you know [uncomfortable laugh, pause]—it's just hard to express. All of them that I've met, that I've been involved with [in the movement], I honestly feel like I could trust them with my life. I do. I feel closer to them [than to a lot of my neighbors]. I do feel like I can trust them—I shouldn't say [this], but I trust them more than [people] here [in my community].

Donetta had a difficult time expressing how kind and caring all of the organizers and activists in the environmental justice movement have been to her.

No matter where I go [with the movement], you know, everybody was like that in New York and everywhere I went. I went to Washington back in May, and Benji [Burrell, with Appalachian Voices], he made a point, no matter what I done, he made sure I was OK with my health and everything the whole time. Even yesterday evening at the [water] hearing, Benji [was supposed to] stay at the hearing so he could finish recording it, but instead, he went ahead and took me to the capitol [to meet country music singer Kathy Mattea, who was holding a press conference against mountaintop-removal mining]. And he kept on asking me if I was OK, he kept on asking me, you know, if I was hungry. I mean, it just [makes me] speechless, how [good] some of these friends really are. And it's not just like that with me. It's like that with my kids, you know? I just can't express it. I just feel like I can't tell you how wonderful they are, and what terrific people they are, and what they're capable of doing. I didn't think they was—especially younger people—I didn't think they was [like that] anymore. I hate to say this, but I guess I needed to get away from here to see that.

When I went to New York, Larry Gibson,[1] he used to tell me all the time that I'm *somebody*. Especially for people like me—a nobody—that's the way I would feel, you know? If I can go and be a part [of this movement]—like I'm starting to see that I'm doing now—being a part of making things better for everybody, then I'm gonna go do it. Trish calls me a community leader. I don't know—she [tells] me that all the time. I don't feel like I am, but she says I am, and other people does, too. [Laughs.] People encouraging me—I think that's what, what makes me want to go [and be a part of this movement]. [Starts to tear up.] And I just have [pauses] so many wonderful, true friends. I, I can't express that enough.

Personal Transformations

Donetta's involvement in the environmental justice movement has deeply affected—even transformed—her life and her view of herself. When I asked Donetta if being involved in this environmental community has changed her life in any particular ways, she described the increased self-efficacy and meaning she has found through her community work.

[Voice shaking.] Me and my therapist talk about this all the time. It has changed me . . . [long pause] . . . in several different ways. One thing . . . [pauses], like I've already said, I have more or less always felt like I'm a nobody. Now I feel like I'm somebody, I, I feel like I can . . . [pauses, sobs softly] do something for somebody—do something for my kids . . . [pauses, crying]. You know, so many people say that they want everything for their kids, they want them to have the things that they didn't have—you know, material things. Material things ain't everything. [Pauses.] You gotta . . . [pauses, crying softly], you gotta go and do everything you can—*fight* for your kids. [Sobs.] You gotta show them you love them . . . [sobs]—because if you don't, they're not gonna know that.

I, I can't express it—it's not just about the water. [Pauses, still crying.] Me and my counselor was talking not too long ago, and that made me realize something [pauses]—about a month ago an incident happened here . . . [voice shakes, pauses], and, um, I, I used to be really depressed. I was so depressed and everything—I thought that my parents could raise my kids, that they'd be fine [if I died]. And in 2005 when [I got sick and was hospitalized] . . . [crying] . . . you know, I was getting *out* of the depression and stuff then. I'd actually come to the point that I wasn't really [thinking] that much about suicide anymore, but I was dying anyway. And about a month ago, when an incident happened here, . . . [pauses, cries, voice shaking] . . . my son asked me, asked me that night—'cause he saw how upset I was—if I'd thought about suicide. And I told him no. I ask him why he asked, and him not wanting to talk much, he just said he didn't know. Next day when I talked to the therapist, I realized at one point I was so depressed [that] I was wanting to die. And now, seeing my son, how he is—an All-American Scholar, and things like that, and seeing my daughter, how she's becoming everything. [Pauses.] You know, thank God I didn't die in 2005 [crying]. I feel like I even need to be here for [my step-daughter]. I wanna be here for my kids. [Sobs.] I really want to—they need me, and now I can see that. [Pauses.] I know this is off the subject a little bit, but I'm, I'm even wanting to write a book now. I'm hoping that if I write a book, that maybe I can help some of these people that feel like I did.

At this moment in the interview, both Donetta and I were crying. We sat crying for a few moments, both of us expressing our gratitude that she had not died and that she could be sitting there in front of me at her kitchen table telling her moving story. I told her that I hoped I could help her share her story with others, because it was such an important story to tell.

Of the women whom I interviewed for this book, Donetta's story of change and personal transformation is perhaps the most dramatic. When I asked her what she was most proud of she responded,

That I can speak out. [Laughs.] That's one thing I've never been able to do. That I'm helping make a difference. I mean, really, I think about it—I can't believe I can say that! But I see all these little events happening, you know, these changes . . . [pauses]. People has actually made me feel like I'm helping to make a difference. And I'm proud to say that, little by little, all my kids are becoming, I guess, activists too! [Laughs.] My step-daughter Christina done her school report presentation on mountaintop removal! [Laughs.] So, I think I'm rubbin' off! I'm proud of that because, maybe, maybe they are caring enough for their community and friends to make a difference, too.

CHAPTER 5

"It's Just a Part of Who I Am"

Maria Lambert and the Movement for Clean Water in Prenter

Maria Lambert enjoying a warm spring day in Boone County, West Virginia. Photo by the author.

Maria Lambert is a lifelong resident of the community of Prenter in Boone County, West Virginia. Born in 1958, Maria lived most of her life in Prenter "Main Camp," which is one of the former coal camps situated in Prenter Hollow. In 2000, she and her family moved a few miles down the road to a piece of family land in Sand Lick, another area of Prenter, where they had hoped to live in peace. This vision was shattered when they—like the residents of Rawl—learned that they and their neighbors had unwittingly been drinking, cooking with, and bathing in well water that was contaminated with coal waste from an underground slurry injection site.

For many years, residents in Prenter—including Maria and her family—suffered high rates of various rare illnesses. In 2008, some of the residents realized that the health issues in their community could be tied to the water problems and began to organize. Since the first community meeting, Maria has been at the forefront of the struggle for water justice in her community.

I conducted this interview with Maria in July of 2008. From 2008 to 2009, she was also one of the participants in the Photovoice project I organized in Southern West Virginia, and a few of her photostories appear in this chapter.

"It's Not Just Us—It's the Whole Community"

We moved down here in 2000. My uncle had just passed away and he left my father the property. So when we moved down here, we thought that the kids—our grandkids—would be able to play in the creek. I think I had it in my mind that this is where I wanted to grow old and relax with my grandchildren, and when my husband retired we could just travel and, you know, not worry about anything. Because at that time, I didn't have anything in my head that anything was going to go wrong—I just knew that this was hid away and it was quiet and peaceful and pretty, a beautiful place.

We had well water, so [we thought] we didn't have to worry about having dirty water. We knew that they were mining back up there in the hollow, but it just didn't seem to be a bad thing, you know, because it had always been kind of clean and everything here. And Mommy started noticing that—she has a nose for everything—she noticed that her water didn't seem right, and she really hated using it. She had to clean her coffee pots really often, and she would have to go and buy new coffee pots often because they'd kind of quit working. So last fall, I don't know where they saw the flyer at, but somehow [my parents] found a flyer that said they were having a water meeting. And [my mom] said, "Maria, I really think that some of us needs to go to this meeting, because there's definitely something wrong with our water. It's not right, something is not right." So, she and my dad and I, we went to the water meeting.

Everybody was showing [samples of] their water. Different people stood up and told about their water and told about what they believed was happening, and told about the different illnesses—the brain tumors, the gallbladder problems, stomach problems, children's teeth falling out, and all of these things. . . . And it's like a light bulb going off all here, there, yonder, everywhere. And it's like my whole life flashing before my eyes, because my children had lost their teeth, my parents had had cancer, we'd had our gallbladders removed, and all of these things was, it's just like, oh no, it's not just us—it's the whole community, and we're not even blood related. There was Jennifer Massey, who had lost her brother to a brain tumor; Kathy Weikle who had a pituitary tumor; Terry Keith who has the triplets and another grandchild who has to bathe in the water, and they were having a rash and everything. They were having to mix their formula with the water and didn't realize it was bad. Oh gosh, let's see. Several people had kidney problems in their family. There's been two kidney transplants—one was a small child and one was an older gentleman—in the past four or five years. People dying from kidney disease, kidney dialysis patients. My mother had to have a third of her lung removed from lung cancer—it wasn't in the bronchial tubes, it was in the fatty part of the lung, the tissuey part of the lung. And then my father come through thyroid cancer. And my husband and I both have had major stomach problems. My sister has major stomach problems and nerve problems, and there's a lot of neuropathy.

My children lost some of their teeth from decaying before [coming] through the skin. I mean, it's just like if it was coming through, breaking through their gums, their teeth was [already] decaying, and they had to have them pulled because of that.[1] And from what I can understand, the dentists get more business from our area than they do any place else, children-wise.

And I'm sure you've read the statistics on the gallbladders. Probably forty-six out of forty-eight people don't have a gallbladder. I knew a lady from across the mountain, across Williams Mountain, who was raised in Prenter, [and] her children have lived in Prenter. She's on well water [and] had to have her gallbladder removed. Their son had to have his gallbladder removed a week or so after his mother did—he's about thirty-five. They squeezed his gallbladder when they took it out, and it was nothing but black stuff come out of it, tarry-looking stuff come out of it. You think of gall as green, you know, and yellow. But it was black.

I sat down with Bobby [Mitchell, a community organizer with Coal River Mountain Watch] here one night right after we had the first meeting, and it's like there was something took hold of my hand and I said, "I can write

"The Changing of the Water Filter"

MARIA LAMBERT

This photo shows what a new water filter should look like (white one) and after only three months (black one), it has become unthinkably black from something lurking in the well. My Dad says it looks like pure coal slurry water—he should know, as he worked at a coal tipple for many years and saw firsthand what it looked and smelled like.

you a list of all these people with all these diseases who died and [those who] are still living with these diseases." So I wrote like twelve pages.

That's how I became involved. It's like it was just overnight. I just got really mad and really upset to realize that our government had kind of blinded everybody for so long—here we thought we were safe tucked back in these mountains, and to wake up one morning and find out that somebody had already been here and invaded us before we even got here. And it's just like a light bulb went off in my head—this is what I have to do. I would stay up all hours of the night, I wouldn't go to bed until daylight, writing letters and writing down thoughts that would come to me. And I would write them so fast I couldn't even read my own handwriting. I would have to go back over it and rewrite it because it's like, no, I can't send that out because you can't read it. But it's like, I felt that God was giving me all this information that I knew, that He was bringing it back to my remembrance to write it down to tell someone else about it. I started writing letters, and I started e-mailing Patty [Sebok] and Judy [Bonds], and they were helping me with the letter writing. I was writing so fast that it was coming out of me like someone throwing up. And I couldn't stop it. It was just happening so fast that I was afraid that if I stopped I would not be able to continue with it. So I just, I would sit up 'til five o'clock in the morning, six o'clock in the morning, sometimes not even go to bed, typing all of this stuff out. Newspapers, senators, TV stations, congressmen. You name it, I sent [letters to them]. I have tons of people on my e-mail list that I've sent them to. It was just an amazing transformation from being totally sedentary, doing nothing, to now I have a calling. Now I have a reason.

We started out as "Concerned Citizens on Prenter Road," because it is the whole ten-mile stretch [of road]. Coal River Mountain Watch has worked very closely with us. If it wasn't for the people at Coal River Mountain Watch, we really wouldn't know where to go. They've been a great help in getting us resources and information, getting testing done, that type of thing. OVEC [Ohio Valley Environmental Coalition] has been a big help. And the Sludge Safety Project, we're working pretty close with them. We try to get more community people involved. We have meetings here at my home and then we have meetings with the lady up the road, at her home, Kathy Weikle. She's real good to open her home for meetings. The last meeting I think we had probably close to twenty people here. So it's getting better and more people are becoming involved. If not openly involved, they're at least showing up for the meetings and getting the information that's out there and they're giving out information. We're trying to get the Health Departments involved. We have had a meeting here with the head of the DEP [Department of Environmental

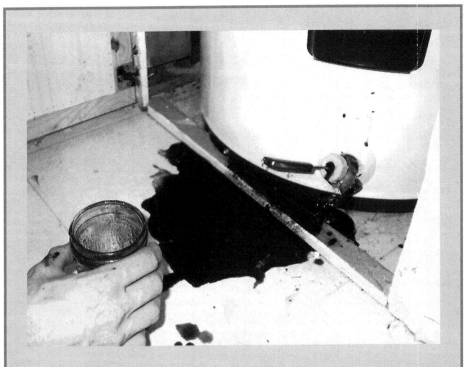

"One Home, Mom, Dad, and Four Children"

MARIA LAMBERT (PHOTO BY BOBBY MITCHELL)

Who would believe that four children had to bathe in this water and no emergency supply was made available! When this touches the skin it burns not from heat but from something in it. The state was asked for emergency water, the county was asked (although they did make it a point to bump this community up on the list to get municipal water), the emergency services was asked, as well as the West Virginia Department of Environmental Protection. They were all shown the bad water supply but nothing was done for the immediate needs. Now after a year of begging, the government is finally stepping in and making a show of concern.

Protection] at my home, and a gentleman from the DHHR [Department of Health and Human Resources] was here that day, and a citizen's advocate with the DEP was here, and we had quite a few people here that day. So we're just kind of making sure that everybody knows that we're here, making our voices heard, getting the word out there to the senators, the congressmen, the TV stations, the radio stations, the newspapers. Whether they print it or air it or not, they know what's going on. They know we're here.

"I Got So Mad": An Emotional Awakening to Injustice

Maria's decision to lead the fight for clean water in Prenter was ignited in large part by her anger at being poisoned by the industry to which her husband, father, grandfather, and great-grandfather had given so much of themselves for so little compensation.

Even though we knew that coal mining was going on all around us, and that's how our husbands and our fathers and grandfathers had all made a living, you didn't think about how dangerous it was, and you didn't know they were injecting this slop underground. I had no idea they were allowed to do that. [Years ago], when we lived in the Main Camp [of Prenter], we would call the DNR [Department of Natural Resources]—because then there was no DEP, it was the DNR—we would call them and say, "You know, the creek's turning black, there's diesel fuel in it, it looks nasty, it's slimy. You need to get somebody up here." They told us, "Well, it wouldn't do us any good to come out because by the time we got there it'd all be gone." That's what they told us. And that happened from the time I was probably about fifteen, sixteen years old, maybe a little younger than that. I got married at sixteen, so it was happening before then.

I'm really not sure when they started injecting, but I know they're still doing it. They're doing it legally and, from what I can understand, illegally. I was told that they are putting barrels and barrels of stuff underground and not reporting it. My dad used to work on the slate dump over at Ashford. No—I don't think they called it a slate dump. But he said they had a couple water holes, what they called—it wasn't really a pond, but it was like a—oh what did he call it? Not a dam, it's like a big mud hole, sort of like the slurry pond up here. He said they could take a fifty-gallon drum and throw it in there, and within five or six hours it would eat that drum up. He worked on that slag, on that, at the tipple, and he ran a dozer. And whenever they would pump that slop back up there, they would have to cover it up or make room for more, you know, that kind of thing. Daddy worked twenty-five years in the mines, in and outside of the mines. He's seventy years old now, and he's

"PSD Water Showing"

MARIA LAMBERT

Our community went to a Boone County Public Service District (PSD) meeting in the late winter of 2008 to show them samples of our water and ask them to consider putting in municipal water in our community. These samples are just a few of what were shown. They were in agreement that the water was really bad. Some of these water samples were taken from the backs of commodes, where nothing is supposed to be except water. But as you can see, something has reached the water, and the only way in is from the well waterline.

come through thyroid cancer. The doctors told him when he was forty-two years old that he had the lungs of an eighty-year-old man. If he hadn't got out then, he would have died. We would have lost him.

I went into the hospital the weekend after that first meeting from intestinal bleeding. All summer long I had been on some medication, and my white blood [cell] count had dropped down to 2.5, and that is not good. They wanted me to go off of some of my medication to see if it could be that that was causing it. And I thought, "Well, since I'm going off of medication, I'm just going to go ahead and try to lose some of this weight," because I weighed over two hundred pounds. I lost fifty pounds by drinking water all summer long—our water—the water that we should not have been drinking. They tell you, "Drink lots of water," you know. So when I found out that what I thought was supposed to be a good thing [made me sick], I got so mad. It was just like an inferno inside of me that was just busting to get out. I was just really, really mad. And about the time I would think that I was going to get over it, I'd get mad all over again.

I never really got that mad about anything [before this], I don't think. I think that was the straw that broke the camel's back. It just infuriated me to think that my husband had spent twenty-three-and-a-half years in the ground [coal mining], my dad had worked for the mining industry for twenty-five years, my grandfather worked for about twenty-something, thirty-something years in the mines. His father was killed in the mines. And to know that they gave their all—*everything* they had, they put into that work. The company had [my husband] believing that—most of the men up there, they believed that if they didn't push that extra hundred ton of coal a night they were going to lose their jobs. They would stand outside and give them this big speech, "Well, tonnage is down and if we don't get this up we're going to have to lay off." They would actually stand and tell them that. And they were running sometimes two and three hundred feet of coal over the safe limit a night—a shift. I think Ralph said they could do a hundred and some feet a night if they would use all of the safety measures that they were required to use. But then he would come home and say, "We run 350-some feet tonight." And you know what they got in return for doing all that? They got two hotdogs and a coke.

My husband got hurt [and stopped working] June 18, 2005. He fell in a hole where they were supposed to keep it leveled off and keep the water pumped out. He slipped and twisted his knee, and he had to have some surgery on his knee. And it was my opinion that he should not go back underground, that if he did, he was just taking his life into his own hands. You know, because he'd already had to give up the roof bolter job because of his neck and his arms. So now he was wearing this big heavy, fifteen-pound box in front of him around his neck to run the continuous miner. It was a remote-control miner, and so that was his job. And you have to stand to do that. You can't sit down, and standing would kill him. I mean it would just—because he'd already had back surgery and he'd had both of his hands and his elbow operated on. His legs was all he had left.

I just know that people are suffering and it's not right for people in power to take advantage of everyday working, taxpaying, breathing citizens. They're taking away from us and trying to make people believe that they're *giving* to us. They have made people believe that for a hundred years, or more—even from the beginning of time. People in power have *always* abused their power.

Maria's Calling

When I asked Maria why she thought it was women like her who were taking up the cause for clean water and a safe environment in Appalachian coal-mining communities, her response echoes a common theme among many local residents: women are protectors.

It's the need to protect, that need inside of most women, and I would say probably 99.9 percent of the women have that need to protect somebody, whether it's a husband, a child, a parent, a neighbor, an animal, whoever. I think women just are born with that nurturing instinct. Women are really the spokespeople. I think it's because women are maternal and they're more passionate about health issues and anything that concerns that nurturing part of people. It comes out more in women than it does men because men have that thing inside of them that just makes them men. It's maybe testosterone, I don't know. They feel that they can't be emotional, and women are more emotional. So, I would think that women don't mind letting their feelings show, and they don't mind telling somebody what they think.

And I think there's a drive to prove something, prove that I can be more than just a housewife, more than just a mother, more than just a daughter or a sister. There's a drive to succeed. I never went to college, I never finished high school. All I wanted to do was have babies and be a wife, you know, be a wife and a mother. That was all I really wanted to do. The year that I quit school, I finished the tenth grade, but that year they were getting ready to open up the vocational school. And my chosen career path would have been social worker. That's what we set up in the counselor's office—I was going into social work classes. So, I thought, you know, that's what I've always done. From the time I was sixteen and quit school and not going into those classes, I've still always been a social worker/advocate, so, *activist*. I think it's brought out the best in me, or brought out what was there that needed bringing out. It kind of works out God's way no matter what you do. If you've been called out to do something, then it always works out His way regardless.

About a year-and-a-half before this all come around, I was sitting in the bedroom on the computer one day, and I looked out the window and I thought, "Here I am sitting here, overweight, tired, growing old and doing nothing." I was kind of shut down as far as society was concerned, as far as the community was concerned. And I thought, "Lord, there's bound to be something out there that I can do. I want to be active the way I used to be. I want to be able to do something meaningful with my life." Nothing happened. Nothing out of the ordinary happened, no big lights went off anywhere or anything. Last summer, 2007, my husband and I were driving somewhere, I don't know where we were, probably coming from a doctor's office somewhere, and we were just riding along being quiet. I was looking out the window, and I started praying, "Lord, please, there's bound to be something out there. I know there's something out there that I can do. I want to make a difference in somebody's life so when I leave here, when I leave this earth, at my funeral I want them to be able to say, 'Maria done what she could.'" Not through me, and not through anything that I did, but because of what God done for me and the impact that He's made in my life. I want to be able to share that with other people, and in the process help people with their physical everyday life. And then it wasn't any time until all of this came about, and it's like, I knew that this is where I was supposed to be.

I never thought of myself as being an activist, just a concerned community person. I think people don't really understand what they're facing, because I didn't really for a long time. It's like inside of me somewhere I knew, but it just had to have the right time to surface.

Staying an Activist: Challenges to Sustaining Involvement

Despite feeling that her community work is answering a calling, Maria still struggles with the stress of being involved in a movement that is not always welcomed by those in her community who fear retaliation for speaking out against coal-related problems or who depend on the coal industry for employment.

We had a meeting at the Prenter Community Center [at Main Camp]. We invited the whole community and, needless to say, when they got there, they were trying to run us off because they were afraid of the coal company. Afraid the coal company was going to turn the power off to their water supply, and they would not have any water, and they couldn't survive without water. [*Unlike the rest of Prenter, where citizens draw their water from wells, the residents living in the Main Camp of Prenter have a community water supply that is provided by the coal company*]. They would rather drink bad water than to fight what was killing them. They even had somebody, I don't know who it was, started a rumor that we were going to come up there and shut the Head Start program down. They had already gotten a Boil Water Advisory from the DHHR, and the Head Start had to buy their water from Tyler Mountain [bottled water company] to keep from boiling their cooking and drinking water. The kids weren't even allowed to brush their teeth in it; [they're] still not. It's a standing order from the Department of Health and Human Resources. And they're on community water up there.

You can't garden, you can't raise your garden and all that stuff if the land is destroyed. The land and the people connect. I don't think people disrespect me, but I don't think they really—well, like I said, they don't understand, so it's like I'm unapproachable: "You don't talk to her because she's one of them." You know, "You don't want to get into too much of a conversation with her because she has joined forces with them"—"them" being the environmental people. People don't, they don't want to kick against anything that's going to stop that almighty dollar from coming home to their pocket.

I think people are so narrow-minded that they can't see that these people are out there, the people that they're fighting against are the people that want to help the most. And they're kissing their government's butt, and they're kissing the people in offices that knows what's happening to them. They know that they're being damaged, these officials know this. But yet, the regular everyday citizens look to these people like they're gods, and they're not. They know exactly what's going on. Because when you get to researching it and you see who their friends are, we're just little peons in a world that don't want us.

Every other day I tell my husband, "I'm not going to do this anymore. I'm done. I'm not going to do this anymore." And then somebody will call me, or I'll get an e-mail and it'll make me mad, and I think, you know, I just can't—if I quit, I'll feel like I've let down a lot of people, and most of all, let myself down for not doing what I've been called out to do.

Why is it worth it to me? Because if I go to bed and not do it, I wouldn't sleep anyway. I'd feel guilty for not doing it. If something that I might say or do would keep one person from being ill, making a difference in one person's life, it's worth it. It's worth it. If whatever we do reaches one person, then it saves one person's life or one person's soul. I think that I finally found my

"Water Testing"

MARIA LAMBERT

No, that's not Kool-Aid! It's a simple Manganese test kit. The water sample was taken from the base of a valley fill. The water immediately turned deep red when the agent was poured in. The water is discharged into Sand Lick Creek after passing through a treatment station that is almost always in need of repair. The place was Chapman Hollow on Sand Lick Road. The former home of my husband's uncle, marked by a lone apple tree.

little niche in life, and I found where I belong, that place of comfort. Maybe a year from now I won't be doing this. I don't know. Whatever comes along that is supposed to be will be, but I feel that I'll always have this in my heart. I don't see me just dropping it because I would feel too guilty. I would feel like I had killed somebody. You know, it's just that strong—it's just a part of who I am, where I came from.

In 2008 Maria and other Prenter residents, with the help of local environmental justice organizations Coal River Mountain Watch, the Sludge Safety Project, and Ohio Valley Environmental Coalition, came together to create the "Prenter Water Fund," which raised enough money to cover the cost of a water truck and plastic water barrels, which were distributed to all of the residents living along Prenter Road. The water truck delivered free water from the community of Racine to residents living along the ten-mile stretch of Prenter Road, so that they did not have to drink or cook with the contaminated well water.

The water barrels were intended to only be a temporary fix, as residents still had to bathe and wash their clothes in the well water. The Concerned Citizens of Prenter Road and their allies lobbied their legislators and other elected officials for a municipal water line to be laid through Prenter and to pass a moratorium on underground slurry injections. Maria used her photostories in these lobbying efforts. Thanks to the hard work of Maria, other Prenter residents, and various organizations, including the Prenter Water Fund, the Sludge Safety Project, Coal River Mountain Watch, and OVEC, the residents of Prenter were awarded a city block grant to have the water line extended into Prenter Hollow.

On August 18, 2009, a groundbreaking ceremony for the water line was held at Hopkins Fork Community Church, which is where we held our Photovoice meetings. At this ceremony, Senator Ron Stollings from Boone County announced that the West Virginia Department of Environmental Protection would be placing a moratorium on all new permits for coal slurry injection sites. As reported in the *Coal Valley News*, Senator Stollings specifically cited Maria's photostories as a reason for his commitment to stop new underground coal slurry injections:

> "There are some health issues in this community," the Senator and local physician said. "There will be no more new slurry injections from here on out," Stollings said to a round of applause. Stollings praised the work of Prenter resident Maria Lambert, whose photo essays helped give a visual voice to the problems plaguing the area. "I appreciate that grassroots approach and it goes to show that the old adage, the squeaky wheel gets the grease, is correct," he said (Newman 2009).

While this was a tremendous success for Prenter residents and for people living in coal-mining communities throughout southern West Virginia, activists are still pushing for a moratorium on permit renewals and modifications for existing slurry injection sites.

CHAPTER 6

"I'm Not an Activist against Coal; I'm an Activist *for* the Preservation of My State"

Teri Blanton and the Fight
for Justice in Kentucky

Teri Blanton at the annual "I Love Mountains Day" at the Kentucky State Capitol
in Frankfort, Kentucky. Photo courtesy of Kentuckians For The Commonwealth.

Teri Blanton is one of the most well-known environmental justice activists in Kentucky. A community leader with Kentuckians For The Commonwealth (KFTC), Teri has been fighting to hold the coal industry accountable to Appalachian communities for more than a decade. In addition to her local community activism, she has spent countless hours lobbying the Kentucky legislature and U.S. Congress and speaking at conferences and panels across the country. Teri is currently a KFTC Fellow through the Canary Leadership Network, and in this position she regularly communicates with fifty-two leaders throughout Kentucky to educate and update them on energy-related issues. She serves on the National Environmental Justice Advisory Council (NEJAC) and takes great pride in being the "first hillbilly ever to sit on the NEJAC." Teri is a founding member of the Coordinating Committee for the Alliance for Appalachia, and Robert Shetterly painted a portrait of Teri for inclusion in his book and exhibit *Americans Who Tell the Truth*. Teri was born in 1957 in Harlan County, Kentucky.

Our interview was conducted in July 2007.When asked to reflect on her biggest motivations for becoming involved and staying involved in the environmental justice movement, Teri describes being driven by a desire to protect a beloved landscape, a way of life, and vital natural resources. In addition, she feels great personal rewards from helping others stand up for their rights and communities.

Speaking Out for Justice

I [grew up] in Harlan County in a little community called Dayhoit. It was like one of those communities that everybody took care of each other, and if somebody had too much of something, then you would share it. So it was a real caring community. Everybody watched out for everybody's kids, that kind of thing. I was about third or fourth generation there—fourth I think.

Watching the mountains around me and my creek being destroyed [has been a big motivation for my activism]. I have a picture of my creek that I grew up on that I loved so well. It runs orange with acid mine drainage, and that makes me mad enough to make me [speak out]. I mean, I grew up on this creek, and creeks were entertainment to poor kids. I was one of six children, and we were extremely poor. We couldn't go to the public pool, we didn't have the money, probably didn't even have the bathing suit. So, the creek was a part of our life, and when I seen them destroying the creek, that really made me angry. I have two grandsons, and I want them to be able to go outside and breathe the air. It's just wrong, for God's sake. The destruction of our land, the destruction of the culture—I embrace the culture, and the destruction of it [makes me angry].

There was this infamous old man George Hereford who owned all this land around our community. I'd heard about [him] my entire life. The rumor in my community was George said he was going to come make his million and then walk away. That's exactly what he did. He did some massive strip mining above my parents' house, and then he walked off and left his sediment ponds and stuff. In 1974 I [got married and] left Dayhoit for eight years. There was this huge flood [while I was gone]—it almost washed our homeplace away. It destroyed our yard, our road, the creek, and everything. The terrain was never the same afterward. I remember coming home visiting one time, and my mom and dad were having to park down the road and walk to their house because the creek was actually running in the road rather than the creek. I called the magistrate, and I asked him, "What kind of car do you drive?" He told me [because] he was all into [his car]. [I asked him,] "Well how would you like to drive your car up and down this road?"

> Teri cites the flood at her family homeplace as the first event that propelled her into activism. After moving back to Dayhoit a few years later, the impacts of the coal industry on the health and safety of residents became more and more apparent to her. With each issue that arose, Teri became more vocal, demanding that the coal companies be held accountable for the harm they were bringing to her community.

I lived in Michigan for eight years. I got a divorce, [and] I came back [to Dayhoit] with two kids. I moved [back] to my community, thinking, "I'm bringing them home to a safe place." [After] this coal company came [in], you would have to drive through coal muck to get in and out of my community. Sometimes it would flood so bad with the coal muck and the runoff from this processing plant that it would be up to your headlights. I was just really mad about it, and I kept going [to the] county government saying, "You need to do something about this road. It's a county road—you ought to do something about it." To shut me up they built a road to my house. There was a county right-of-way that was supposed to go across my property to the graveyard, so they built this paved road up to my house so I wouldn't have to drive through that coal company place.

[Another] time I called [the road department] because my kids had to walk to the bottom of the hill [through coal muck] to get on the school bus. Rather than the road department coming and cleaning up the mess, which they should have done, the guy at the road department called the mining company and told them that I complained. The mining company sent a truck up to circle my house to frighten me. So, I called the guy back at the road department [and asked], "Did you do that?" I said, "Did you call them?" And he said, "Yeah." I said, "Well, I want to talk to your supervisor." Then he told me that it was something I had to learn to live with [because I lived] in a coal-mining community. I told him I begged to differ with him, [and] my kids didn't want coal muck up to their knees to get on the school bus.

[Then] I called the mining company and told them that if they thought they could intimidate me, they'd better think again; I'd fought with bigger dogs than them.

From Individual Action to Collective Action

Up until the early 1990s, Teri's activism was individual; she had taken it upon herself to act as a watchdog over the local coal company, making phone calls to the authorities when a problem arose. However, when she learned her community's water was contaminated with PCBs and other toxic chemicals, she began to see the importance of collective action in struggles for justice.

I found out in 1989 that this company from Houston, Texas, had dumped toxic waste into my community from 1951 to 1987 and then sold it as "environmentally clean" to a local company. They dumped hazardous waste on the ground and also burned transformer oil, which [contains] PCBs, in a fuel-burning furnace for seven years. My community was a federal superfund site, so it's one of the most contaminated areas in the nation. When a community group first started, they kept calling me, you know, "Teri you got to get involved." So, I went to my first public hearing with the community group in '90, '91, or something like that. My well was listed as one of the contaminated wells. Over two hundred volatile and semi-volatile organics, about six different carcinogens, and then all the heavy metals. It's a chemical soup, for God's sake.

I jumped right into [the community group] because my kids were sick all the time. I have two children, and they would just like break out in these rashes all over their body, and my daughter had lots of breathing problems and stuff. I would take them to the doctor and it's like, you know, they have this rash, and the doctor would say, "It's an allergic reaction and a measle-type rash." I [was] always racking my brain [for what caused it]. I didn't bring anything new into my house, you know, because they were so allergic to everything. When I found out that what was coming out of the faucet was what poisoned my children, it just made me mad as hell.

You grow up thinking, "Environmental Protection Agency—OK, they're going to protect me as a citizen." They had sent me a notice and told me my well water was good. I mean, the EPA sent me a letter and said it was good, so I continued to use it to wash my car and water my gardens and stuff. I paid a lot of money for that well—it was like $75 a month forever, and I [had] just got it paid off, and maybe ten months later they told me it was contaminated.

My niece is about twenty-four years old, [and] she has endometriosis really, really bad. Endometriosis is one of the side effects from the exposure to the chemicals. We call ourselves "the uterus-free community" because we have to have hysterectomies at a very young age here [from] endometriosis. Being a part of that [community] group and studying, learning—at one point I felt like a chemist. I could tell all of these chemicals and how many people will die out of one hundred thousand.

Sometime along the way, I read *Balancing the Scales*, which is [Kentuckians For The Commonwealth's] newspaper, and I thought, "Wow, these people think the same way I do." I've been a member and a leader in the organization ever since. [Kentuckians For The Commonwealth] was founded in the '80s [to make] the coal companies pay their fair share of taxes. That's how the organization actually came to be in the first place. It was called Kentucky Fair Tax Coalition. The message we try to portray is pro-Kentucky: we are *for* happy communities, we are *for* a sustainable economy, we are *for* clean water and healthcare for everyone. I'm not an activist against coal, I'm an activist *for* the preservation of my state, clean water, and clean air. Of course [the coal supporters] do really good at calling us anti-coal or anti-this, and so it's been really hard to change that whole frame. We have this project called the "Canary Project" and "Kentucky Beyond Coal." The canary project helps us talk about [the problems] in a different frame of mind: OK, when they get finished [mining coal], what are they going to leave us? [The point of the project is] trying to work *toward* something.

Community Challenges to Speaking Out

While Teri does not hesitate to speak out about irresponsible coal-industry practices herself, she recognizes that many local residents are afraid to speak out—or even report—problems related to coal mining.

My brother was on the mining side for years and years, and he [was] actually part of opening this processing plant in the community and [ran] it for awhile. My brother lived in this community, [and when he] ran this processing plant, the people of the community was constantly on him about cleaning the muck. He had to make sure that there was no runoff onto the road— they was calling him on his butt all the time about it. But then the outside operators come in. When these other thugs came in and took over, it was a whole different ballgame, [and people stopped reporting the problems]. I had creek watchers that would watch the creek [for coal-mining runoff]. This little old lady that lived way up the hollow from me was terrified to call, so when something would happen to the creek, she would call me, and I would call and complain about it. I didn't really care if they got upset at me.

Coal has been crippling Kentucky. Some people [say], "Well, we just want them to do it right; we know we have to have coal." [But] when we just narrowly focus on stopping mountaintop removal, then we're losing sight of the big picture. We have this movement afoot across the nation to stop mountaintop removal, [but if] we had a federal law passed tomorrow that said, "No more mountaintop removal," does that mean our movement is going to end? [That thought] really frightens me. Mountaintop removal is just a [part] of this huge, bigger problem—coal is an outlaw industry, and it's *always* operated above the law. Mountaintop removal is just one of the ways that they do it. What I keep screaming right now is, we have this global warming thing that is front-page news, and this is our window of opportunity to say, "Hey, this is what's happening and the destruction." We've lost six hundred thousand acres in Kentucky alone to surface mining. The whole impact of extraction is not part of the conversation about global warming, so I think I've taken that on as my responsibility to tell the rest of the world that, by God, this *has* to be a part of it.

In some of the communities coal is all we got, and [people think] it's like biting the hand that feeds you [to complain]. It's always been this boom or bust cycle, so there is either a whole lot of coal mining or it stops, and I think a lot of people are just waiting for that next time [coal is booming]. Some people are really frightened that if they stand up, then no one in their family is ever going to get a job in coal. And if that's their only choice—and I think we've been fed this line so much all of our lives, you know, "You can't fight city hall, you can't stand up against big business, you can't fight corporate America, your vote don't count, and a woman's place is in the home," and all—I think we've just been fed this stuff so much to the point that we believe it. I mean, it's just been engrained in us so much that we don't even realize that it's there until we really start challenging it. Appalachian people are humble, and they don't want to make waves, they just want to live and let live. They don't want somebody else telling them how to live, and they don't want to tell nobody else how to live. They're just too good to a fault.

Inspiration and Motivations for Activism

Despite the reluctance and fear many in her community feel about speaking against the coal industry, Teri has somehow been able to overcome her community's propensity toward silence. She attributes much of her strength and willingness to speak out about the injustices of the coal industry to the role model she had in her mother and to growing up during the politically charged years of the late 1960s and early 1970s.

My mother was just this really strong woman and strong willed, and I think that was always in the back of my head. I remember when I was a little-bitty kid, and we still lived on a dirt road and had to walk to school. We had a two-room schoolhouse in the community—the first through the eighth [grades] went to this school. Then they consolidated all the little two-room schools and sent us to another bigger school, [but] we didn't have a school bus. Some of the kids that lived way up the hollow, they would have to walk three or four miles to school. So my mom and one of the other ladies in town went to the school board and asked for a school bus. The school bus people decided we couldn't have a school bus [because] we didn't have a road. My mom [then] went to the road department and said, "We need a road." She *got* the road, and then once she got us a road, she went back to get us a school bus.

My mother worked her butt off. My father was an alcoholic for about the first fourteen years of my life, and my mother had six kids. She was orphaned when she was about five years old and was just raised by whoever in the family needed a slave. So family was really important to her. She worked at any job she could possibly get to make money to give us things. I never remember us being on any kind of social services whatsoever—not that there's anything wrong with it, but I guess her pride just wouldn't allow it. My mother was always into politics, and our income was supplemented by [her] political work. Ever since I was a little kid, we would go hanging [campaign] signs on the telephone poles. So, politics was always a part of our life. I also think maybe the Vietnam War had a lot to do with knowing that you could stand up. Watching the protests was exciting to me as a young girl. [My mother] would be so proud of me right now, she really would. She's been dead since about '91. She would be glad, she would love [what I am doing].

You know, there's been times that I think, "Oh my God, I need a normal life." All my life I've heard, "Ignorance is bliss." [You] never quite understand that until you really aren't ignorant anymore; [then] you learn exactly what that means. So a couple times I tried to say, "OK, I just need a normal life, I just need to go get a regular job. My worries need to be, 'What am I going to do this weekend?' or 'How am I going to spend my summer vacation?'" You know, most people, that's how they spend their lives. But then they got a permit to do mountaintop removal on Black Mountain, the highest point in the state of Kentucky—you have to fight that. And then another time there was the Martin County coal sludge spill. It's like, "OK, you got to do something about that."

[Also] just empowering the people [is a motivation], helping people find their voice—and democracy, for God's sake. I want democracy back in this country. I want people to start voting and holding people accountable when they vote for them. So, [it's] just knowing that there is a better way. I think I do feed on, like when [a community member] stood up and spoke for herself [for the first time], that does do something for me inside. Maybe that's a little bit selfish, but it excites me.

I know I'm not going to live very long because of my exposures to all the chemicals. Everybody in my community dies by the time they're about fifty-five years old, and very few of them last to sixty. I've come to grips with that. You don't drink five carcinogens in your drinking water your entire life [and live a long time]. I had cancer when I was twenty-nine, and I've watched so many of my friends and neighbors [die]. Right before I moved here [to Berea, Kentucky], I had five neighbors die at the same time—*five*. In my mother's family, they all die very young—I am the oldest generation in my mother's family. I want my life to really stand for something. When I'm dead and gone, I want [my grandsons] to say, "My grandmother did this," and it mean something. I want to make my mark in history, I guess. I just want to make a difference. I think if we all made a difference and we all stood for what we believed in, how much better this world would be.

"Just Being 'Emotional' and 'Passionate'": Gender and Activism

Like the other women in this book, Teri has seen through her years as an activist that many Appalachian women tend to be more willing to speak out about environmental justice issues than Appalachian men. When asked to reflect on why that might be, she responded,

Men's too chicken, I guess! That was a joke. I don't know, I think [women are] caregivers, we're the nurturers, we're the ones that worry about our homeplace, we're the one that worries about feeding our children. I think that's a part of us. I mean, if I had to, I could feed you a meal out of this yard, [from] the weeds and stuff that's growing here. I think that women are the caregivers, the nurturers, and they realize that to destroy your own home is destroying your future.

In addition to the determination and strength that Teri sees in Appalachian women activists, she also recognizes that women activists are frequently

I've been called passionate many times—I'm just being "emotional" and "passionate" because I'm a woman. That is dismissive of the actual—of what I'm saying. They [dismiss] my actions by saying I'm passionate: "Oh, you're, like, really *passionate* about this issue, aren't you?" I was in Frankfort [the capital of Kentucky] two years ago, and I was talking to one of the representatives that was writing a bill about mine safety. The biggest thing that came out of that bill that year was drug testing the miners. So of course it's the *miners'* fault that they get killed, not the fact that the company's not obeying the law. I got really upset over the drug-testing thing because I felt that it was just the company's way of getting out of being responsible. Me and him were sitting there debating this. I said, "Oh, does that mean if someone smokes a joint last week and it still shows up in their system this week and they're killed in an accident, their widow and children's not going to get anything because [the miner tested positive for drugs]?" So me and him argued about it. My youngest brother died at the age of forty-one as the result of a mining accident in those same mines—Darby mines—that the guys were killed in last year in Kentucky. You know, all of that sort of opened up wounds for me. And so we're debating this issue, and I told him that my brother was killed, and his answer was, "You're really emotional about this." You know, I watched my father smother to death from black lung, my brother die, and people around me get injured—their lives are worth nothing. They go to the doctor, and the only thing the doctors do for them is drug them rather than treat them. So yeah, his answer to all of it is like, "Oh you're just really passionate about this," rather than, "Let's address the issue." [Saying] I'm just really passionate about it [is] a way they think they can dismiss me and what I say.

Finding Strength through the Activist Community

You know, sometimes it's quite isolating [being an activist]. I think my children took a lot of crap in school. You know, "Your mother is a radical." It's like, "Oh yeah, [I'm] asking for clean air and clean water—that's really a radical idea." It can get worse than that, you know, we've been called communist and hysterical housewives and the whole thing. Popovich, who is the spokesperson for the National Mining Association, said that environmental extremists were waging "jihad" on the coal industry. Now it's jihad! *They* are the real terrorists—the only people bombing America is the coal industry!

While Teri often feels isolated from others in her hometown because of her environmental justice activism, she finds belonging and support through her activist community. It is these connections that sustain her and keep her strong despite the challenges she faces.

My "community" is my activist friends. I love them. I mean, I could go and climb on an airplane and go anywhere, and you walk in the room, whether it be twenty people or two hundred people, and you're at home. You could not know a soul there, [but] you know you're walking into *your community* because you know those people would not be there unless they had the same heart you did. So it's like you never feel like you walk into a room full of strangers. You know that you're walking into a room full of love, because those people love what they do or else they wouldn't be doing it. That's really the great part about it.

Since our interview in 2007, Teri has been involved in numerous protests and events to raise awareness about the true cost of cheap energy. She has been arrested three times for her acts of civil disobedience. The first time she was arrested was in September 2010 at the first Appalachia Rising event in Washington, D.C., which was a mass mobilization calling for the end to mountaintop-removal mining. Her second arrest occurred in September 2011, when she participated in the Tar Sands Action at the White House to call on President Obama to deny the TransCanada Keystone pipeline permit. Teri believes this to have been an important act of solidarity, telling me during a phone conversation in 2012,

I believe we must all stand together. It would be a hollow victory if we stop mountaintop removal in Appalachia and just moved the resource extraction to another community. I believe we should all join hands to move our nation to a new energy economy. Changing deck chairs on the Titanic isn't going to save you.

Teri's most recent arrest was again in Washington, D.C., during Appalachia Rising in June 2012. As Teri explains, she and other Kentucky activists have been trying to meet with Representative Hal Rogers for the past seven years, but he has repeatedly refused. During Appalachia Rising, about twenty people occupied Representative Rogers's office with hopes of meeting with him, but yet again, he denied their request. Teri and six other Kentuckians were arrested that day and "faced misdemeanor charges for singing Amazing Grace in Hal Rogers's office." Other Appalachia Rising participants were also arrested in the offices of Representative Nick Rahall from West Virginia, Morgan Griffith from Virginia, and Jimmy Duncan from Tennessee.

CHAPTER 7

"I'm Not Going to Be Run Out, I'm Not Going to Be Run Over, I'm Not Going Out without a Fight"

Patty Sebok's Battle against Monster Coal Trucks

Patty Sebok wearing a shirt printed with her favorite quote, "Well behaved women seldom make history" (Laurel Thatcher Ulrich). Photo by the author.

Patty Sebok is a lifelong resident of the Coal River Valley in Boone County, West Virginia, and has been an outspoken activist against overweight coal trucks and irresponsible mining practices for more than a decade. Born in 1955, Patty spent most of her adult life living in the community of Prenter. Patty's husband, Butch, worked as an underground union coal miner for almost thirty years and has always supported her community and activist work.

I conducted interviews with Patty during the summers of 2006, 2007, and 2008. Patty was also a participant in the Photovoice project I organized in Southern West Virginia from 2008 to 2009, and some of her photostories are included at the end of this chapter.

Patty's entry into community activism began in 1989, when she and other women in her community set up a multi-day roadblock with their own bodies to protest the dust problems speeding coal trucks were causing in their hollow. This protest coincided with (but was separate from) the Pittston Coal Strike in Virginia.

The Coal Truck Protest of '89

There's a little side hollow in my hollow—it's a branch, a dirt road, and it's right below our house. That's where these coal trucks were coming out of, and when [the Massey mine] first went in there, they promised everybody that they would keep the road watered because you had retired miners with breathing problems, black lung, kids with asthma, and different things like that. They told the people that they'd water the roads—they had the water truck, and they promised that they would do that. Well, that summer was really dry, and for some reason, they quit watering. I got a phone call from some of the women that lived there; they had asked [Massey] to water [the road], and they out-and-out refused to do it. So, [the women] said, "Do you want to come and join us? We're going to stand here in the road and we're going to block these trucks." I said, "Well, I might come down that way and see what's going on." So, I walked down that road and joined them one day. We stood in the road and blocked the road with just, you know, us standing there.

When [the coal trucks] came, we had already decided [we would] walk them down the road, make them drive real slow because they were speeding, too. That ticked 'em off real bad. We [spread] all the way across the road, and when a car would come up the road we would get into the middle line and let that one go up, and then we'd spread back out, because [the coal trucks] did try to rush us and go around us. We found out later that some of the drivers was like, talking on their CBs, talking about how much extra money [the coal company would] pay them, you know, they'd pay 'em three hundred dollars for every load they could get by us—coal was probably twenty or thirty dollars a ton then. The longer it goes on, the more it builds and the madder they get at ya. We marched probably a good two miles before the law came. Then we just turned around and walked back up the road and did it again. So, it built and built and built.

After we had done it a few days, they were getting madder and madder at us. They [finally] said, "We'll water the roads." They'd sporadically water it, but they were still *flying up* the mountain. And like I said, it being a little hollow and a dirt road, people live real close [to the road]. Your kids is always wanting to ride their bike or play or whatever—well, they couldn't.

I don't even know how it came about, all I know is we got a phone call that said, "The union's gonna bring some people down, and how would you all like to get arrested?" I was like, "I don't know, I've never been arrested in my life. I don't really want to go to jail." And they're like, "No, they'll set it up, they'll take care of it, they'll take care of everybody's bail, it will be all right." It was like, "Well, maybe then."

So, the morning that [the arrest] was to be, it was pourin' rain, of course. [The union miners] told us, "We went down there, and there was a whole bunch of men in camouflage. We want you women up front when the law gets here." And we were like, "OK." Five hundred of us went to jail over the coal trucks.

Later we heard that the reason that they were rushing and didn't want to water the road, didn't want to slow down, didn't want to do nothing was they were trying to fill the supply for Pittston Coal, because Pittston was on strike. We heard that Pittston had made an agreement with Massey to buy their coal in order to fill an order they couldn't fill because of the strike. A lot of people said, "You just did it for the union." And we were like, "No, we didn't know that when it started." It started over something as simple as [the coal company] not wanting to water our road.

Fighting Monster Coal Trucks

Over the next ten years, the coal truck problem steadily intensified. The trucks became larger and larger, and it became common practice for these coal trucks to carry loads that were more than double the legal weight limit. In 2000 and 2001, there was a rash of deaths caused by out-of-control, overweight coal trucks, resulting in a public outcry. There were a series of community meetings about the coal truck problem, and it was through one of these meetings that Patty met Judy Bonds and found her way to Coal River Mountain Watch.

From '89 to 2000, [coal trucks] went from what they call the tandem dump trucks to the eighteen-wheelers. They've gotten bigger, there's more of them,

[and] no law enforcement. We were told [by law enforcement], "If they pull off the side of the road, we can't weigh 'em." For speeding, if you would call, it's like, "Well, by the time I get there, they're gonna be gone—what do you want me to do about it?" You know, that was the enforcement. We had no enforcement. It done absolutely no good to complain because nobody cared—nobody was gonna do anything.

I absolutely had coal trucks going by [my house] 24–7. The only time there was a break in the traffic was if there was an accident, if DOT [Department of Transportation] came out with the scales to weigh them, or at shift change sometimes there would be a half an hour, forty-five minutes that you wouldn't see a lot of trucks out. Other than that, it was 24–7. I lived up the hollow, approximately three-and-a-half miles, and it was nothing for me to be ran off the road three times in each direction just trying to get out or back up to where I lived.

I didn't want [the coal trucks] driving through my community like they were doing. How would they feel if I came to their community in a big *tank* like that with their kids out playing or trying to learn how to drive and run down the road like that—how would they like it? These roads are narrow, especially the hollows, and they have stiff curves. Of course the faster and the more weight [the trucks] have on them, they can't keep on their side [of the road]—there's no way humanly possible. So, anytime that you came up to a curve, there might be a truck right in the middle of your lane [coming the opposite direction]. The other thing was they would tailgate so close that you look in your rearview—I was driving a full-size Bronco at the time—and all I could see was the grill of their truck. [I would be thinking], "I gotta pull off down the road here, and I don't know if this guy's brakes are gonna work. If I have to cross a lane of traffic, I might not be able to just pull straight off the road, I might have to stop and sit there. I might end up like those people in Hernshaw."[1] So it was pretty scary. I told people, "You haven't known fear until you look in your rearview and all you see is that grill, and you know you've got to pull off right down the road there, and you don't know if that guy's gonna be able to stop." So that's why I decided I don't care what they think, and I don't care what they do—I'm gonna speak out until they stop doing what they've been doing.

So that's why I stood up and started fighting, because I thought, "What have I got to lose?" They're going to kill me or my kids on the road, and it wasn't just in my hollow. Anytime I would do my errands it was just very, very dangerous. I was just, you know, a housewife and a mother doing my thing, taking care of my home and my kids. It had got to the point that when I walked to my gate, my chest got really tight because I dreaded to have to go out on the road with these people. And I said, "When I step out on the road in my vehicle, every time I go out, my life is in their hands." That's the way I felt about it. My life was truly in their hands.

They told us that they actually felt like it was their God-given right to haul overloaded and speed and drive on the wrong side of the road, even though it was against the law, because they were bigger than us and they work for the coal industry, and they had to make a living—like the rest of us don't! The way I see it, it was *not* their God-given right. Their rights stop when they start to infringe on *my* rights. I don't care who it is—right's right and wrong's wrong. I thought I lived in the United States and that I had some rights. I thought I had the right to be safe on my road and that they should enforce the law to make these trucks stay on their side and do the speed limit like I've always done. But it wasn't happening. I've always heard the squeaky wheel gets the oil, so I had to squeak real loud!

Patty Finds Coal River Mountain Watch

[Public] meetings [about the coal-truck problem] started to happen in the communities of Hernshaw and Marmet after the death of an older brother and sister in 2001. They were killed right in front of their family member's home. It's a very strange story—they were on their way to another family member's funeral, and they had stopped to turn left across the lane of traffic. So they were sitting there, minding their own business with their turn signal light on, making a last-minute stop to [the house of] one of their family members. A coal truck that was overloaded [behind them] could not stop. He ran off the edge of the road [but] caught the corner of their bumper. And when he caught the corner of their bumper, he knocked them over into the other lane, and an empty coal truck hit them and killed them. It was just terrible. Everyone was outraged because it wasn't just one or two people—everybody had to face this that lived in the coalfields. The trucks were like that everywhere.

Marmet City Council [called] a meeting. The guys on city council, several of them worked at Kroger [grocery store] with [a woman named] Ruth Cooper. In '89, the day after Christmas, she had lost her daughter, son-in-law, and two grandbabies to one coal truck that ran over them. It wasn't far from her house, and it was the day after Christmas. She had mounted a big campaign after that—it was all over the news, in the newspaper, and we really, really thought that, you know, somethin' would happen because it was such a big thing in the news and lasted so long. Well, she had petitions signed and everything else, and it was presented to the legislature. They told her they would "do a study." If they studied it, they didn't do anything about it.

The guys on city council knew Ruth and what happened [in 1989], so they called Ruth and asked her if she knew anybody from over this way that she could bring to their meeting. My sons lifted weights with her sons. She knew that I had been outspoken [about the coal trucks in the past], and she called me up and asked me if I'd like to go to that meeting with her. So, that's how I got started with the first meeting at Marmet. Then at that [meeting], some gentleman stood up and said, "Next week Hernshaw's gonna have a meeting." I met Judy [Bonds] at the Hernshaw meeting. When she stood up and spoke, she talked about an office there in Whitesville, and I'm like, "I don't know who that is, and I don't know anything about an office in Whitesville, but let's find out." We were in a little church basement, and you couldn't put a sheet of paper in there between the people. So, I sent my friend Lori—I'm like, "I can't get up there, Lori, so you work your way through there and grab her and don't let her get away." [Judy and I] exchanged information, and that's when I found out about the office [Coal River Mountain Watch].

Like most people, I knew that there was mountaintop-removal mining, but I had no idea how extensive it was. I mean, I knew it was happening, but I had no idea how many sites, how many acres, I didn't know about the blasting and the flooding problems that were associated with it, but I did learn that the coal trucks were coming off of these mountaintop-removal sites, [and] that that was part of my problem. I didn't become an employee at Coal River 'til 2002, but even before that, I worked with Judy going to meetings and to the Capitol, and we went to lots of meetings together and did things. So that's when I learned more about mountaintop removal. When I started to work [at Coal River Mountain Watch], I worked on basically just coal-truck stuff. I told her with my husband being an underground coal miner, "I don't really know how I feel about this." And she said, "Well, you don't have to do anything that you don't feel comfortable doing." So I thought, "Well, that sounds OK," and I started in April of 2002.

The Statewide Battle against Overweight Coal Trucks

In response to the public outcry against dangerous coal trucks, Delegate Mike Caputo (D-Marion) introduced a bill in the West Virginia legislature in 2002 to increase enforcement of the coal-truck weight limits. Coal-industry-supporting legislators quickly introduced retaliatory legislation to raise maximum legal weight limits for coal trucks from 80,000 pounds to 132,000 pounds (with a 5 percent variance) (Nyden 2002). Neither bill passed during the 2002 session, but the topic reemerged in the 2003 legislative session. Activists continued to push for stronger enforcement of coal-truck weight limits, while the opposition called for an increase in weight limits. Patty and Judy spent many hours lobbying at the capitol for stricter enforcement of coal-truck weight limits during both the 2002 and 2003 legislative sessions. Patty and Judy could always be spotted with poster-sized photographs of coal truck accidents, along with stickers that played off of the popular coal industry slogan, "Coal Keeps the Lights On." Their stickers retorted, "Coal Keeps the Lights on in West Virginia Funeral Homes. Stop Over-loaded Trucks."

Patty, Judy, and the other activists fighting overweight coal trucks often felt threatened and outnumbered at the capitol, especially in 2003 when the coal industry urged coal-truck drivers to show up in droves to protest stricter enforce-ment measures. Below Patty describes one particularly intimidating run-in that she and Judy had in the downstairs lobby of the capitol while they were waiting for a meeting to start.

We're standing there and Hoppy Kercheval, the Metronews talk show radio host, was interviewing Bill Raney, the president of the West Virginia Coal Association. They're not six feet from where we're standing, and about six foot around on the other side of the fountain [is a] state trooper. We thought, "Well these [coal-truck drivers] won't bother us because they've got cameras all over this place." But they [kept] circling us like sharks, I felt like the bloody fish in the water [with] the sharks circling it. Well, little did we know, that was the only place that didn't have a camera. These men [were] circling us and getting in closer and closer. There's just me and Judy there, and we had our posters up against the wall, and like I said, talk-show radio host about six foot away, state trooper not six foot away on the other side. Next thing I know, these guys keep moving in closer and closer. The state trooper looks over at them and looks at us, [and] takes off, takes a walk—yeah. We were standing there talking, and I see this one [guy] get this ["Coal Keeps the Lights On"] sticker out. And I said, "Judy, they're going to put that on our poster, I know they are." She said, "No they're not." I said, "Yes they are." Then he comes over and he's ripping it off [the backing], and he's looking at the poster. And she's going, "No, sir, please don't do that, please don't do that!" And he rips it off and sticks it on there. When he did that, when [Judy] kept telling him, "No!" and he did it, she went, "Security!" and it echoed off the wall. Everyone shut up 'til you could have heard a pin drop, echoing off those walls. And it was funny because, you know, the guy's go-ing, "Security? Where? Where?" And I'm standing with my back against this wall, you know, both of us, and she looks over at Bill Raney and Hoppy, and Hoppy, he's finished the interview and he's packing up his shit. He wants to get the hell out of there, he don't want nothing to do with us. So Judy goes, "One of us is going to go downstairs and get security." [The coal-truck driver] said, "I've got every right to be here." And I looked him right dead in the eye and I said, "Yes you do. But you don't have the right to touch our property. How disrespectful is it to these two dead people [in the photograph], what you just done," I said. And it shocked him. He didn't know what to say because I said, "Yes, you have the right to be here." [He said], "Well, I'll just plaster these [stickers] all over the wall." I said, "You know what? That's a great idea. If I was you, I'd do that." I said, "Go right ahead. If I was you, I'd go downstairs and I'd put them everywhere." I tried to get him to do it right in front of the governor's office.

Judy said, "Well you stay here and I'll go and look [for security]." "I don't want to stay here," [I said]. And she said, "Somebody has to stay here." I said, "Yeah, you're right, because we'd never be able to show our faces back." So I was standing up against the rotunda wall watching, and the head of the trucker's association comes by, and all these guys gathered around on each side of him, you know. And I held up [the poster], and I said, "Look what they done to our poster, Corky!" He went, "Who done it? Which one of them done it?" And I looked around because the guy [had] ran out the door and went outside. By that time, I went from fear to anger, and I said, "How am I supposed to know? The chicken-shit ran out the door when he done it." And they all started [making clucking sounds]. They wanted to get me so bad—slam me over that wall—but I knew they wouldn't with him standing there, though. I said, "Yeah, the chicken-shit ran out the door."

I really didn't want to fight them—I thought that we could all help each other, that they would get, you know, better wages, and their trucks would be taken care of better, the wear and tear on them, because of the weight. But they'd listen to the other side, and I guess some of them were truly scared. And some of them, I have to say, they must've just been ignorant—if they would have used their brain and thought it over, they would have seen that we were right. But, they didn't want to hear it from us, and of course the other side that was holdin' their paycheck was tellin' them, "These people want to take your job!" You know, but we really wanted them to make more money, and haul less, and be safer. That's what we really wanted. We did talk to a few of them and say, "Look, we'll stand with you. We'll stand right in the road and we'll block those other trucks. We won't let them have your job. But you have to stand up with us, we're not gonna do it for you, but we'll help you." And it just flew right out the other ear.

They held these meetings [about the coal-truck problem] all over the state. [Coal-truck drivers] kept going, "We can't make a living if we don't haul [overweight]." And we said, "Well, ask them how the northern truckers can haul less and make a living if the southern truckers can't. We want to know that, we really think it's a good question."

> The coal trucks used in the northern part of the state were notably smaller than those in the southern coal-mining region, and, as a result, the northern region did not have the same problem with overweight coal trucks as did southern West Virginia.

[Delegate] Caputo asked [why truckers in the north don't have to haul overloaded to make a living]. This [coal-truck driver from northern West Virginia] stood up there and stuttered around a little bit, and he said, "It's a cultural difference between the north and the south." Cultural difference? I looked at Judy and I said, "What the hell does that mean?" I thought for a little bit, and then it hit me. I said, "He's calling us ignorant." He is, he's calling us ignorant. "It's a *cultural* difference." If that's not a slap in the face, I don't know what is. They always say, "South of U.S. 60, don't go there. They're ignorant hillbillies." Well, I think that the answer was that the southern truck drivers are stupid, they were calling them uneducated. Because when they wanted to bid for a job contract [to truck coal from a particular coal mine], it was whoever bid the lowest [per ton] got the job. So they would underbid and keep cut-throating each other 'til they weren't making anything. And of course, you know, the coal companies said, "Well, the stupid idiots."

> Because it was common practice in southern West Virginia for trucking companies that hauled coal to underbid each other so aggressively for a coal-company contract, hauling more coal with each load (by hauling overweight) and hauling coal faster (by speeding) became the only way for these companies, and their drivers, to turn a profit. Patty was quick to assert, though, that the problem was not simply a "cultural" problem; it was a structural problem. The "billion dollar coalfields" of southern West Virginia have intentionally been kept a monoeconomy since the early 1900s, and as such, the region has long been plagued by political corruption. The coal companies in southern West Virginia accepted (and encouraged) trucking bids that they knew were too low to be legal. Furthermore, Patty and Judy learned through their investigations that the Department of Transportation (DOT) was employing a "turn-the-other-way" approach to coal-truck weight-limit enforcement in southern West Virginia.

[The coal trucks] had what they called "spotters." They would get on their cell phones or their CBs and let the truckers [on the other side of the mountain] know where DOT was [with] the scales. They [would] pull off the side of the road and lock their truck up. [DOT] told us the law is they legally can't weigh [a truck if it's already pulled over on the side of the road], which was a lie. The way they had to weigh it was say, "You pull it up on the scales or I'm going to bring a tow truck and I'll pull it up on the scales and weigh it." But they wouldn't do that, the law wouldn't do that. When Governor Underwood was in office, he actually told [the DOT], "Go up north and leave the southern coalfields alone" with the weight crews. It doesn't get much more blatant than that.

"They Had a Hit Out on Me": The Backlash

It was very, very dangerous before we started to fight them, but after we started to fight them, that's when they started to swerve at us on purpose. A few of the drivers knew me, and a lot of them went by my home. The ones that were haulin' by my house every day, they saw me. I had a Bronco that was one-of-a-kind. They knew I had been in the newspaper, they knew I had been in the news. But before that, I had been out in my yard holding up a sign, "School starts tomorrow, the speed limit's thirty-five." There was two coal-truck accidents at the high school where both my sons went. One of [the coal trucks] hit the other one, rear-ended him right in front of the school. I held the poster up right there from my yard and from my driveway. The news came and interviewed me in my driveway one day, and [the coal trucks] were all coming by. Then here come one of the truck bosses, and he made four or five trips by—oh, I was rantin' and ravin' because I was so ticked! "Who does he think he is to come trottin' by here like that when I'm in my driveway, think[ing] he can intimidate me and the news here?"

It's three to three-and-a-half miles up this hollow, and I couldn't go out that three-and-a-half miles without being run off the road a minimum of three times by a coal truck. At first it was just because they were speeding and overloaded and stuff like that. Then after I started to speak out, it got worse because they knew who I was and [that] I was speaking out. We got a portable CB for my birthday so I could listen and see if they were trying to run over me. I have set here and listened to them late at night with my lights off, and I've listened to them say, "I'd like to just let my truck go plumb through that trailer right there." "Well I would just like to back up there and dump my whole load on them." I've heard them say, "I'd like to catch that [Bronco] behind my truck and just open my gate and let it all out on them."

Well, that portable CB would [only] pick up so far within the hollow, but [Butch's] friend had a base CB, and he told him a year after the coal-truck deal was passed that they had a hit out on me. They were going to catch me between two coal trucks and crush me to smithereens. They were saying that on the CB. I pretty much know about the time that it happened. When you went up Lens Creek Mountain, [the coal trucks] were so loaded then, they could barely do five miles an hour up that mountain. It made it really dangerous because everybody was trying to get out and around them [because] nobody wanted to follow them up and down that mountain. They didn't have a third lane there then, and so if you were passing and you were trying to pass three to five coal trucks all in a caravan bumper-to-bumper, and here comes a coal truck down [the opposite side] coming to get its load—just flying because it's empty—you're hurting. So they started to flag me out, and there was traffic coming. Put [their] signal on, wave me around, and traffic was coming. I wouldn't go—I just shook my head and looked at them like, "You're stupid, I wouldn't pass you."

[Butch has] been talking about it for a couple of years, but I'm about ready to go take me a weapons course and get me a concealed weapons permit. I'll just put it right under here on a shoulder harness and pack it with me. And if they got something to say, I'll put it right in their face. "Talk to my gun, I don't want to hear your voice yet." Because I'm not going to be run out, I'm not going to be run over, I'm not going out without a fight.

> After a two-year battle, the West Virginia legislature finally passed a coal-truck safety bill. Senate Bill 583 mandated stricter monitoring and enforcement of coal-truck weight limits and speed limits. The bill transferred enforcement responsibility from the Department of Transportation to the Public Service Commission, and a public complaint hotline (1–866-SEE-TRUX) was initiated. While these measures were an important step forward for improving the safety of the roadways in southern West Virginia, the coal industry was also granted a big victory with the passage of this bill. Senate Bill 583 also increased weight limits on designated coal transportation routes from 80,000 pounds to 120,000 pounds, with a 5 percent variance (in other words, up to 126,000 pounds). Patty and other coal truck activists were disappointed with the weight limit increase, but thankfully, they have seen significant improvements in monitoring and enforcement of the new law.

A Highly Gendered Experience

> Patty recognizes that her gender has played a significant role in many facets of her activism, from how she has been treated by government agencies and coal-company executives to the names she and other women activists have been called. During her earlier activism against dangerous coal trucks, Patty was called "The Blonde Bitch" by coal-truck drivers. In her later activism, gendered insults and threats have continued to be used against her and the other women activists.

[For] one of the [protest] trips with the union, we met over at the Magic Mart parking lot. They had vans they rented and hauled us down [to the capitol].

A friend of mine named Lori was planning on going, [but] she didn't go. When we got back, her husband found a note on his truck windshield that said, "Bobby, keep your bitch off the road or she could be run over. You know, brakes fail on these trucks all the time." So she filed a report with the state police, but what are you going to do? It's not signed, you don't know who put it on there. So then she and I both went to [Attorney General] Darrell McGraw's office to show them and give them a copy of [the note] to make sure they were aware of it. We both told them, "If we die, we want you to investigate. We don't want the state police to investigate." They were like, "Well, what do you mean?" [We said], "You heard what I said. If I come up dead, I don't want the state police to investigate in any way, shape, or form." And so we tried to protect ourselves the best way we knew how—we decided that it would be to our advantage [to talk to the media] because that way we [would be] high profile.

They said Judy and I were "media whores"—we were just out to be in the news and be in the media. I'm not that stupid. Doing a story on the local news and my local papers is not going to get me anywhere. The reason that Judy and I did step out to the forefront and did do so many of those interviews was for two reasons. Number one, it was the only way to get a bill passed and make our roads safer. Number two, it was to protect our asses because we were flopping in the wind out there on our own. When they want to come after us, who was going to protect us? Nobody but ourselves. And yes, we've been known, Judy and I, as the "Babes of the coal-truck issue," but it wasn't because we wanted the media attention. It was to get the job done and to protect ourselves.

[Being a woman] can go against you, [or] it can work for you. I think sometimes doors might open a little easier for women. I think that most of the state legislators and Bill Raney and people like that in the coal industry, I think that they thought we would just be there for a day or two and we would go away and listen to whatever they said. I think that it opened the door, in a way, because they thought that it would be a revolving door. But then, to tip the scale back the other way, when you're dealing with government agencies or coal companies and stuff, I don't think they take a woman as seriously as they do a man, especially when it comes to the coal industry thing. Just like with the coal-truck issue. They'd say, "Well, how do you know that truck's overweight?" And, "How do you know this, and how do you know that?" I said, "Well I'm not completely stupid. I have eyes, I can see. When we see loads of coal humped up above the truck, we know it's overweight, and when I see the wires sticking out of the back of the tire, it's pretty obvious that that tire is unsafe."

They accused us of being "emotional." That was all it was—it was just emotion. It had nothin' to do with the law being broke, or anything—it was just emotion! Well, that came back and it bit [them]. In the heat of the two-year [battle] to get the safety bill passed, I believe it was Channel 8 news, they had went over to the Kanawha River Terminals over around [the] Marmet area. One of the camera guys was filming—all he was doing was standing beside the road filming what they call their "B footage," just to show on the news. He was filming a truck going in [the terminal], didn't say anything, didn't try to interview him or anything, and the driver gets mad. It was just great—[the driver] aims that truck right at that guy, and the guy had to literally jump out of the way with the camera! And [with] him filming it! They put that on the news—it was on the news for a long time. That was good enough, but the best part of it all was they made this truck driver go and meet with this cameraman and apologize. They filmed it all. And he said, "I don't know what happened, my *emotions* just overtook me." [Claps her hands] It was great! I loved it! That was the last time they used that word "emotional" with *us*!

There may be a few activists that have the little letters Ph.D. and things like that after their name, and that sometimes will give you more clout as a woman. [But] most of us living in the coalfields don't have those degrees. So sometimes we're not taken as seriously. When it comes to people in power places in government and stuff, I don't think they take women as seriously. As a matter of fact, being on the picket line, I've had a state trooper tell me, "You need to go home and do your dishes and [look after] your kids, where you should be." I said, "I do have some dirty dishes down there. You volunteering to do them?!" But then again, on the other hand, we're not seen as much of a threat as a man would be, especially in this area. So I think it can work for you or against you. Women are used to being told "No," so we don't usually stop at the first no. I [also] think that, as a woman, we were easier to approach than [men]. I think it made it easier for the people that were having problems with coal trucks [to talk with us]. So it's really a balancing act, because it can go either way.

The Fight for Clean Water in Prenter

In 2007, a new issue of concern surfaced in Patty's community: water contamination.

After residents of Rawl in Mingo County, West Virginia, discovered that their well water was contaminated with coal waste from a leaking underground slurry injection site, Patty and others living in the Prenter area began questioning whether the same thing was happening in their community. Patty and other employees and volunteers from Coal River Mountain Watch began to investigate the water problems that were emerging in the community of Prenter, where Patty had lived her entire adult life. Patty is certain that her husband's kidney problems were tied to the water problems in Prenter. In the fall of 2007, Patty helped organize the first community meetings about the water problems in Prenter. She and Maria Lambert—whose story is told in chapter 5—were integral to the fight that ultimately brought clean water to Prenter Hollow three years later.

Most recently, Patty has moved on to working with another community group, called the Boone-Raleigh Community Group, which was started by Lorelei Scarboro (whose story is also in this book).

Patty recognizes that over the past ten years of activism, her perspective on the coal industry has changed dramatically. When she first started working for Coal River Mountain Watch in 2002, she limited her work to the coal-truck issue because she was not sure how she felt about fighting mountaintop-removal mining, since her husband was a long-time underground union coal miner. However, as she learned more about the devastation of mountaintop-removal mining, she became one of the most outspoken activists against the practice and now sees her activism as reaching even beyond issues just related to coal extraction.

[My activism has] opened up my knowledge of different things that I never knew about before. It's really made me aware of [what] some people call a "web of life," how everything's connected. Everything from our food supply to our water supply [to] all the pollution. Everything is connected. [My] dad always gardened, and he would always keep seeds to restart his garden the next year. Well, now through genetic engineering, those seeds are not of any use whatsoever. Not only that, but they don't know what it's going to do to you down the line. I never knew this before I became an activist—that the growth hormones and the steroids and the antibiotics that they feed the animals are coming down our food line. I mean, it's just setting up a whole world of bad. Who would have ever thought, you know, that you'd be learning about stuff like that when you started out fighting your own little battle here about coal? It has become a battle [about] everything.

"Nature's Beauty"

PATTY SEBOK

We rescued this orange honeysuckle from Williams Mountain before a strip mine site buried it under tons of rubble. I wanted to make sure it would be available for future generations to see. It smells so wonderful in the spring—I see why it's called "honeysuckle." Honeysuckle grows wild in the most rugged, rocky, and sandy soil on top of mountain ridges, like the yellow honeysuckle in the upper left.

"Loss of Access"

PATTY SEBOK

This is a picture of Georgie Branch, which we can no longer get to because of Mountaintop Removal mining. There are a lot of places we used to go mollymoocher hunting, berry picking, and four-wheeling that we can't get to anymore because they've either been mined over or the access is closed off.

"Coal Fork"

PATTY SEBOK

We had to stop four-wheeling here, as it was strip-mined again, and coal trucks were hauling through here. Guards would stop you and ask you to not even stop to take photos. This photo was taken in Laurel Creek hollow at the bottom of the mountain.

"Pink Sunset at the Mouth of Prenter Hollow"

PATTY SEBOK

This is a beautiful sunset over the mouth of Prenter Hollow. I have to wonder if the blasting and destruction also causes some of the most beautiful sunsets we have today. I have read that the U.S. Geological Survey says our pink sunsets are caused by dust and smoke in the air. To me this means that even though we are destroying some of our most fertile and beautiful mountains and streams, God still gives us beauty even in the wake of destruction.

CHAPTER 8

"Our Roots Run So Deep, You Can't Distinguish Us from the Earth We Live On"

Debbie Jarrell and the Campaign to Move Marsh Fork Elementary School

Debbie Jarrell being arrested at a 2005 protest against Massey Energy's Goals Coal Processing Plant and Edwight Surface Mine, both located next to Marsh Fork Elementary School. Photo courtesy of Vivian Stockman/Ohio Valley Environmental Coalition.

Debbie Jarrell and her husband Ed Wiley became involved in the environmental justice movement when they initiated a campaign to move the students of Marsh Fork Elementary School to a safer learning environment. The children who attended this school, one of whom was their granddaughter Kayla, played in a playground that stood in the shadow of a massive coal preparation plant with a coal silo looming a mere 225 feet from the school building. At this facility (run by Goals Coal Company, a subsidiary of Massey Energy [now Alpha Resources]), coal is pulverized into a fine powder and "washed" with carcinogenic chemicals to remove the noncombustible materials, such as sulfur. The processed coal is then loaded into trains and is shipped to coal-fired power plants all over the country. The classrooms at Marsh Fork Elementary School were found to be contaminated with coal dust, the inhalation of which is linked to respiratory problems and other health conditions. In addition to its proximity to the coal-processing plant, the elementary school was also situated four hundred yards from the Brushy Fork Slurry Impoundment, which is a gargantuan industry-created lake storing 2.8 billion gallons of coal waste produced by the preparation plant during the coal-washing process. Just beyond the impoundment is the Marfork mountaintop removal mining operation (also a Massey subsidiary). Concerns about the safety of their granddaughter and the other 230 children attending Marsh Fork Elementary was the motivating force that drew both Debbie and Ed into the environmental justice movement.

I interviewed Debbie at her home in Rock Creek, West Virginia, in August 2006.

In October of 2000, there was a sludge-impoundment break in Kentucky,[1] and that was considered the worst disaster in the eastern United States. It was bigger than the Valdez [oil] spill. My husband Ed, he was working for a contracting company at that time that had done contract work on all the strip mines in our area—and of course, most of those are owned by Massey. He was called to go to Kentucky to help clean this sludge spill up, so they spent a couple of days down there doing that work. Right after he returned home from doing that, he got a call from his boss stating that there was a 911 down at the Goals Coal Company. A 911 meant, "Come now, we need you *now*." That's where the school [Marsh Fork Elementary] was at. [The coal facility] is located right beside the school down there. He got down there, and due to some heavy rains that we'd had, they were afraid that the [sludge] dam was going to fail at that time. They had to put pumps in that sludge impoundment to divert water out of it. [The dam] has a capacity of 2.8 billion gallons, [and] it's 385 foot tall. Now in Buffalo Creek,[2] that [slurry impoundment] was only [132] million gallons, [and it] killed 125 [people], mostly children. So this is a capacity of 2.8 billion. Apparently, it was full to capacity at that time or they wouldn't have put that 911 out for [Ed] to come down there.

Ever since [that event], there has been numerous days that we couldn't allow our granddaughter to go [to school] out of our fear. It was totally our fear that something was going to happen [if it] rained too much, [or] she'd go to school, and it'd start raining too hard. You know, a lot of days she missed because of that. So that is basically what got me involved in the issue about the school and the coal-mining site around it.

It is important to note that there was a school at this site long before there was a coal-sludge impoundment or a coal mine.

The original school was [built] in the 1940s. It burned down in '76 or '77, and of course they rebuilt it right back. So that has been a school site since 1940. The prep plant was permitted in 1982. The sludge-impoundment was permitted in 1985. When I went to school there, it was a junior high. The only thing that I can recall being at that area was plumb up to the upper end—a coal load-out—and it was based at the mouth of a hollow which is no longer there. But that's the only mining facility at that site that I can recall. There was no processing plant. [At the] processing plant, coal is crushed. It's fine powdered. It's cleaned with chemicals and stuff—it's not just coal [in the sludge].

[In] 2003 the first silo [was built] there. [Locating the silo so close to the school] was truly the biggest sign of arrogance that I have ever seen—"Look here what we can do." Totally arrogance on Massey's side, if you ask my opinion about it. I mean, they have a great big bottom there to work with, and they have to put it directly behind the school.

Initially [the DEP] gave them a permit for a second silo. That permit was rescinded, and, of course, Massey appealed that ruling. At that appeal hearing, the lawyer for Massey made the statement, "We could have put it closer." Two-hundred-and-some-odd feet [away from the school] and, "We could have put it closer"! And this is in court—now talk about arrogant! According to SMCRA [Surface Mining Control and Reclamation Act] laws, [it was supposed to be] three hundred feet [away]. But of course DEP wasn't looking at SMCRA laws. They have not looked at SMCRA laws until this last hearing. You know, here we are fighting for two years over a law that's—they should have laughed at them and said, "No way you're going to put that there." Same thing with this sludge impoundment, letting it get that big. They should have looked at them and laughed, "There ain't no way." But instead, "No, go right ahead, it's OK."

In 2003 not only did the [first] silo go up, but a 1,847-acre surface-mine permit was also OK'd. And this is above the sludge impoundment. The sludge impoundment, when it was originally permitted in 1985, was at the height of sixty foot. That was the original permit for that dam. It is currently—of course this is an old number [and] I don't know if it's grown more—385 foot tall. In 1999, they was permitted to use that sludge impoundment as a drain-off for water and stuff. In 2003, they put an 1,847-acre strip job, or surface mine, right on top of it. And this was *after* 2000 when Ed had to go down there and diverted that water off of it. DEP is allowing them to do this. They said, "Yeah, go ahead. Use this as a drain-off [for the surface mine]."

As Debbie indicates, allowing a surface mine to be built above an already-stressed slurry impoundment may have put the children at Marsh Fork Elementary at even further risk. In a Department of Environmental Protection study of the massive flooding that devastated southern West Virginia in 2001, researchers found that mining and logging contributed significantly to runoff, increasing the overspill up to 21 percent in some cases (Flood Advisory Taskforce 2002).

Debbie expressed indignation at the fact that, despite the tremendous risks associated with a slurry-impoundment failure, there was not a realistic evacuation plan in place for the students, teachers, and staff at Marsh Fork Elementary.

Evacuation plan? You've seen what that looks like down there. You have a river on one side of the school, you have a cliff on the other side of the school. I read—I'm not sure exactly what formal document it was—that it would take approximately eleven minutes once the dam started failing for [the school] to be totally gone. You understand what I'm saying? Eleven minutes. That's not saying you're even going to catch it that first one or two minutes. That's eleven total minutes you've got altogether. What are you going to do with two hundred little kids? Their evacuation plan is: get a bull horn out, yell, let these people know buses are going to transport them upriver. Where are [the buses] coming from? And they're going upriver—now how are they going to get upriver?

I asked Debbie if the school administrators had ever run an evacuation drill at the school. Debbie responded,

Absolutely not. Absolutely not, and I don't foresee them doing that either, because they would see what a totally ridiculous thing they have there. You know, totally ridiculous. If I'm not mistaken, the teachers now have transmitters that are on the same frequency as that mine. So they do have communication, but once again, there's that eleven minutes. And what are you going to do with two hundred little kids? You know? Even if you do a drill, what are you going to do? Put them up the cliff? I mean, seriously, two hundred little kids. You couldn't get them out front in that amount of time. Look where it's sitting at: you've got a river and you've got a cliff. Once you're outside, what are you going to do? There's no way they can get buses there in that time. It's ridiculous, but as far as I understand, that's the evacuation plan.

Denial of the Danger

Despite the overwhelming evidence pointing to the danger that the sludge impoundment, the coal-preparation plant, and the mountaintop-removal mine posed to those who worked at and attended Marsh Fork Elementary School, Debbie and other activists faced challenges from a number of community members and Massey workers, who argued that there was no risk associated with the Massey facility.

Last summer [we] had a little community sustainability fair, a very small one—first one we've ever had in this area. And a couple of these Massey supporters come down, of course, and stood around. There was a [few] verbal disagreements and stuff. One couple that I spoke to, though, I was watching. [The man] was listening and really wasn't saying too much—he worked on the surface mine there. He really wasn't going to open his mouth too much, because you could tell that he was thinking about all these things, and, you know, [he's thinking],"Maybe they're right."I pull out a fly-over picture [an aerial photograph of the Marsh Fork site showing the school's close proximity to the coal facility, impoundment, and mountaintop-removal mine], and his wife was standing there talking and everything. I said, "Now you look at this and tell me that's a safe playground for our kids." "Yep, yep, looks OK to me," [she said]. He didn't open his mouth. You could tell by the look in his eyes that he knew [it was not safe]. But this is their livelihood. I understand that these companies are putting these people in this position.

One look at a fly-over picture of that site, and there's no one using their correct facilities in their head [that] can say that that's OK. [People rationalize it by saying], "My husband works there. He said it's OK." "The DEP, we have to trust in what they say. They're the experts. They'll take care of us." "If it was that bad, my husband wouldn't work there. He wouldn't endanger our children's lives." But I don't blame [them] for working—got to work. That's all we do have, you know.

Additional dangers also faced the children and staff at Marsh Fork Elementary School. In 2006, Dr. D. Scott Simonton, vice chair of West Virginia's Environmental Quality Board, collected dust samples from classrooms at Marsh Fork Elementary School and found unsafe levels of coal dust present.[3] After this study was conducted, Debbie's husband Ed Wiley, along with Bo Webb, another local activist, conducted a survey of households proximal to the school to determine whether local children were experiencing health problems that could be linked to coal dust inhalation.

Bo and Ed went house-to-house asking about the kids being sick and everything. Out of 125 homes, sixty homes [had] kids. Fifty-five of those homes stated there was asthma, some kind of breathing problem, or something like that. I think it came out to be like 80 percent. All this information, [we] of course give it to the governor, give it to the health department—just whoever we could give it to. The [coal dust] report of Dr. Simonton, they're trying to brush that off like it ain't nothing.

At that silo hearing, [after presenting this information], some of the [teachers] was asking, "Why haven't you given us information?"—talking about the coal dust or this or that. Well, we *did* give the principal a packet. [The teachers said], "He didn't say nothing. He didn't tell us." I don't know why. [The principal has] just been [at the school] this past year, so I don't know. I don't know what the reason behind that was, but you would think that he would share that with the teachers down there.

Many of the school administrators, teachers, and parents refused to publicly speak in favor of the campaign to build a new school in a safer location. Debbie cited many reasons for the lack of public support:

[Losing] the school, [losing] the job, [losing] your home, you know. Or let's say even if you're a grandparent, you've got a grandson working on one of these mine sites. One lady that I know, she lives half a mile from the school site there. She has three small children, the youngest one is three. All three of them [have] asthma. And the oldest one, I think he even has some type of heart problem—I'm not sure exactly what—as well as asthma. She will not open her mouth [about the school issue]. The house she lives in is owned by Massey.

I went over the transcripts from the last DEP [meeting]—the silo hearing that we had—to see exactly what was said. If you listen to these tapes, what you hear is [the teachers and administrators saying], "We're not getting a new school. Raleigh County Board of Education won't give us a new school—they told us we won't get a new school." "We don't get nothing down on this end of the county. We always get the short end of the stick in this county." They're afraid we're going to *lose* our school—that is what that is. That's their jobs. And just like the teachers or Massey supporters stated down there, we get the short end of the stick every time—because we are known as "the coalfields." You turn the TV on, "Well, the weather in the coalfields today is. . . ." you know. But that's what we are—"the coalfields." I don't know if our political figures don't realize that we're also *communities,* not just coalfields, but we're a community as well. Or, they just don't give a shit.

[The town of Glen Daniel is] getting a new school. They just got almost six million dollars to get them a new school. They *needed* one; [said sarcastically] *theirs* is in bad shape. Raleigh County ends there—we're *the coalfields* down here.

> Debbie articulated that she and the other activists fighting for a new elementary school were very clear that the new school needed to be built in their community and that it was not acceptable for the children to be bused to Glen Daniel.

If you live along the route here, that would be thirty minutes [to Glen Daniel]. If you live up the hollow, how long is that going to be? Because we've got some big hollows that these kids have to come out of to go to school. Our junior high and our high school both go up there [to Glen Daniel]. They closed [those schools] down. Same with Clear Fork. The Clear Fork kids, they have to go up there too—closed their high school down. There was a big, big court battle over closing that school down. I wasn't involved in the fight, but the fight that the ladies put on, I mean they worked hard to keep that school open. But Raleigh County Board of Education did not deem it fit to keep it open. They say [it was] because of enrollment drop. You have these mountaintop-removal sites going in the head of the hollows, moving the families out—yeah, you're going to have a drop in enrollment.

> Debbie discussed her opinion, which is shared among most in the activist community, that the coal companies are trying to push people out of the area so that they can have easier access to the coal.

I do believe that's how they work. I swear I believe that's how they work. It's their mindset. You look what they would gain. [If that school closed], not only would they gain that site that they could work at, but they could put anything that they wanted to down there then. I mean, who's going to stop them and what's to prevent them? There would be nothing to prevent them from doing just that. Roland Land Company owns the biggest part of our mountains back in the hollows. Roland Land Company, their main objective is money, period. They [don't] give a shit about the people here—they never have. Years ago they began gobbling all this land up from everybody. A lot of people aren't willing or don't have the health to fight that.

Gender and Activism

> Debbie's husband Ed Wiley is one of the few but notable local men who is at the front lines of the movement for environmental justice in the Central Appalachia.[4] In 2006, Ed set out on a well-publicized walk from Raleigh County, West Virginia,

to Washington, D.C., to raise funds and awareness about Marsh Fork Elementary School. The campaign that he, Debbie, and other concerned southern West Virginia citizens initiated was called the Pennies of Promise Campaign.

In describing what Ed has done for the children of their community, Debbie professes, "I admire his strength and his determination so much." While expressing her respect and appreciation for the few local men, like Ed Wiley, Bo Webb, and the late Larry Gibson, who have taken a stand against the injustices of the coal industry, Debbie recognizes that there are far more women who are involved in the environmental justice movement than men. Reflecting on the reasons for the women-dominated character of the movement, Debbie asserts,

> We are Appalachian women, and I believe that I can speak for them as well—our roots run so deep, you can't distinguish us from the earth we live on. It's just a part of us. So, you know, this is us, when you talk about Appalachia you're talking about us. That, plus the fact that the mothering instinct that women have, I think—it's wanting to make things right, wanting to correct something, not wanting the children to be harmed, you know. I think a mothering instinct may have a lot to do with that as well.

In April 2010, after a six-year campaign, the hard work and dedication of environmental justice organizations and local residents finally paid off. The Pennies of Promise campaign mobilized $8.6 million in donations and grants from concerned citizens, the Annenberg Foundation, the Raleigh County School Board, the School Building Authority, Coal River Mountain Watch, and Massey Energy (now Alpha Resources). A site for the new school was purchased in Rock Creek, approximately three miles from the original Marsh Fork Elementary, and a groundbreaking ceremony took place in October 2011. The new Marsh Fork Elementary School opened its doors on January 7, 2013. Marsh Fork students are now learning in a healthy environment that is located a safe distance from the slurry impoundment and coal-preparation plant.

CHAPTER 9

"It's Not Just What I Choose to Do, It's Also, I Think, What I *Have* to Do"

Lorelei Scarboro's Drive to Save Coal River Mountain

Figure 24. Lorelei Scarboro at the Central Appalachian Women's Tribunal on Climate Justice. Charleston, West Virginia; May 10, 2012. Photo by the author.

For many years, Lorelei Scarboro has been involved in local struggles for justice in her community. She has been an activist and leader in the movement against school consolidation, she has fought to protect Coal River Mountain from mountaintop-removal mining through advocating for a wind farm to be constructed in place of surface mining, and most recently, she has created a community space for residents in the Coal River Valley to come together and work toward building a thriving local economy and sustainable future. I interviewed Lorelei in July of 2008.

Lorelei has long seen the injustices of the coal industry in and around her community. As a member of a family dependent on coal, she has firsthand knowledge of the benefits and costs associated with this industry.

My husband spent thirty-five years as an underground union coal miner. My father was a coal miner, my grandfather was a coal miner, I have brothers that are coal miners. Living in southern West Virginia, you of course grow up around coal. My husband was a very, very proud coal miner. I believe that coal mining has been an honorable profession; I just believe that the time for coal has come and gone. As I become more aware of the damage that fossil fuels are doing to the climate, and as I think of the generations to come—what will be left for them? I feel a really desperate need to try to do something to change it.

I have heard it said by members of the Coal Association that God didn't make a mistake when He put the coal in the ground, and I agree with that. But I think there's a right way and a wrong way. There is a reason that God put it there, but the way that it's being extracted and used at this point, I don't believe is what God originally intended. I remember when I was a little girl growing up in Lincoln County, my daddy used to take his pick and his bucket, and I would go along behind him. We would go around the hill from where we lived—we had about seventeen acres there—and he would go to what we called "the coal bank." He'd take the little pick and dig the coal out and put it in the bucket and bring it back home, and we would put it in our pot-belly stove—our warm morning stove—and that's what we used to heat our home with. I was one of nine children, and we desperately needed the coal as a heat source. I think that's why God put the coal there; I don't believe God put the coal there for the greed and the wide profit margin of the coal industry. Like I said, I think the time for coal has come and gone because burning fossil fuels is definitely the major reason for our climate crisis. I believe in "carbon sequestration": it's *already* sequestered, leave it there!

I'm not against coal mining, [but] I think there's a drastic difference between coal mining and mountaintop removal, you know, from the way it's mined to the environmental impact. I don't believe mountaintop removal is strip mining—it's strip mining on steroids. There are many, many people who live in the southern coalfields of West Virginia that have either been driven out or they're very, very sick because of the effects of what goes on around them, whether it be that their wells are contaminated, the blasting, the rock dust, the silica, the coal dust. That [all] comes with the territory of mountaintop removal, the coal-mining industry, and the fact that we are truly in their way.

I have watched for several years the devastation of mountaintop removal. I have gotten to know people whose life and health is dramatically impacted by the negative things that go along with coal mining. And then Massey Energy applied for a very large permit [for a mountaintop-removal mine] right behind my house. The house that I live in, I raised my four kids in, [that] my husband built from the ground up. He is buried in the family cemetery right next door. I've got almost ten acres, which goes to the top of Coal River Mountain. It's a very peaceful place. I can sit in my living room and watch the deer with velvet still on their antlers jump the fence next door. This morning, I was looking out my bathroom window, and I saw the groundhog that lives under the building out back that my granddaughter named "Rocky." Yesterday, on the way home, we had to stop twice on the way in Rock Creek for the turkey to cross the road. There's a freshwater stream that runs right by my driveway. It's a very quiet, peaceful, serene place that I don't believe *anybody* has the right to drive me out of.

My home's threatened. The family cemetery is threatened. The stream that runs by my house, the deer that I sit there and watch leap across the fence—everything, because of Eagle 2 [mine], is now threatened. So I really don't have a choice. You know, life would be so much easier for the coal companies if they could totally depopulate southern West Virginia and they could do whatever they wanted and nobody could see. But we're not leaving, and that makes their life a little harder.

[Massey Energy] applied for the Eagle 2 permit sometime in the summer of 2007. There was a hearing requested, and the hearing was August 2, 2007. There were eighty-nine people who signed in to speak. Everybody that spoke, spoke *against* that permit, and it took the DEP until June 6 of this year [2008] to approve that permit. [The Eagle 2 permit] will come in right behind my house and is for about twenty-four hundred acres of Coal River Mountain. That's one of four permits that would total sixty-six hundred acres, which will destroy Coal River Mountain. I spoke out at the hearing, [and] came to work at Coal River [Mountain Watch] in August of 2007. I have been aggressively involved in the fight against mountaintop removal since that time.

"I Always Grieved for Green":
The Connection to Place

> While Lorelei has visited and lived in other parts of the country, her connection to southern West Virginia has always pulled her back home. In her travels, she has found it difficult to make others understand her connection to place and why she and other local activists feel that "simply moving" away from the coal industry's destruction is not an option.

I grew up in Lincoln County, [West Virginia,] which is a couple of hours from here. My father was killed when I was eleven, and the guy that killed him served three years [in prison]. My mother knew she had to get her children out of Lincoln County, so we moved to Raleigh County. I had six brothers and two sisters. I finished high school in Raleigh County, graduated from Trap Hill High School.

In 1980 I got married to a guy from southern California and moved to Palm Springs, spent nine years there. Nine years and three kids later, I boarded a plane and headed back to Raleigh County. Five days after I got here, I found out I was pregnant—so, four kids. I spent nine years in the desert of southern California and never, never, ever got used to it—always grieved for green. There's nothing there but dirt, rock, and cactus, so I always grieved for green.

[After moving back], I tried working a couple of times, but with four kids it's really, really difficult. I realized that I had two jobs, one I was doing well and one I wasn't, and the most important one, which was being a mommy, I wasn't. So I made the decision to stay home and have less, but I was there for my kids.

Then in '94 I met my second husband, and, like I said, he spent thirty-five years as an underground union coal miner. I was at home, we were living on welfare, I had four kids. My total income was $360 a month, my rent was $200, and I had four little kids. The day I met my husband he said, "That's the girl I'm going to marry," and I'm going, "That ain't happening!" A few days later, he showed up in front of my house with a whole truck-full of groceries. And I said, "What do you want?" and he said, "Nothing." And I said, "I don't have time in my life to work on a relationship." He said, "I'm not here to make your life harder, I'm here to make it easier." And he did. He told me that he wanted to help me raise my kids, and he would give me a home and an income to raise them in. I told him that I would take care of him as long as he let me, and he did—and I did. He died of black lung in '99. That's a horrible way to go. It's very difficult to watch somebody slowly suffocate to death, and that's one of the reasons why it's hard not to have a measurable amount of respect for a coal miner. They know when they go in [the mines] what the cost is. Even with all that, I can't stand by and allow the coal company to destroy everything. When I married my husband and moved into my home, I had planned to spend the rest of my life peacefully there and probably leave that to my kids. If mountaintop removal continues, that's just not possible.

Everywhere we go, when we talk to people about how life is here, they say, "Why don't you just move?" I went all the way to Reno [Nevada] for a training session. We were at South Lake Tahoe for a Patagonia grassroots training session the first week in May, and one of the people that I spent a good amount of time with is a vice president for Patagonia, his name's Robert Cohen, and he had a really big heart. As they listened, Robert just kept sitting there looking at me, and he said, "The easiest thing in the world to do would be to move." But it wouldn't. That would be the *hardest* thing to do, because that's the house I raised my kids in, that's the house my husband built. He's buried next door. The land that he loved has been in his family for generations, and I can't imagine driving out of the driveway for the last time and leaving him in the cemetery and everything else there. That would be the *hardest* thing to do. It's easier to fight and to try to, to try to save all that, because if I walk away from it, it's certainly destroyed. It's certainly blown apart and destroyed. So it's a whole lot easier to stay there and fight.

It's difficult to explain the attachment, the sense of place that Appalachians have. It's a connectedness to the land, to your surroundings. It's not the value of the house, it's not the price of the ten acres. It's the memories. It's what you have there. It's the life you share with the people you love. There's a whole range of emotions that go through me when people say, "Why don't you just move?" I mean, it's everything from anger to sadness. Patty [Sebok] and I and Maria Gunnoe went to Baltimore after Thanksgiving last year. We were checking out of the hotel, and we were standing there talking to the bellhop, and we were telling this story, and he said the same thing. There are some times that it's all you could do just not to want to take people and shake them and try to make them understand, because it *wouldn't* be the easiest thing to do. It would be very, very difficult to walk away and allow it to be totally destroyed. It really *wouldn't* be easier to leave. It really wouldn't.

At one point I considered selling. I said, you know, "I'm going to sell, I'm going to move closer to town." It didn't take long for that idea to go away, because when I think about driving out of the driveway for the last time, I just don't believe I could do it. I don't believe I could do it because I know where I am and what I have there—that's the only place that I will ever have that. I remember when we were in Baltimore, and I looked out the hotel window, and I listened to the sirens, and I listened to the traffic, and I saw the people and all the buildings and all the pollution, and it's just, I just wanted to *scream*! I heard somebody say one time, "I've never been really comfortable when the horizon stretches out too far in front of me." And that's the way I am—there's a sense of security where I am that I just, I haven't found anywhere else. And it's not that I haven't been anywhere. I've been to Chicago and New York and Atlanta and L.A. and lived in southern California. It's just a sense of place that's very difficult to describe.

Lorelei's Path to Coal River Mountain Watch

I had done a lot of work on the fringes of this movement for a long time. I had a good friend [Judy Bonds] that's one of the co-directors [of Coal River Mountain Watch]. For a number of years, I [wrote] letters to the editor, spoke at DEP hearings for mountaintop-removal permits, things like that. I had planned for several years to go back into the workforce. My husband had passed away, my last child of four turned eighteen and moved out of the house. It just so happened that there was an opening at Coal River [Mountain Watch], and Judy asked me to submit a résumé. I did, and I was hired. I started part time—two days a week—and that quickly went to four days a week and five and six and, you know, it has snowballed. I really, really enjoy what I'm doing. When I interviewed with Janice [Nease], Vernon [Haltom], and Judy [Bonds], they asked me why I wanted to work here. I said, "Well I'm doing all this anyway." And I really was, you know—speaking at hearings, sending letters to the editor, researching and submitting information to Coal River. So, I might as well get paid for it.

One of the reasons that coal has such a strong hold on West Virginia politicians is they believe that if we stop burning coal that the bottom will literally fall out of the whole economic market for the whole state. And I agree with that—I believe that we have to create new jobs. I believe we definitely need to stop coal mining, but we need to create new jobs—we need to transition into renewables. We don't want to see anybody out of work. I certainly don't want the father of my only grandchild, [who is a coal miner for Massey Energy], to be unemployed. I want him to take care of my daughter and my granddaughter in the best way that he possibly can. The problem is, we live in a mono-economy. The only jobs here are coal, and I blame that on the politicians. I believe that the politicians in this state—the delegates, the senators, the congressmen, and the governor—all have a responsibility to create jobs here post-coal. We need to start doing that now. What we need to do today, yesterday, last week is to start transitioning into green jobs, into renewable energy, into things that are sustainable. The wind's going to blow forever, coal is going to be gone. No matter *when* we stop, you know, coal *is* going to be gone. There's only a few years of coal left, and we need to start transitioning into renewables. We need to take the coal miners and start training them in green jobs. We need good-paying jobs with good retirement, good health benefits for the people who work here. We have a responsibility to retrain those people. The politicians have a responsibility to create jobs in the renewable energy field in the state of West Virginia. I believe that. And they're not doing it.

Part of our mission statement [at Coal River Mountain Watch] is rebuilding sustainable communities, and the only option that I see for us right here, right now, would be a wind farm. That's the alternative [to mining coal] that the Coal Association says we never offer, and of course we do now. We're working very hard to see to it that that happens. This is a monumental struggle. It's a very, very difficult fight. We win some and we lose some, you know, but we can't quit.

> Lorelei traces the roots of her environmental justice activism with Coal River Mountain Watch to her earlier efforts against school consolidation in the Coal River Valley. In fact, she views both of these movements as being intimately linked to the same social problems caused by the coal industry.

In January of 2001, I got involved with Challenge West Virginia when the local Board of Education decided to implement a plan of closure for our local high school. I was the vice chair of a committee called Citizens Preserving Marsh Fork and Clear Fork Community. We had a seven-person steering committee, and Judy [Bonds] sat on that committee. The chair was a teacher at the school, and I was the most vocal person on that committee. I was the one with my picture on the front page of the paper, and I was on the six o'clock news and quoted in the paper. That's when I was first labeled an "activist." I was really, really shocked when a local newspaper reporter actually labeled me as an activist. I never really thought of myself as an activist.

Because of that fight, because it was just such a monumental struggle to try to save our local high school, somebody in the neighboring county gave me the name of the statewide organization [Challenge West Virginia]. I went to a meeting and immediately became the representative for this county, for Raleigh County. Challenge is a statewide organization that advocates for small rural community schools. We believe—and it's true—when you close the last remaining school in a very rural area, that's the death of the community. Of course, this area is living proof of that. Clear Fork High School is gone, Marsh Fork High School is gone, and you can see that we lose the last few remaining businesses all the time. It is the death of the community.

We had a pretty tough fight for about two-and-a-half years. We won in court on the local level, but when we got to the state [level], of course they won the decision [to close Marsh Fork High School]. In this very, very rural area, there were 750 people [who] showed up for our closure hearing. It was what they labeled a "marathon" closure hearing. That hearing started at six o'clock at night, and it ended about 2:45 in the morning. They rewrote a lot of laws [because of] us. One of the laws they wrote was if you have a closure hearing that's going to carry past midnight on any given day, you adjourn by midnight and you set another date to finish the hearing.

We appealed to the Supreme Court, and [they] refused to hear [our case]. We believed then, and I still believe today, that the reason that school was closed, along with many, many others in the coalfields of West Virginia, is because they're in the way of the coal mines. The evidence is on the side of the mountaintop up there. If you drive up Route 3 today and you look up on the hill above what used to be the site of Marsh Fork High School, you can see that they take a little bit more of that mountain every day, and you can see that really is the reason why Marsh Fork High School was closed. We knew at that time that they wanted that last ridge next to where the high school was. It would be a public relations nightmare if they were blasting on the mountain and a boulder went through a high school with two hundred kids in it.

I guess one of the things that really connected the dots for me was the day that the decision was handed down—the day we got word that the Supreme Court had refused to hear our appeal. Our school colors were orange and black, and I remember we were standing up by the road across from the site that was Marsh Fork High School. It was also the same day of the Massey annual picnic that's held in Logan County. They make T-shirts [for the picnic] every year, and they're different colors every year. As we stood there discussing the fact that the Supreme Court had refused to hear our appeal—which meant that our fight was over—we saw all of these [Massey Energy] people driving down the road on their way to the picnic in Logan County. The colors that they had chosen for their T-shirts that year were *our school colors.* I really think that that did something to me that day. I think that's part of what really helped connect the dots, because some of us believed that the main reason that that school was being closed was because it was in the way of the coal mines. It made me really understand the enormous impact that the coal companies have on the lives of the people here. It made me angry. I was angry, and I had a hunger then to learn more about the things that I knew they were doing wrong. I knew that there were a lot of injustices that were being done that I just hadn't opened my eyes to yet. And that was actually about four years before I started working [at Coal River Mountain Watch].

I used to say years ago, before I really got involved in this, that Judy Bonds knew things that I didn't want to know. But now I know, and you can't not know now. The more you know, the harder it is to understand why, and the more of a sense of urgency you feel to try to do something about it. It's very difficult to look at people like Patty [Sebok] and know that what's wrong with her husband is because of the coal mines. I cannot imagine how angry she has to be [knowing] that her husband is dying, and they intentionally do that stuff. I mean, they had permits to inject that toxic sludge underground knowing it's not going to stay there—it will make it to the water table, and those people in Prenter Hollow had well water. Unbelievable. Unbelievable. And the government allows it. It's tough to know that those people are sick, dead, and dying so the coal companies can make more money. There's something wrong with that, and our politicians know it. When we went to meet with [U.S. Representative] Nick Rahall, we gave him a picture of the water, the quality of water that people in southern West Virginia have. He just tossed the picture back across the table and said, "It's like that throughout southern West Virginia." How can he not feel responsibility to do something about that? How could he ignore that or how could he act like that's OK? It's not OK. These are people, these are his constituents, these are people he's responsible for, and he has the nerve to toss a picture of rusty, contaminated water coming out of somebody's sink back across the table and ignore it?

"The Majority of the Appalachian Women that I Know Were Born Fighting and Protecting"

Lorelei speaks of having a strong identity as a protector—a protector of her children, of her homeplace, and of her community. While she believes this "protector" identity is an attribute of Appalachian women generally, she sees some men in the movement embodying this identity as well.

I guess my purpose changed when I had my first child. I spent twenty-six years being a mommy, and I was committed to that. I did my job—they're all eighteen and graduated from school. What they make of their lives after that is up to them. I was a mommy for twenty-six years, and now it's my turn [to] go and do what I want to do. I see different stages of my life: I was a wife, I was mother, and I was a wife and a homemaker. And now I can do what I choose to do, and what I choose to do is here.

It's not just what I choose to do, it's also, I think, what I *have* to do. I've always been a very fierce protector of my kids, and I'm still doing that. I'm still protecting what I have left there [at my home]. Not only [my house and land], but the mountain behind it and the environment and the wildlife and the vegetation. I think I'm still a very fierce protector. I don't think that's something that I created. I think that's something that was handed down—my mother was [a protector] too. I think that's part of me. The majority of the Appalachian women that I know were born fighting and protecting. I think Judy's a protector, too, Maria is a protector. There are men in this movement, too—there's Larry Gibson and Julian Martin. I don't know if it's that we have that sense to take care of or protect what's ours, or if there's so many things that we've lost, and we feel the need to fight to hang on to what we have left. Judy was driven out of her home and has moved to another. They're trying to drive Maria out. I think we get to a point to where we consciously make a decision that here's the line in the sand. The majority of the people that I know in this fight just had so much taken away that they'd had enough—they decided to stand firm. That's probably the point that I got to—I never really thought of it—but when [Massey] applied for a permit behind my house, everything that I have [was put] at risk. And it's not just that it's my backyard. I spent years leading up to this—I can't let them take any more. At one point, I had decided to sell my house and move, and then the day came when I said, "I can't let them have another ten acres." Right beside my driveway, the edge of my property, is Roland Land company property. I thought, "I can't let them have another ten acres," because if they get that ten acres, they'll come in and get the next [property] and not very far down there is the family cemetery.

> While Lorelei observes that there are more local women involved in the move-ment than local men, she has seen that as young people from college campuses across the nation join the struggle against mountaintop-removal mining, the gender dynamic within the movement seems to be changing.

I've never really thought about why there are more women in this [move-ment] than there are men. I think it's the job market. I think it's the mono-economy. I think it's no options, no other options. Maybe it's the brother-hood. I'm not sure. Maybe there are just more of us than there are of them.

There was a hearing last September—the hearing that Maria [Gunnoe] was the only witness in, where they stopped the valley-fill permit behind her house. There was an article in the paper after that hearing that said the only [people] that were there [at the hearing] was a bunch of gray-haired ladies that didn't have anything better to do with their life. But that's not true. There were a lot of men there, too. The movement is changing with the youth movement across the nation, with the student-environmental coalition, with Power Shift. We have tirelessly gone to college campuses [to recruit for] the student movement. There's a major youth movement across the nation that is bringing forth a lot of young men and women into this movement. My son is probably one of the few people that you will meet that actually grew up here that's young and fighting against [the coal industry].

Challenges in the Struggle

Like the other activist women in this book, Lorelei has faced many difficulties because of her choice to speak out against the injustices of the coal industry. A number of residents in her community, including her own son-in-law, are employed by the very company that is threatening to destroy her homeplace. Maintaining these relationships in the midst of fighting against coal-related injustices has been a constant challenge.

My next-door neighbor works for Massey. He works for Elk Run right down here. He was one of my son's best friends in high school. He does his job, we do ours. And a lot of the people that live in Rock Creek, a lot of the younger guys with new homes and new wives and new little kids, you know, have been hired by Massey. They're hiring a lot more local people now than they have in the past. I don't know if that's a calculated effort to turn neighbor against neighbor or if it's the increase in the demand for coal.

When you sign on with Massey, you don't become a Massey *employee,* you immediately become a Massey "member." They have a major membership drive. Not only are you a Massey member, but every member of your immediate family is a Massey member. My only granddaughter is a Massey member. I was working for Coal River before [my son-in-law] went to work for Massey. He knew what my position was when he put his application in. The day he had his orientation, he came to me and said, "What do you think?" and I said, "You're asking the wrong person." I said, "Whether or not you take this job has absolutely nothing to do with me. That's between you and your wife and your child. That's a decision for your family." He knew my position, but, you know, I want him to take care of them in the best possible way. I would hope that he would go to work for somebody else, but it's like I said, we have a mono-economy, I blame that on the politicians. They need to start doing something to change this.

I'm at their house on a regular basis, they're at my house on a regular basis. He goes to work right up here, [and] when the weather's bad, instead of driving an hour back to Beckley, he's at my house. We had a Massey miner come through the door at nine o'clock and an environmentalist go out the door at nine o'clock. And it's OK. I don't have a right to tell him what to do. I would prefer that he didn't [work for Massey], and he knows. I don't tell people his name. Given the history of Massey Energy and the way they can treat their employees, I'm concerned that if people find out—when he went to work there, I said, "Don't tell people who you're related to." You know, "Do not tell people that your mother-in-law is—" Because he could get hurt. You know, I'm concerned. I know there's a strong possibility that if you're not a real good soldier to Massey, that you could end up in the most labor-intensive jobs and the jobs that you would break down in the quickest—the most dangerous jobs. If your boss tells you that's where you got to work, you've got to work. I don't want to be the reason for my grand-daughter's daddy to be put in harm's way. So, I have strongly advised him not to let anybody know who he's related to, and I never mention his name. So he does his job and I do mine.

So yeah, that helps you to better understand the intensity of the situation because, like if your mother-in-law is an environmentalist and you work for Massey and you think your job's at risk, that's going to make life a little tougher. Given the mono-economy, given the political climate, given the fact that our legislators are not changing the situation, are not creating green jobs, are not bringing in other industry—there are some people who work for the coal company that are arrogant, but then there's an awful lot of those guys that are just out there trying to support their family and they have nowhere to go. My son-in-law didn't graduate high school, and this is the best that he could do. He could go to work for Walmart, you know. A lot of them just don't have a choice, given where we live and the fact that our politicians won't do anything to change it.

One of the things that really helped my son-in-law to understand my position—because when you work for Massey, you're fed all of this crap about "those environmentalists"—he was laying on my living room floor one day, and I told him, I said, "The reason I do what I do is, when I look at [my granddaughter], I try to think about the quality of water she's going to have to drink when she's of child-bearing age. What I do is about the water. It's not against mining, it's for the water. Of all of the really, really bad things that they do, the worst that they do is destroy the water. You can't look at her and not think about the quality of water that she's going to have." That really, really helped him to understand—because we can live without electricity, but we've got three days without water. She's got three days without safe drinking water.

Suppressing Emotions for Power-Holders

One of the biggest challenges Lorelei faces as an activist has been feeling that she
has had to mute her interactional style in ways that mask her very real emotions
about the injustices she and the residents of her community have experienced. As
is common in struggles for environmental justice, women activists in particular
are often accused of being "overly emotional" or "irrational" in their interactions
with politicians or others in positions of power, who most often are men. These
accusations become a justification to dismiss women activists' claims as "unscien-
tific" or exaggerated.

Whether it's through Challenge West Virginia or whether it's through Coal
River Mountain Watch or whether it's through the environmental movement,
one of the things that we have to do is find a way to deal with the people who
are in control of what we do. Those are the politicians, the people in power
are the politicians. We haven't [been able to come to the table] with a lot of
the people who have the power over us. We had the head of the DEP sitting
at the table there a few weeks ago, and he was talking about the fact that
some of the people in this movement get very emotional. Sarah [Haltom]
told him, "Where we live this is a very, very emotional thing." Not too long
ago, we didn't have a relationship with the head of the DEP where we could
all come to the table and talk civilly. One of the things [the head of DEP] said
was, "I'm really glad that we've had an opportunity to sit down here and talk
like this, and I want you to know that as long as we can sit and talk like this,
my door's always open. But if things are different, if you have very negative
protest signs outside my door, you might not get a meeting that day." One
of the things that happened was there was somebody in this movement that
called him a murderer. We realized that he used that [as an excuse] not to
deal with any of us. Because he could say, you know, "Those people are too
unreasonable, they're too irrational, you don't know what they're going to
do, we're afraid of them, they called me a murderer. I can't deal with those
people." And they can get by with that, so they don't have to deal with us.

It's been very difficult for me. Judy Bonds and I are built very much
alike—we're that in-your-face, screaming and yelling and letting you know
exactly how it is. That's the way I conducted myself through the fight to
save the schools. You know, it's like I said, I was always on the front page
of the paper, always on the six o'clock news, always the in-your-face kind of
thing. Since I started working for Coal River, I have taken a different approach—hence, I'm being very good, and it's *really* hard. I'm the one that
they put out there when they need somebody to sit and in a monotone,
civilized, polite, diplomatic way, talk about it. It's like the meeting that we

had with [Representative Nick] Rahall. I would have loved to have just torn into him, but I had to make a decision before I went in there that if it goes wrong, I don't want that to be my fault. I don't want to give him anything that he can use to justify not working with us.

I was on the phone earlier today trying to set up a meeting with Senator Rockefeller's office to do a presentation about the wind campaign, and his aide was saying, "Well, you have to do this and you have to do this, and you got to do this." And all of the things that he said, we had already done. He, of course, was not—to sum it up—he was not interested in having a meeting with us. But he decided he was going to tell us, and it was in a very condescending tone. I kind of got the impression that he felt as though we were just these stupid little people down here with these visions of windmills on the mountain, and I really, really wanted to just really tell him—in not a kind way—but I knew I couldn't do that. I knew that I had to be good.

So, that's how I've changed. That's the biggest change that I see in me, and it's difficult because it goes against my standard operating procedure. But I see that it's the way you have to be if we're going to accomplish [our goals]. We had a meeting on Kayford Mountain[1] Friday a week ago with these top executives from a very large bank that is one of the primary funders of mountaintop removal. We [went] to Kayford Mountain, and I had to be very well behaved to tell my story and all that. So, I cried all the way down there because it's that whole range of emotions again. Like I say, it's tough to be good, and it makes me really, really angry that we have to fit into this mold in order to try to get them to listen, to do the right thing—to stop killing people. So, I got all cried out before I got to Kayford [because] I have learned that's the way I'm going to have to operate, at least in my foreseeable future, in order to accomplish the goal that we want. I hate that, you know, because it goes against my nature. It really, really does. I see it as a means to an end, and I see it as just playing politics, and I hate it. But I don't see any other way that I can operate for now because Judy's always right there ready to just crawl up one side of them, down the other. Like I said, I'm perfectly capable of that and have operated that way in the past. But somebody has to be good here. Somebody has to be the voice of reason, and right now I guess I have been nominated to be that, and, like I said, it goes against my grain to do that. There's just so much rage. I honestly don't know how long I can go on holding this in. I really don't.

There are times when I hesitate to speak because I'm afraid I'm just going to fall apart. There's just so much intensity in this, and there's so much sacrifice, and there's so much to lose, and there's so much injustice. I don't care to[2] show my emotions, I'm just afraid sometimes I'm not going to be able to finish [what I am saying]. In February, Senator Hunter from the West Virginia legislature introduced a bill to stop mountaintop removal, and I was asked to speak at that hearing. That was one of those times when I was just terrified. But I learned with that one that if I read it—and it's hard to do that because it doesn't seem as genuine if you're reading it—but I'm not as emotional if I read it, rather than if I'm sitting there thinking about it. If I read it—just read—then I can sometimes maintain it.

I think one of the most powerful things [from] my statement when I spoke at the Hunter hearing was, "We don't live where they mine coal, they mine coal where we live." A lot of people really got that. I talked about the turkey and the stream, and that my husband built the house, that he's buried in the cemetery next door, that I saw him die of black lung—"We don't live where they mine coal, they mine coal where we live." There seems to be this idea that if all of us people below [Interstate] 64 would just disappear, you know, [the coal executives' lives] would be so much easier. Then they could go in there and continue to rape Appalachia and nobody would say anything. But you've got Judy Bonds and Larry Gibson and Maria Gunnoe in the way, screaming—we're telling. Our homes shake, our foundations crack, they mine under and around our family cemeteries. We live at ground zero for mountaintop removal.

> In 2010, after fighting for three years to save Coal River Mountain from mountaintop-removal mining through promoting the development of a large-scale wind farm, Lorelei moved on to initiate a new venture: the Boone-Raleigh Community Group, which is working to provide a neutral community space in a region that is very divided between those who want to end destructive coal-mining practices and those whose paychecks come from the coal industry.
>
> The Boone-Raleigh Community Group is working toward the goals of "binding the community together, empowering local residents, and honoring the culture of the Coal River Valley and Appalachia while passing it on to the next generation." Since the organization's inception in 2010, the members have built a community greenhouse, which provides a space for residents to grow their own food, a place to host workshops on sustainable agriculture, and a site for strengthening the local economy through plant sales. In addition, the organization is starting a small business incubator, a community center with a commercial kitchen for canning and cooking, and a crafts store for local artisans. While Lorelei continues to advocate for an end to mountaintop-removal mining in her community and throughout Central Appalachia, she sees an urgent need to help create an environment where the wounds of community conflict can be healed.

CHAPTER 10

"Money Cannot Recreate What Nature Gives You"

Donna Branham's Struggle against Mountaintop Removal

Donna Branham at the Central Appalachian Women's Tribunal on Climate Justice. Charleston, West Virginia; May 10, 2012. Photo by the author.

Donna Branham lives in the community of Lenore in Mingo County, West Virginia. She lives on a small subsistence farm where she and her husband Charlie raise chickens, keep bees, and grow vegetables and grapes. She became active in the environmental justice movement when permits for mountaintop-removal mines began to threaten her community and farm. I interviewed Donna at her home in July 2007 and July 2008.

I've lived in Mingo County, West Virginia, for the biggest portion of my life. I was raised in what you'd consider a coal camp. I don't know if you've ever seen the slate dumps on the side of the road or not, but that's the way the community looked that I grew up in. Even then I didn't feel it was right.

[I grew up in] Trace Creek, it was a little hollow called Twenty-Seventh Hollow—I think now they call it Garnet Road. There's a tipple there at the mouth of the hollow, and we lived beside it. [My husband] worked for twenty-five years in the coal mines—underground and strip. He worked union when he started out, [but] in the early '80s, the union started going downhill. So he worked wherever he could. He's been told he has black lung. My dad worked in the coal mines for thirty-nine years. His dad worked in the coal mines for twenty-seven years, so we have a big history of coal mining. I'm not ashamed of a coal miner's life, but there's a right way and a wrong way to do it. You would think and should hope that with today's technology we should be going forward, where it's more environmentally friendly, where it's got less impact on the environment, where it's safer for the men. But instead, it's just going backward. You want to say, "What's wrong here?" You know, we've been going to the moon forever, stem cell research, and that's great stuff—but we need to watch where our industrial future is. As I got older, I got more involved with nature and the things that we need to do to protect it instead of harm it.

When we got married in '70, we moved up here [to Lenore]. My husband was raised up here. The mining that had been here was long gone, so there was no effects of the mining [that we could see]. [But] as we'd read the newspaper, we would notice that there was advertisements for permits that was getting closer and closer to the area. We also heard about a lot of our friends that lived up [Route] 119 and down [Routes] 52 and 65, that their homes and communities and waters was beginning to get spoiled and polluted from the mines. And they had very little recourse; even the ones that did file lawsuits didn't get proper compensation. We just thought that was so totally unfair. You really can't get compensation for a place you call home because home is special. Once you ruin it, it's not the same.

Maybe four years ago, Delbarton Mining Company, a subdivision of Massey, affected all those little hollows that run off [Route] 119 between here and Logan. A lot of their wells was sunk, and even the ones that wasn't sunk was just so contaminated they couldn't use [the water]. People were getting sick, a lot of stomach problems, skin rashes, even a lot of respiratory problems. A lot of friends lived up those roads. As a matter of fact, my daughter was renting a house in that community. She had a baby [during] the time, and she had to go buy special water and soap to bathe her baby in, because she couldn't use [the well water]. So, I knew firsthand it wasn't just talk or hearsay. I knew what the water was like because she lived there and I visited there, and I'd seen the baby's rash.

What it boiled down to, Delbarton Mining Company had sort of lost their way underneath the earth, and they was mining coal in an area where they wasn't supposed to go, and it affected the community. [They were] mining underneath the people's property. They didn't have a permit for that particular area, which I think happens a lot in Mingo County because people cannot afford their own geologist—[they] can't afford to get somebody here to do a core sample and to see where these [mines] are at. Unless you feel a vibration underneath your home continuously, how are you to know? They do blast and you do have quivers and quakes and things in the ground [even if they aren't directly beneath you]. So how are you to know?

It took the citizens the longest time to get any kind of assistance. Once they did, the mines brought these big plastic tanks and would fill them up with water. You could look inside the tank—it was just plastic you could see through—[and] you could see stuff floating around in there. People were getting all these skin rashes, and if they drank the water, there was all the G.I. problems. People were losing weight. People that was already slim was beginning to look like cancer patients. Then they started supplying them with bottled water. A lot of people signed up for a class action [lawsuit]. There are still a few individuals that's out there that hasn't yet been compensated or heard. That [case is] going to the Supreme Court.

After seeing that happen and knowing that mine permits [were being submitted] closer and closer to our area, we just started watching real vigilant and trying to stay aware of what they were doing. Anytime the DEP would advertise in the newspaper that someone had submitted an application for a permit that was close to my home or in my watershed I would write the DEP a letter wanting to know exactly where it was at, what kind of impact it was going to have on the community, [asking] if they'd done impact studies, environmental studies, you know, all that kind of stuff. I don't think they really appreciated that.

[There were] at least five informal conferences that I request[ed] and [tried] to get the people in the community to go. It's not so much that [local people] don't care—everybody's just sort of been brow-beaten or they just sort of [believe] it's not going to do any good to try to fight. I didn't like that attitude, and I didn't want to take that attitude. So that's how I got started in the movement.

Fighting for Her Homeplace

At the time of our interview, Donna was deep in a fight against one permit in particular: Laurel Creek Coal Company's underground mining permit that would mine the land directly behind her home. To make matters worse, Donna learned that there were plans for a mountaintop-removal mining operation to come in behind the underground mine to extract the remaining coal. Donna and her husband Charlie depend on the stream that flows from the mountain behind their home for their small farm, and they fear that the mining operations will destroy their source of water and way of life.

This most recent application really hits home. It's right above my home, up the holler that runs through my property. The creek and the holler they're talking about [are] right down the middle of my property. They're going to mine right down to my property line, and they say [there's] not going to be no impact, but I know there will be. I have animals here, we have fish ponds, gardens, all these things rely on the fresh water that flows through there. We've worked for years to get a stream coming down with the water hoses that I was describing yesterday at the hearing. I'm just real worried that it's going to affect that. And even if it wasn't my stream being polluted, no more streams in West Virginia need to be polluted. No streams *anywhere* needs to be polluted, but people need to be more vigilant about this area and quit letting coal mines get away with what they do, and make the DEP stand up. There are laws and rules, you just have to make sure that someone looks at them. Just make enough noise so they know you're not going away, and they'll be more vigilant in it.

Throughout the appeals process for this mining permit, Donna had to confront multiple obstacles, including inadequate notice of the application for this permit, uncooperative regulatory agency (DEP) staff, inflexible scheduling procedures, last-minute cancelations, vague answers to her inquiries, and intimidating and manipulative coal-company executives. The difficulties she encountered with this most recent permit are illustrative of the challenges most Central Appalachian residents face when they attempt to insert themselves into decision-making processes over the fate of their homes.

They advertised an application for this mine [in] August of '06 or the first of September [in the local newspaper]. They're supposed to [include] a little map [of the proposed site], and you're supposed to be able to read that map—it's supposed to be legible. Well, on this map, you couldn't see anything—it looked like just two little curved sticks. I read [the text], and I knew where Ashcamp Branch was. My husband was real ill then, he'd just had heart surgery. I went over to the DEP [in Logan], and I asked them [about the permit]. Like I say, I'd been over there numerous times before, so they knew me. This particular [DEP official] was Haskel Boytek. He said, "I knew you'd be in here, Donna. I knew that you'd do this. Where's your husband?" I said, "He just had heart surgery." He said, "What are you doing over here?" I said, "I'm over here to protect my community." "Well, shouldn't you be with him?" I said, "I've *been* with him, and I'm going *back* to him. It's just Logan." He said, "I told them this wouldn't fly. We're going to re-advertise it." I said, "Well, you better." So like in two weeks or so they re-advertised [the permit] and it was correct, you know, the way that they were supposed to do it.

So then I wrote a letter, because that's what you have to do—it has to be in writing. You have thirty days from the first day that it's advertised to get your letter in [stating] that you're opposed or concerned, and just to list your concerns or whatever. So I done that. I wrote them a letter stating that we feared that this would affect our community and our immediate area. I got a couple of letters [in response]—one from the DEP stating that they would make [my letter] part of their permanent record, and [stating] that nothing had been done, except applications had been submitted. Then I got a letter from Laurel Creek Coal Company stating that they appreciate my concern; however, [the mine] is not going to impact me, and [asking] if I would like to remove or rescind my letter. I said, "No." Then they scheduled the informal hearing for the public, and I told everybody about it. November 30, [2006] was the first informal hearing.

My husband was sick and had gotten worse, and we couldn't attend the meeting. So I called. Before, whenever we would have these meetings, sometimes we'd go and the roads would be really, really icy or whatever, and Haskel Boytek said, "Anytime you can't make it, just call us." He said, "For whatever reason—if the roads are bad, you can't get a babysitter or whatever, just let us know, we can reschedule." So that's exactly what I done. I called, and I said, "Listen, Charlie is really sick and I don't want to leave. I can't make it. Can we reschedule?" His answer was, "No, it's already been advertised. We have to have it." They didn't take into consideration that like a year before that, I had requested a hearing [for another permit], and we went over there [for the hearing], and they forgot about it. The door was locked, everything. They rescheduled it, and I went. Anyway, that's beside the point. He said, "I'll see if I can get a [second] meeting set up here, just an informal one, and have the coal company here." I said, "Well, that would be fine."

Charlie was still recuperating, so me and [my daughter] Kelly went [to the informal meeting Haskel Boytek arranged]. Laurel Creek was there. Haskel said, "We don't really need to record this, do we Donna? Because it's just an informal meeting." I knew better, but I said, "I don't guess so." Kelly did say, "Yeah, I think we ought to," but still yet, I didn't [record the meeting]. There were like maybe ten of those men, like six from Laurel Creek and a couple of geologists and stuff. I kept asking them questions, you know, showing them where I lived on the map. My house was wrong on their map, so they had to fix that. They kept saying there would be "minimal damage." I said, "Well listen, my husband's sick. He's been going through surgeries and stuff." I said, "Right now he's real anxious and upset. He really can't stand the stress, nor would you really want to put more on him at this time." I said, "You'll need to be real careful with your dust. He has breathing problems already." [They said], "Oh, there will be minimal dust, if any at all." And Kelly said, "Well, what about our creek?" I had already told them how I use it for the farm and all that stuff. At first they said it [would be] "minimal damage," just minimal, and I kept saying, "Can you give me some kind of a statement, you know, compass for 'minimal'?" I said, "Give me a rule. Show me what minimal is." "Nobody can define minimal," they would say. This one guy from the mining company, it's like he was just trying to woo me, I thought. [Speaking in a soft voice], "Donna, I *promise* you, we will not harm you in any way. Our reputation, we're the best company there [is]. Our reputation speaks for itself. I promise you—your creek, your way of life, will *not* be impacted." And that's whenever I said, "Well, you need to define 'minimal.'" He said, "Don't worry about Laurel Creek [Coal Company]. You need to worry about Consol [Coal Company], because they're going to come in behind us after we do this deep mining. They'll do complete, total mountaintop removal." We kept insisting with these same questions, because we wanted an answer that we could hold to. And that's whenever [one of them] got mad and said, "You're not going to have a creek for two-and-a-half years! It's going to be completely stopped up because we're going to be mining up there!" Kelly said, "You can't do that!" He said, "Yes we can." Kelly was getting riled up, and I was kicking [her] under the table because I wanted her to hush, you know, didn't want it to turn into a shouting match. I didn't want it to be put on the record that I was hostile or unruly or anything like that, because you just can't get to your objective that way.

I said, "Well, I think it's time for us to go." And again I told them about the map being wrong. I said, "I wish my husband was here because he knows more about this than I do," and I said, "Would it be possible for you to come to my home and talk to him?" [They said], "Oh yes, it will be possible. We'll come." I said, "I'll get the people that's concerned in the community. We'll have a little meeting at my house. You can answer questions, you can put our mind to rest. We can tell you what we're worried about." "Yes, ma'am, we'll do that. I'll call you, we'll set it up." "OK," I said, "You all make this appointment to come to my home and talk to us." I never heard another thing from them.

That was that, and then I got the papers stating [the permit] was approved. I petitioned the board, you know, appealed to the board [to rescind the permit], and that was where we was at yesterday. I think it's been proven that you can't trust them. I've got a stack of articles of things that they've done wrong since I've been watching them for the last six years. It's just mind blowing. And then you go in front of the board, or go to the DEP and you try to tell your plight and your worries, and it's almost like it's news to them that anything there has happened. Because somehow you're not allowed to talk about what [the coal companies] have done in the past. You have to say "*this* permit" [and not talk about their history with past mining operations].

We were supposed to have this hearing in June [a month ago]. It was scheduled for June 10, [2007], and by law they have to give you ten-day notice. That's exactly what I got—ten-day notice. I got the notice on a Saturday, and it was the day before Memorial weekend, so I couldn't call [the DEP hearing scheduler] on Monday because it was their holiday. I called Tuesday, and I said, "This date isn't good for us. My husband has some appointments with specialists." I said, "Whenever I have to reschedule [these appointments], sometimes it's three months out before you can get back in with the specialist." I said, "He's getting better. I really hate to miss these appointments. [Is] there any way we can change this date?" "No, there [is] not. These dates are set the first of the year in January. Therefore, there's no way that we can change this date." "OK," I said, "I'll be there. I'll see you the 10th," and I left it at that.

At 3:30 the day before my hearing, [the scheduler] called and said [the hearing] had to be cancelled because one of the board members could not make it. I was just trying to hold my temper. I said, "Well, do you remember whenever I called you and asked if we could reschedule it, and you said we couldn't because these things are scheduled in January?" I said, "Which, I don't know how you knew in January I'd be requesting a hearing at this particular time." That's when she told me all the hearings were done on the second Tuesday or Wednesday of each month—they're only two days a month. And I didn't say anything. I didn't say whether I agreed with the change or not—it wasn't up to me, anyway. She said, "It doesn't matter if you come down here or not, there will be no hearing. There will be no one here to have a hearing because all the members cannot make it." I said, "OK. You know my plight about my husband and our appointments and stuff." I said, "Can you go ahead and set the date now? That gives me a whole month to work on it." "Well, it'll either be July the 10th or 11th or August 12th or 13th." And I said, "OK, I'll see you then." I think I got the hearing letter with the date on it like twenty-one days in advance, so I called her and thanked her for that and said that I appreciated it. Give me a little bit more time than the ten days before. So we went to the hearing [yesterday—July 10, 2007].

There were eight [community people at the hearing], not counting me and Kelly. I think there would have been more in June, because a lot of people work, and they'd already requested that day off. You know, you just can't keep doing that. A lot of people has vacations this time of year, especially around the Fourth of July is when most people try to do their summer vacations. That had a lot to do with [the low turn-out]. So we had eight people, and we had ninety-some signatures on the petition. I wished more of our people could have went. But with all the other people that appeared [environmental justice organizers and other activists], I still feel that it was a good number.

Fear and Mistrust in the Community

Despite all of the efforts that Donna put into fighting the permit, the DEP did not vote to rescind it. While she and her allies did not win this battle, Donna still feels that there were positive outcomes. At the same time, however, she also learned that there are significant barriers to convincing local residents to become involved in speaking out against harmful coal industry activities. Fear and mistrust are two of the biggest obstacles she has faced in her efforts to organize her community.

Very few people find out in time what's going to happen to their community. That was one reason why I was so gung-ho to get to the hearing. This situation was sort of unique because they haven't started mining—they haven't done anything up there. So it's sort of like we could prevent all this stuff from happening, and that's what I intend to do. Even though the permit wasn't rescinded, they made it plain in the hearing that I should have no problems, and they'll be held to that 100 percent. I will have a court record of that, and that should hold up anywhere.

As I went up and down this holler, I did meet most of the people that I never met before. That was one good thing that come [from this]. [I told] them about this permit and how we all needed to get involved and come out to the meetings and things. At first a lot of people were really interested in it.

When I took the petition around, we got ninety-three signatures. That's a lot of signatures! And that was just grownups, you know, I didn't ask children or anything like that, and there were some people that I just simply couldn't catch because of their schedules because they worked, or, you know, I tried to be respectful if I thought they was asleep, like if they worked nights. But as we got more into it, and I was having these little community meetings about what we were concerned about and what we was going to present before the board, [fewer and fewer] people kept showing up. It went from people saying, "I hope we win," you know—"we" and "our," and then two or three days before the hearing, it's, "I do hope you win your case." That's what they said—it was "your" case. It wasn't "ours" or "our fight" or "our community," "our rights." Now it's just mine.

I [also] think we have a history of always worrying about what "bigger" people's going to do to the people of West Virginia. Sometimes you wonder if the mining companies plant people with little ideas to spread in the community. I don't know. Someone [said to] me, "You're totally against coal mining, you want all the coal mines to shut down. You want us to lose our medical benefits and our pensions." I said, "I don't think so—you know, I depend on the same thing!" I said, "No. I am not against coal mining, I have stated that from the beginning. But we need to make sure that they're doing it *responsibly*."

> Donna recalled one recent incident with a long-time friend that is illustrative of the conflict and fear that has pervaded her community. This friend was the preacher of a nearby church and offered to let Donna hold her meetings in his church. Donna's husband Charlie had known this man his entire life; in fact, he even lived with Charlie's family for a time when they were in high school.

We've been best friends forever, or thought we were. You know, we graduated from school [together]. He lives on this creek a mile-and-a-half down the road. I asked him if we could have a community meeting down there, and he said, "Sure, would you like the fellowship hall?" So I made flyers up and passed them around. The *night before* [the meeting], he [called and] said that he was getting too many threatening phone calls. He said that he'd been getting a lot of calls from church people that works in the mines. He said, "I'm a preacher, I can't play politics." I said, "We're not playing politics," I said, "We're playing environment." He said he was afraid of losing his tax-exempt license for his church. I said, "Well, OK." So that meant I had to stay up that night, [make] flyers, get up at six o'clock in the morning, go put them in everybody's boxes. That just shows that we started stepping on some toes real early on.

Personal Losses and Gains

Donna has found that her activism can be very isolating at times and that it has led to a breakdown in some friendships and social ties in her community. At the same time that it can be isolating, however, Donna's activism has also expanded her network to include many new friends outside her geographic community from whom she draws strength and a great deal of personal satisfaction.

I think I've lost some friends. In just this short period of time, this last permit that I've been working diligently on, I feel I've lost some friends. [But] I've gained many *new* friends, I mean *many*, and that's good. According to Indian legend, you have to lose something to gain something, so that's good. It's a tradeoff.

I first met Trish [Feeney, organizer with Ohio Valley Environmental Coalition] whenever I went to Rawl for one of their community meetings about the water. She was just so upbeat. I thought, "This is good that someone is trying to help, trying to organize." And then I just got a call one day from Jordan Freeman [a Mountain Justice activist and filmmaker]. He just called out of the blue and [asked], could he come out and talk to me and my husband about mountaintop removal, mining in general, [and] about the environment and stuff. He come out and interviewed us. He was just so nice, and to see that these people are not from our area, but they've read of our plight and our fight [and want to help]. They know that there's something that needs to be done here and they have all this energy, and it just makes you renew yourself in, I guess, the feeling that great things can be done.

The day I went to Kayford Mountain [for the Mountainkeepers Fourth of July Celebration], I had never been there—that was my first time up there. Most of these people I had never met—I think there were only four people there that I had ever met before, and I was able to give a short speech [about what was going on with the mining permit]. I was so nervous at the time, [but] people was coming to me and introducing [themselves] and just wanting to be so helpful and so friendly. I had never ever been in a more friendlier atmosphere. You know, when complete strangers come up to you and identify themselves and tell you what they're trying to do and how we can all join together—it was just great. It's so humbling. "What can I do to help?" They'll say, "I could do so-and-so and so-and-so, is that OK?" And then they just jump in and do it. It is humbling and it is amazing, and it's wonderful. It shows you how the world could be, it really does. It just renewed, it just give me the energy and the drive I needed.

From that point on, I think I sort of changed a little bit. I mean, I think I was always sort of strong and stuff, but now I just feel I can do this. I can do this. I'm going to leave something behind, something good behind. So I'm in it, I'm in it, I'm here. I've always been in it, but now I have the time and the energy, and I'm going to do it. So it's, like I say, I think just going to Kayford Mountain and meeting all the people involved, I've been able to draw from that strength. I hope that they understand what I was able to get from them, and I just hope I'm able to help other people, to radiate it or however you want to put it. Sort of like, "Yeah, I'm going to let this light shine." It's worth it.

Women's Leadership in the Movement and Donna's Personal Motivations

While Donna's husband Charlie has been extremely supportive of her activism, she has been the one to take the lead in fighting against the mining permits and protecting their farm. In our interview she reflected on why it so often is the women, and not the men, who are the ones to take action to protect their homes and communities from environmental harm in coal-mining communities.

To be honest, most of the men, they've made their living with the coal mines. And I think the women sit back all their lives and [have] seen their husband come in dirty and treated wrongly, and I think we've had enough of it. I'm not against coal mining, I am *not* against coal mining—but I think it's up to us to step up to the plate because the men, for whatever reason, they're not quite as vocal as women. They've worked all their life *in* that, and I think it's up to us [the women] to do our own thing now.

I always loved nature. I just think it's terrific, to me. And it does sound, I guess, like I'm on a soapbox, but to be able to plant a seed and have enough faith to know that it's going to grow and flourish, and you can use it for whatever purpose you put it there, whether it's shelter, food, or just aesthetically. To me, that's just wonderful. I mean, who can produce something like that? Only nature. And I want my children, my grandchildren especially—you get energized just looking at things through their eyes. Like this summer, they found all these baby turtles, and they were cute, and to them that was just the best thing. I mean, to me, people need to be more aware of that. That makes me just as happy to see as it would be to get a ring. You know, I can buy a ring any day, really, as long as I have the money. But even if I had the money, I can't produce that turtle. Unless nature does it for me, there's no amount of money that could do that. There's just a lot of things, not just the turtles—money cannot recreate what nature gives you. Material things you can buy anytime if you have the money, or get enough credit to sign your name to. I mean, really, it's no problem. There's always a way of getting material things, but you cannot bring back nature. You cannot. And once these mountains is flattened—and I know you've had to see them, it looks so pitiful to look up there and see nothing. They have never, ever, ever done reclaiming and put it back. The law says it should be put back as good as or better than before, but there's just no way. They don't even attempt to do it. There's just no attempt made—they just throw out a bunch of vegetative seeds, and that's it. Well, it takes hundreds of years for the forest to grow. And with global warming and just the need for oxygen, I mean, you just feel like going, "Duh!" It's just so simple. That may be why they can't see it.

I'm really not an articulate person, but I can tell my story. You just feel it inside that what you're doing is right, and it needs to be done, and you're so afraid if you *don't* do it, it's not going to be done. That's the way I feel. I wanted to make sure that the children growing up, our teenagers, not just mine, but everybody's, says, "Hey wait a minute." In a way it's sad, a lot of the younger children, the fourteen- and fifteen-year-old boys, you can ask them what they're going to do [when they grow up], and they'll say, "I guess I'll just work in the mines." Even if they wanted to, there are not going to be the jobs [in the mines]. Even if they keep fifteen thousand jobs 'til these children get old enough to work, there're not going to be enough jobs [in the mines] for our children. If they don't understand now that they need to get out and do different things and change the system around here, the way we're going, they're going to be stuck in a rut. You always want to see young people aspire. You know, even if you work in the coal mines, you still need to get an education, you still need to know what's out in the world, you need to look at your surroundings as a whole. Take the whole thing in, not just have blinders on.

I do feel real passionate about this. Even if I didn't have children, which I'm glad I do, but I would still be doing this at this point in my life because I'm able to give the amount of time that it requires, and I'm able now to get out and enjoy these things that I've always loved, since I'm not so busy rearing a family and working at the home. You know, we got married young, had four daughters, I went back to college, I got my R.N. degree and I worked for twenty-five years, and we were blessed to get the girls through college and everybody's doing good. It's time for me to do something that I want to do. Well, I wanted to raise children and all that, but right now is a really good time for me to do something that I've always loved and to help preserve.

We can't get away from it entirely right now, but I think in the future we need to be away from coal entirely because it is a fossil fuel. It's always going to have some potential for polluting. The fossil fuels [are] going to run out. There are so many more clean ways of getting energy—that's where they need to put more research in. The people that own the coal—not the people in the community, but the coal companies—*they're* the ones that are getting rich from this area. The other men that work, they'll get a paycheck, but at the end of the work period, their health is gone, they're unable to enjoy their retirement, you know, the rest of the days of their life.

Transformations through Activism

Like other women in this book, Donna feels that her activism has brought about positive changes in her ability to speak out for what she feels is right.

I'm more assertive than I used to be. I thought really, really hard before I took a big, firm step here. I just feel like I'm standing here, and I'm not going to take a step back. I plan to go forward, and when I can't go forward I'll just stand firm. And for me to do that is really hard because I'm not a really articulate person. I've never spoken out like this in my life. I'm proud of myself because I took a stand and I'm not going to back down. I've always been timid. [But] I found out that you're just as timid and as strong as you'll let yourself be.

I expect to win, and if I quit before I win I haven't done what I started out to do. I still expect to win, [despite the set-backs]. I'll take small wins because they'll add up. That'll keep me going. Sometimes a fall gives you the energies that you need to get back up. Sometimes you can surprise yourself. I think the basis for [my strength] is because I *know* I'm right.

CHAPTER 11

"I WANT MY GREAT-GREAT-GRANDCHILDREN TO BE ABLE TO LIVE ON THIS EARTH!"

The Legacy of the Courageous Julia "Judy" Bonds
August 27, 1952 – January 3, 2011

Judy Bonds on Kayford Mountain, August 2006.
A moment before I took this photograph, Judy
reached down and picked up the handful of leaves
and soil shown in her hand. Bringing the handful
to her nose, she inhaled deeply, exclaiming over the
wonderful smell of the earth on her beloved West
Virginia mountains. Photo by the author.

Winner of the Goldman Environmental Prize in 2003 and appearing in dozens of films, books, and articles, Julia "Judy" Bonds is one of the most well-known faces of the anti–mountaintop-removal movement. The Appalachian activist family suffered a heart-breaking loss on January 3, 2011, when Judy died of cancer. Hundreds—if not thousands—grieved her passing across the nation. Fierce and strong, brave and proud, Judy tirelessly defended her mountains, her community, her heritage, and her family from the injustices of the coal industry.

Judy lived in the community of Rock Creek in Raleigh County, West Virginia. I had the honor of formally interviewing her in July and August 2006. As a testament to the incredible impact she had on so many people, I have also included excerpts from her memorial service in Beckley, West Virginia, which was held on January 15, 2011.

We have lost a brilliant and beautiful light in this world with Judy's passing.

From Coal Miner's Daughter to Environmental Justice Activist

I was just a regular person minding my business. I'm used to coal mining—I had an *intimate* relationship with the coal-mining industry. My father and grandfather, my brother was a coal miner, cousins, my ex-husband was a coal miner. They've been mining at Marfork—my homeplace—for forever. When Marfork Coal Company and Massey [Energy] moved in [in the 1990s], I thought it was just going to be a regular old [underground] coal mine.

[After the mining began], I started to notice my neighbors above me there moving out. I noticed coal trucks twenty-four hours a day, seven days a week. They built a helicopter landing pad all of, oh, I'd say six hundred yards from my house, and there was coal dust all over everything. The way [the coal companies] treated the people that lived in Marfork Holler and in Packsville and up in Birch Holler—they wanted people out of there. They bought out a few people and gave them good prices, and then they just ran over top of everybody else.

Every morning I'd get up, I'd see dust all over my cars, it was all over our house, it was in everything. My grandson started to get sicker and sicker with asthma and childhood diseases, mostly colds and things like that. And more and more of my neighbors were moving out. The train started loadin' [coal] right in front of our house. It loaded so loud, it shook our whole trailer—it set off alarm clocks. Like I said, coal dust was *everywhere*. And I was just *frustrated*. I made a phone call to a lawyer to see if I couldn't get them to cover [up] the coal trucks, to cover the railroads, to keep the railroad cars from loading at certain hours of the day. The lawyer told me, "Well, Ms. Bonds, this is a coal-mining town." I said, "Well, Mr. Atkins, you ain't the lawyer I'm lookin' for, I reckon."

My cousin Micky told me, "You need to look at the water, they're start-ing to get black water spills." There was fish kills—there was two fish kills up there. My grandson was standing in the stream when one of the fish kills happened. He was six years old, standing in a stream full of dead fish. He asked me, "What's wrong with all these fish?" That was the stream that my family had been going to for generations. [Massey Energy] blasted out the side of the hill [above our community], and I remember watchin' my grand-son playing in the alley there the day they blasted off the hill. And when the first blast sound went off, he dropped his toys and ran in the house. I had been around mining all my life. *All* my life. But I had never seen anything like this—the most aggressive, irresponsible mining I've ever seen.

That's how I got started—out of frustration. One day I was walking in Whitesville, and I saw a flyer that said there's a rally at Orgas about irrespon-sible mining and mountaintop removal. I went to that rally and then I found Coal River Mountain Watch's office.

[Coal River Mountain Watch] had just started; in February [they had] gotten their 501(c)3. I think the rally was in July. That's how I got started. I met Randy [Sprouse] and Janice [Nease] at the rally [the individuals who started Coal River Mountain Watch]. I saw that they were having a meeting, so I attended that meeting, and that's how I got started.

I volunteered [with Coal River Mountain Watch] for a year, and then I went on staff. I worked for Pizza Hut and for a convenience store up the road here—Country General. It was December of '99 or January of 2000 when I quit my other jobs and went to work for Coal River Mountain Watch. My very first event with Coal River Mountain Watch was a reenactment of [the miners' march to] Blair Mountain, which was a seven-day march that started in Hernshaw. That was before I even was on staff.

> The Battle of Blair Mountain was one of the most important—and deadly—events in the movement to unionize the Central Appalachian coal mines. It was also the United States' largest labor uprising (Shogan 2004). In 1921, more than ten thousand coal miners took up arms and set out to unionize the coalfields of southwestern West Virginia. As the miners marched toward Logan and Mingo Counties, they were confronted on Blair Mountain by anti-unionists, and a bloody battle ensued. After the combat continued for more than a week, Presi-dent Harding sent twenty-five hundred troops and fourteen bombing planes to end the rebellion of the West Virginia miners (McNeil 2005). In 1999, Coal River Mountain Watch organized a reenactment of the miners' march to Blair Mountain to raise awareness about this historically important landmark, which was being threatened by the Hobet mountaintop-removal mine. The march was intended to be a nonviolent event, but anti-union and pro-coal supporters physically assaulted the peaceful marchers.

[At the start of the march], when the news cameras just had left us after our press conference, we got to the Church of the Nazerene at Hernshaw. Right up above there on the right where the post office is, there were some coal miners, coal executives, Logan County Commissioners, and some UMWA [United Mine Workers of America] members. They attacked [former senator] Ken Heckler, Larry Gibson, and us—and that's well documented. They *physically* attacked us! I watched men belly-bump Janice Nease—little old ladies. Grandmas! I watched them push eighty-six-year-old Ken Heckler around like a bunch of schoolyard bullies. It was *sickening* to watch the violence that they perpetrated on little old ladies and old men. That was my first experience [with Coal River Mountain Watch]. And it wasn't just that one day we were attacked. We had to have a police escort *every day* that we marched after that.

[The march was] seven days. I was only going to walk for four days. That's all I had time off of my job, but [after the first day], I negotiated with my boss to be able to walk the rest of the time. So instead of scaring me and intimidating me, [the antagonists] pissed me off. [Their actions] only backfired on them. But it did keep other people from walking with us because of the intimidation.

We made headlines—we could not have bought the publicity that we got from this walk. We had a police escort every day that we marched, we walked through gauntlets. What [the antagonists] would do is they would set up on each side of the road, and as we walked by, they would scream and yell bad things at us. They spit on us, they threw eggs at us, they cussed us. My grandson walked with us one day, and he was like eight years old at that time—him and one of my girlfriend's daughters. They wanted to be a part of this reenactment. There was a man that followed us and cussed us while the kids were here—just screaming! It was pretty hectic. So after we walked past them, they would get in their cars and go down to the next wide spot and set up again. So we walked a gauntlet every day. We got death threats—we were told that we would never, *ever* see Blair Mountain.

We were against mountaintop removal and the Hobet mine, and so [the miners] were told that we were marching to get rid of their jobs. So it's the same old story: jobs versus the environment. They had signs like "Lizard lovers go home."

"The hardest thing I ever did was to leave Marfork": Making the Difficult Decision to Move

When Judy started volunteering at Coal River Mountain Watch, she began to learn more about the hidden dangers associated with living in the shadow of a mountaintop-removal mining operation. While she did not want to move away from her family homeplace, her fears for her grandson's health and safety eventually gave her no other option but to leave.

I moved at the end of December 1999, about when I started this job. What really, really topped it all off was when I found out that they was in the process of building the nine-billion-gallon, nine-hundred-and-some-foot-tall Brushy Fork Sludge Dam [above our homes]. My grandson, he had asthma, and the coal dust was everywhere. Everyone in that holler had moved out. I was the last one left in that holler—myself and my neighbor. This sludge dam was the last straw. We would lay awake at night, wondering, "Is this the night?" On a rainy night, "Is this the night that we'll all be washed away?" You know, no sleep.

A couple of months after I found out about the sludge dam, the more I investigated it, I found out what could happen to me is what is happening to the people in Mingo County.[1] The Department of Environmental Protection started to test my well water, and I said, "What are you testing my well water for?" "Well, that stuff could leach out [of the sludge dam] into it. It usually won't, but we just test it, because it could." So that really did it for me. I knew, of course, that water is your lifeblood. Your water supply is your lifeblood. So that's what did it for me—that sludge dam [looming] above us and the fact that it could leach into my well water.

The hardest thing I ever did was to leave Marfork. That's where I was raised, and we've been up there for over six generations that I know of. That sludge dam really did it. The property was an heirship property, and the others in my family wanted to sell. They were worried about our safety. I finally did find a lawyer to take my case on the dust and all that, and that was the solution to the lawsuit—that they bought us out. So that was it—the family wanted to sell, and so we decided that it would be in everyone's best interest [to sell]. If it had been just me, you know, I don't think I would have sold. But my grandson was involved, my daughter was involved, and that kind of sealed it.

The coal company bought everyone out up there. They own that holler now, except I do have the right—anybody [has the right]—to go to their guard shacks to [gain permission to] go to the cemetery. There's three cemeteries up there. So I go back up there and visit the cemetery. But it's hard—it's really hard when you realize that your holler's turned into a toxic waste dump. It's real hard.

[I only received a fair price for the property] *because* I had complained, *because* they knew they were in the wrong. But of course, all that money didn't go into my pocket. The price that we got had to be split seven ways [among all of the family members who jointly owned the property]. So I went from a home that was paid for but wasn't safe to using my part of the money after it was split seven ways to make a down payment on the house where I live at now. We wanted to move up into Horse Creek—into a holler—but I knew it wouldn't be safe until we stopped mountaintop removal. To live in a holler, it would be the same thing—we would be blasted, we would be flooded, it would be the same thing forever. By that time, I already knew what was going to happen. So we picked Rock Creek right off the road because it had a good amount of land there; the house was a good, solid-built house. It was a good price, $65,000, and it was what I could afford, you know, after all, I have a house payment now. My part of that money would never have paid for a house. It would have paid for a piece of land, but I had to use it as a down payment.

So I didn't win, you know. What I had was a home that was paid for, to now a home that I have to make payments on. So I lost—literally. I didn't gain, I lost. The only thing I gained was a safe feeling for my family, for my grandson, getting away from the coal dust and the sludge dam and everything up there. That's all I got out of that. You know, after studying a little bit about the Vietnam War, I was thinking about the Vietnamese—"Run away, live to fight another day." I couldn't see my grandson suffering any more from coal dust and breathing, as young as he was, because it's worse on young kids than it is adults. My grandson didn't want to move because he didn't fully realize all the dangers he was in. I realized it, though.

The Silent Majority:
Why Aren't Others Speaking Out?

I remember we took an air conditioner out of the trailer that we lived in down there [in Marfork] to put it in the upstairs window up where I live at now. The room's painted white. I turned the air conditioner on, and it blew out *black* dust *all* over that room. I just looked at that, thinking, "That's what we were breathing!" It went all over—it took me four hours to wash that black coal dust off my walls. And that just let me know what I'm dealing with. I already knew it, but that solidified it. I could never go back to dumb-and-in-the-dark again. You know, some people don't want to move from that position. Some people are smart enough to realize what's going on, they just choose not to move into that position because they know it will cost a change in their life and in their lifestyle.

Some people, of course, have allegiance to the coal companies because they're getting paid by the coal companies, which I still don't think is an excuse. It is a mono-economy here, and it is a *deliberate* mono-economy. If you control people's livelihoods, then you can take away their choices. When you take away their choices, it's like battered-wife-syndrome. [They think], "I know that I'm going to work in the coal mines, and it's going to kill me. I'm poisoning my children's water, I'm flooding my neighbors out, I'm blasting my neighbor's home, I'm sending my kid to a school where my own job is poisoning that child. But, I don't want to leave that coal baron, because that's where I get my paycheck."

Some people are afraid of the intimidation and the violence and are older, and I can understand that, in a way, because you are older. But then there are those that just don't want to do anything. I have a hard time dealing with these people because if Pauline Canterberry and Mary Miller in their seventies, and Janice [Nease], can stand up and be counted for, why can't they? You know, what makes them any different? If you're making a living by destroying other people and destroying God's creation, then that's not called a living. You're making *death*, is what you're making. You're making death and destruction, so it's no longer a living. And it's *not* OK to make a living in that way. I do realize that the coal industry has put some people in some situations. The problem is, though, you can't use that as a crutch. When they're done with this area, they're going to move out, and they're going to pull out, and leave everybody hanging. It's not a matter of *if* it happens, it's just *when* it happens. It's inevitable that it's going to happen, so why should we allow them to destroy what we have left for the last remaining tons of coal? It's ridiculous. It is ridiculous.

Women in the Movement

I asked Judy if she felt that there were more women than men at the forefront of the movement against mountaintop-removal mining. She told me that she did see more women on the front lines and cited a number of reasons for women's prominence relative to men.

In my opinion, it's because Appalachian women usually keep down the violence. They've always been on the front line. When you have a woman on the front line, that keeps down violence from people on the other side because there is a woman there. You'll find in history, look back through history and you'll see—in the movements, they put the women up front, like in the Civil Rights movement and the Vietnam War movement. Also, [it is because] women are the protectors, the mother figure. They protect their children, they want to protect their grandchildren, and they want to protect their communities. People say that ironweed is the symbol for Appalachian women.

You know that tall purple flower that's all over the mountains at the end of summer? Have you ever tried to pull it out of the ground? It's called iron-weed because its roots won't budge. That's like Appalachian women—their roots are deep and strong in these mountains, and they will fight to stay put.

Personal Costs of Activism

Judy's decision to start speaking out against irresponsible mining in Appalachia has not been without personal costs.

[My activism] has definitely affected my relationships. It drew the line on some relationships. Not all of them—I would say those that were my closest friends are still my close friends, but there are some people, you know, that won't talk to me now, just go on, walk on by—which is fine. You know, I would rather not be in with someone [if it's] going to end up in an argument. [Some in the community have had] straight-up confrontations with me. But a lot of them will just look away. It's been half and half—a lot of people just turn their head and won't even look.

I'm aware, every time that I go to a store or that I'm out alone, I'm always aware of my surroundings. I'm always aware of the fact that at any moment someone could say something to me. I have to be aware of that fact. But am I afraid? No. It makes me sad, in a way, to know that there could be people out there. I'm not worried about *my* personal safety, I'm worried about my friends and my family. I can't be worried about my personal safety. I just have to be aware that it could happen, you know, that it *could* happen. And it's something I just choose to put out of my mind, other than being aware of my surroundings. Basically, that's just how you live with it. Knowing that what I'm doing is the right thing to do is also helpful to [my] fight. It helps alleviate some of the stress from it. That's how I pay my rent for living on this planet—by being an activist and doing what I'm doing.

The last threat [against me] was a man that said there was rumors going around that they were gonna kill me and Bo [Webb] and throw us down a mine crack. We reported it to the police, but you know what? There's nothing I can do about that, other than be aware of where I'm at, you know? I carry pepper spray with me, I got a stick in the back trunk, but there's nothing I can do about that. If a coal truck wants to run me off the road—if they want to run over top of me, there's nothing I can do about it. You just have to be aware of what's going on, you have to raise your head up, look people in the eye, and know where you're at, know what your options are. Yeah, somebody could jump you, but you can't live your life afraid.

The only thing I worry about is having my grandson in the car with me if that would happen. That's why [he] rarely travels with me; that's why I'm reluctant to be seen with my grandson. See, that's how it affects me—it doesn't really affect me by making me afraid that they're gonna hurt me. What else can they do to me? There's not much else they can do to me besides kill me. But, I am afraid for my family. You have to worry about your close relatives, you know, and that's why I don't really want to be seen with [them]. I really don't like for [my grandson] to be in the vehicle with me, or attend places where there's going to be functions. I'm worried that someone will poison my dog, but as for myself, no, I'm not [worried].

Despite the threats she has experienced and the ways she has had to adjust her life to deal with dangers to her family, Judy feels her activism is a calling she must answer.

Why is it worth it to me? It's because of the future of our children and God's creation, and my soul. It's my soul, too. I look at this, this creation—God loves His creation. Who am I to *not* protect what He gave us? And I would think, why would God or Jesus want anybody in heaven that destroyed His creation here on earth—why would they want somebody like that in heaven? And I turn around and I look, and I see it's not just these mountains—it's our culture and our heritage. It's everyone's child. Everyone's child has to have clean air, and everyone's child has to have clean water, and I want my great-great-grandchildren to be able to live on this earth. Why shouldn't they? Why *shouldn't* they be able to live on this earth? It's my *duty* to protect it for them. And that's what I'm doing.

The environmental justice movement suffered a tremendous loss on January 3, 2011, when Judy died of cancer. Judy's spirit and light will continue to shine and inspire as we remember, mourn, and rejoice for the gift of this great woman. A beautiful celebration of Judy's life was held on Saturday, January 15, 2011, at the Tamarack Center in Beckley, West Virginia. The memorial service itself lasted for more than three hours and included nineteen speakers, five singers (three of whom wrote songs about Judy for her memorial), and one film tribute to her life and work. Hundreds of people from all over the country filled the large room of the convention center, leaving standing room only at the back of the hall.

In the pages that follow, I have included the program for the memorial service, as well as four of the speakers' memories and reflections on Judy's life. This section closes with a song that Andy Mahler wrote for Judy, titled "Fight Harder! (What Would Judy Do?)," which he performed during the service. We all rose to this song, raising our fists and joining in the call to "fight harder" against the environmental injustices and irresponsible practices of the coal industry.

Memorial Service for Judy Bonds
January 15, 2011 2:00–5:15 pm
Tamarack, Beckley, W.V.

Invocation—Rev. Jim Lewis
Eulogy—Vernon Haltom
Song "Black Water"—Kathy Mattea

Reflections:
Speaker—Denise Giardina
Speaker—Lisa Henderson (Judy's daughter)
Speaker—Mari-Lynn Evans
Film—A tribute to Judy Bonds

Speaker—Janet Keating
Speaker—Julian Martin
Speaker—Janice Nease
Speaker—Bob Kincaid
Song—"Hillbilly Angel"—Shirley Stewart Burns

Speaker—Larry Gibson
Speaker—Bill Price
Speaker—Debbie Jarrell (due to a family emergency Debbie Jarrell
   could not attend. An activist from New York City spoke in her place)
Song—"Beautiful Judy (Judy's Song)"—T. Paige Dalporto
Speaker—Bo Webb
Speaker—Maria Gunnoe
Speaker—John Johnson
Song—"Fight Harder (What Would Judy Do?)"—Andy Mahler

Speaker—Kathy Mattea
Speaker—Jeff Biggers and Chris Hill
Speaker—Chuck Nelson
Song—"Amazing Grace"—Jen Osha

Inspiration—Rev. Allan Johnson
Song—"Now is the Cool of the Day"—Kathy Mattea
Benediction—Rev. Jim Lewis

Eulogy: Vernon Haltom,
Coal River Mountain Watch

There aren't enough words to express what Judy Bonds has meant to the people not only of Appalachia and the United States, but the world, and what she has meant to so many of us here who knew her closely. . . . There are so many people in this room who knew her longer than I did and knew her better than I did, and her family that she loved so dearly, who really inspired her to become a leader of this movement. Not that she woke up one day and said, "I'm going to be a leader of this movement," but the heartbreak of seeing an injustice of a grandchild holding dead fish, saying, "Maw-maw, what's wrong with these fish?" She did what she had to do. She didn't have to become an activist—it was thrust upon her.

You can look around you, and probably every person in this room has some story about Judy. She inspired people from the very old to the very young, family members, new acquaintances, people that she had never met before. And she didn't have to do it in person; people would see her in a documentary and become involved in this movement. Her passion and her drive were not a normal human passion and drive. It was God-given. It was truly inspired—and very inspiring.

Judy often said, "You are the ones you've been waiting for." That was one of the things she nearly always said, whether it was to an audience of one person stopping by in the office to visit, or to a group of six thousand or more students at Power Shift. "You are the one that you've been waiting for." Judy took that mantle and that torch and carried it bravely. People who have baser gods, i.e., dirty, filthy, toxic rocks for their idols—would speak bad words about Judy. And they would threaten her, they would threaten her life, and in some cases physically attack her. But she held her head up, and she kept moving, she kept marching on.

One of the many things that Judy said that was so inspiring was, "Save the baby humans." And, having recently fathered another baby human [myself], those words have even more importance now. . . . Judy has left something in every person here. That's why we're all here—because she left a piece of herself with everybody here. She replicated herself, she expanded, she grew this movement and grew her family, which is really what this movement has become—is family. . . .

The words that Judy left us are probably more than sufficient to carry on a movement. And we have them well documented in lots of documentaries, books, magazine articles, newspaper articles, memories. Those words will always be with us, and that spirit that Judy left with us will always be with us. We need to hold that close to us and hold it dear, and do as Judy asked—to fight harder. Last summer [when Judy was diagnosed with cancer], I asked her, "Judy, what do you want me to tell people?" She said, "We've got 'em on the ropes, fight harder and finish them off!" And just this week we had good news—the EPA has vetoed the Spruce Mine [cheers from the audience]. I think Judy had no small hand in that—a lot to do with that! I figure

Judy would remind us that that's one mountain. We've got a lot more to save, too. So, enjoy that victory, and fight harder for the rest of them—fight harder for the rest of the baby humans. Judy knew that this wasn't just about her backyard, it was not just about Coal River Valley, it was about the world. This is a worldwide struggle. And I think people being here from California and New York attests somewhat to that fact. . . . In the days to come, we do need to stay strong and fight harder because when those who worship a toxic black rock are dealt a blow, they come back violently. So, I ask everyone to stay strong, stay courageous, stay together, united, stay in solidarity. And for Judy's sake and the baby humans, fight harder.

Personal Reflection:
Lisa Henderson Snodgrass, Judy's daughter

First, I would like to say hello to all of you—friends, family, and environmental family of my mother Julia Bonds. . . . Some of you I have met, and some of you I have only heard stories about, but most of you I read cards and letters from that were sent to my mom while she was sick. We sat almost daily and read over her letters and cards. And I'm sure this made her feel close to you all and kept her in touch with her work. I told Mom that I always knew that her environmental family were wonderful people, but I never really knew what extraordinary people you all were until her life took this awful, unexpected turn. And it touched us all so much that she meant so much to you. And again, thank you all for your gifts, cards, prayers, donations, and well-wishes that have continued toward our family even after my mom's death.

I'd like to tell you a little about my mother before she became the person that you all knew. She was born August 27, 1952, the sixth child to Oliver "Cobb" Thompson and Sarah Easton Hannah Thompson, but one of her sisters was stillborn and a brother only lived a few days. She was not born in a hospital, but at home in Birch Hollow. My grandfather was a coal miner that began working in the mines in his early teens. Mom told many stories about growing up in Birch Hollow where she was born, and some would say that these were the poorest and hardest conditions in her family's life. But her siblings and her always spoke of Birch Hollow as though they were describing paradise. Surrounded by clear streams and untouched mountains full of wildlife, I'm sure [it provided] many adventures for a child. And in case you are wondering, no, at times they didn't have an indoor toilet—or running water!

With their family still growing, and the addition of two more children, my grandmother and grandfather moved their family toward the mouth of the hollow, but never completely leaving Packsville Hollow. I grew up in this hollow, and my son grew up here until he was ten. My mom and I watched him climb the same hills that we did as kids, play in the same mud puddles, ride the same bike path, take the same walks down the same little dirt roads, and build little dams in the stream like we did. This is why we loved our little hollow so much, and these hard times and good times are what shaped us as a family and as human beings. This is part of the fire that burned in my mother to defend her family memories, home, and hollow, and the rest of the homes on Coal River Valley.

As I said before, my grandfather was an underground coal miner from his early teens until he retired, and he died six months later from black lung. Many of you know the story of how my grandmother obtained my grandfather's black lung [benefits]. I heard my mother tell the story several times. My grandfather filed for his black lung benefits, and of course was denied. My grandmother tried to obtain a life insurance policy on him, to which the insurance company put him through many tests. They came to visit my grandparents' home in Packsville afterward, only to deny him because *their* test results showed that he *did* have black lung, rather extensively. My grandmother sent her youngest child next door to visit her elder sister and proceeded to demand from the insurance agent the test results proving my grandfather had lung disease. He declined to give them to her, to which she asked him again a little more forcefully by removing her pistol from her house coat pocket—proving her point to the insurance agent that she needed those papers a little more than he did!

This is the type of grit that my mother had in her, so when Massey Energy came to Packsville in the 1990s and proceeded to remove some of the residents out of their way, they had no idea that the daughter of Easton Thompson lived there. They didn't know any of the names or the faces of residents of Packsville, nor did they care. And, boy, would they come to regret that! You see, most of the time in history great warriors are created when they are forced—when the battle is forced upon them. Trains screeched by our house all hours of the night, coal trucks rumbled and splashed mud and coal dust on our fences, porches, houses, and lawn furniture. Helicopters buzzed the big man in and out of the landing pad only a few hundred feet from our house. Traffic from miners commuting from Madison, Beckley, Logan, and places even farther away, zoomed past our house all hours of the day and night. The long walks that my mom, my son, and me took on lazy summer days were now all but impossible to enjoy. And just living there was becoming increasingly difficult. Traffic constantly zoomed by us, trash littered our little hollow road, and the smell of diesel fuel choked us. The final poke in the eye came when we walked across our road to let Andrew dip his feet in the stream and our little dog Daisy get a few gulps from the stream as well. And Andrew and Daisy reached the edge of the stream first, of course, and plunged right in. As Mom and me reached the stream, we were horrified at the sight of a child standing in the middle of a grey-black stream with his dog, surrounded by dead fish and holding them in his little hands. He looked up at us and asked her, "What's wrong with these fish?" We knew that Whitesville's drinking water intake was less than three miles down the river, and whatever was coming from the mines that ate the gills and the eyes out of these fish was being drank by *hundreds* of people.

The DEP of course came and issued violations, but the spills never stopped the *entire* time we lived there. Once my mom even called in a violation to the DEP and the operator asked her what it was to her—she lived above the contaminated water. Were we supposed to shut up and say nothing while hundreds of people were slowly being poisoned to death below us? If we did, we were as much to blame, and we knew that somehow, somewhere we were being poisoned also, and we would soon have to leave our little hollow.

This was how a true pioneer was made—a defender and a tree hugger. Mom began checking into our neighbors and became aware of the plans they had to strip every mountain on Coal River, therefore affecting every hollow, house, and stream the way we were being affected. Suddenly, our eyes were open to the effects of global warming and polluted waters in other communities. This woman educated herself. She became a volunteer at Coal River Mountain Watch while she worked several minimum-wage jobs. She was eventually offered a job at Coal River Mountain Watch and became a part of your environmental family.

This journey for her was a true struggle in every sense of the word. She traveled far from her family and home to other states to bring attention to her cause. She was made fun of in her community, shunned by many neighbors and so-called friends, members of our own church, and physically attacked. This even caused strife at home between her and I. Although I was proud of her and supported her and loved her, I was also treated badly by many people in the community—by some of my so-called friends—and I was physically attacked also.

I was always terrified that physical harm would come to her, and I was worried—but was it worth it? Absolutely. This little five-foot-one, one-hundred-forty-pound, poor, high-school-educated woman kept mighty King Coal on his toes. And for what? Her family, their future, her community and its future, and God's Creation. She armed herself with a protest sign, her voice, the truth, and the purest of intentions. And if you have the truth on your side and your intentions are pure and not self-serving, God is also on your side. And what else do you need? That's why she never backed down from a debate or a challenge—because she knew that she was right and that He was on her side. Her eyes were opened at a time in her life when I'm sure she was reflecting on her own past. The imprint she left on so many lives I'm sure will be felt for generations.

Oftentimes, when me and her would encounter someone flaunting their riches, she would say, "Why can't people live simply so others can just simply live?" She wasn't at all impressed by their money, and she had the quote plastered on her walls that read, "The comfort of the rich depends on the abundant supply of the poor." To many of you she was a mentor and hero and a true patriot. To me she was this also. She made our little family laugh and cry and see things in all lights. She raised me and Andrew, educated us, sheltered and clothed us, and at times drove us crazy! She was the last face I seen in the night and the first one I seen in the morning. And I'm now at a point in my life where I'm sure many of you have been—or you will be—when you wake up and say, "Oh my God, my mother was right about *everything.*" I lived in the same house with her all of my life, and I knew her better than any of you, and I'm still in awe of her courage and passion. She was my mother, and I miss her so much. [Begins crying.]

She was passionate to the very end. One day she received a letter from Senator Rockefeller when she was sick, and it *infuriated* her! She went to work right away in response to this letter, but for his sake, she never got to finish it. I told her I would type it for her, but she only had time to put a few broken, unfinished lines on paper that contained what she seen as disgust, that a man with his education and stature [had] *zero* vision and *zero* ingenuity when it came to creating new clean energy jobs for his fellow West Virginians that would greatly benefit our state. It amazed her that politicians and fellow West Virginians could gather in a dome in Morgantown and cheer for the mighty Mountaineers but could not—and would not—protect the mountains for which they are named.

Mom once inspired you all not to give up and to keep fighting. Let a fire be ignited in all of us, that we could bring good to the world with pure intentions, the truth, a loud voice, and a protest sign. A friend of Mom's wrote comforting words to me. [He] wanted to pass along to you that my Mom is in a wonderful place now, where the mountains are undisturbed, wild, and beautiful as God intended them.

Thank you all, and God bless.

Personal Reflection: Bill Price, Sierra Club, West Virginia Chapter

Over the past several days, I read e-mails, blog posts, articles, and even today some of the remarks—so many people when they were reflecting on Judy Bonds, talked about "the first time." "The first time I met Judy Bonds." "The first time I heard Judy Bonds speak." "The first time that I saw Judy Bonds on film." So that got me to thinking about that phrase, "the first time." And how it is reserved for special people and special times. Perhaps we remember the first time we saw our child. The first time we met our wife, or husband, or life partner. Perhaps it's the first time we met that special teacher or that special minister. Sometimes those memories of the first times are sad because it's tied to tragedy. Some of us in this room will always remember the first time and where we were when we heard that President Kennedy had been assassinated, even though we may have been very young. Or where we were the first time we heard that Martin Luther King had been killed. Many of us will remember where we were when we first heard about 9/11. And I dare say that most of us will remember where we were when we first heard about the shootings in Tuscon a week ago today.

Those first times, both the ones that are joyful and the ones that are heartbreaking, are remembered because they are about moments that change our life. And that's what meeting Judy Bonds was—life changing. I first met Judy when I walked into the office of Coal River Mountain Watch after having attended the Coal Summit in Charleston, West Virginia, and having gone up to Kayford Mountain to see Larry Gibson. Judy was in her usual state. She was on her computer, checking e-mail, answering the lies—the latest lies of the coal barons, or the politicians that are in their hip pockets. Going over to her little desk in the corner, looking for something that she couldn't find, going back to the big table in the middle of the room, sorting through articles. Judy was always busy. Never still, even before the Goldman Prize.

Back in those days, the office was basically Judy Bonds, Janice Nease, and Patty Sebok. And Judy was busy, but she took the time to sit down with me. Now, I have to admit, I didn't realize just how life changing it was going to be. But what I did realize was that Judy was a kindred spirit. At the time, I was dealing with coming to the realization that the same industry that put food on my table when I was a child, gave my father a way to allow my parents to send me to college, was also the same industry—the coal industry—that had destroyed my community in Dorothy, West Virginia, and was destroying community after community all over Appalachia. Judy, who came from a family of coal miners, had been through that realization herself, and one of those moments was when she saw her grandson in that stream in Marfork Holler, holding those dead fish. And Judy knew, as Martin Luther King said, "There comes a time when silence is betrayal." And Judy would never be silent again, and she would help so many people—including me—find our voice.

Judy always loved and showed that love by keeping us true to our mission. I remember back in the days when we were first looking at Mountain Justice Summer—the first one. Having those sometimes-difficult discussions—Were we ready to ramp this up? Were we ready to step up to nonviolent civil disobedience? What would that mean to other communities that we worked in? What would be their reaction? How would it impact people's safety? One concern was that we didn't have that Martin Luther King type of leader—the one person who could electrify people. I remember meeting at the Unitarian Church with many of you in this room. And Judy listened to those concerns, and then she leaned forward, and with those blazing eyes she said, "Guys! Let me tell you something!" Judy often started with that phrase. And then she used the quote that you've heard today that has been attributed to Gandhi and that's also been attributed to the elders of the Hopi Nation. She said, "We are the ones we've been waiting for!"

You see, Judy understood—and helped so many people understand—that this movement is not about a single person. This movement is not about one organization. This movement is about a vision. A vision for Appalachia and a vision for this nation, indeed, for this earth. It's a vision for clean water, clean air, healthy grandchildren, prosperous people, and a vision of justice. And if we are to attain that vision, we all must be working to achieve it. We must organize. And she knew that all of us could do our part. And to quote Judy, as you heard today, "If a short, gray-haired grandmother from West Virginia can do it, so can you!"

We come here today to remember and to honor and to mourn Judy. She was an encouraging and inspiring individual. And that encouragement and inspiration will continue into future generations. Let's remember what Judy would want us to do. I'll close with this—with deep respect and admiration for Judy—"Hey guys, let me tell you something! You want to be the one? Then go out this week and talk to somebody who's not in this movement right now, and get them to TAKE ACTION to stop the terror that is mountaintop-removal coal mining. Go! Fight Harder! ORGANIZE!"

Thank you.

Maria Gunnoe, Southern West Virginia Resident and Organizer, Ohio Valley Environmental Coalition

When I first heard of Judy's passing [crying], I was setting in front of the computer. I put on my hiking boots, and I hit the hills with everything I had. And you know what I found there? I found peace. I found the peace that Judy fought for. Judy's with us in everything we do. She left a little piece of her with everyone she met. And when you take a stand, when you dig in your heels, when you say, "It stops here," that's that piece of Judy. That's that piece of Judy that she left with everyone in this room.

Judy was an inspiration to me, beyond an inspiration that anyone could put words to. She educated me, she helped me to be proud of something that I had always been somewhat ashamed of. I had been taught to be ashamed of being a hillbilly. Judy was the first person that ever looked me in the face and said, "There's nothing wrong with being a hillbilly. Being a hillbilly is a good thing! Being a hillbilly is a good thing. We've survived everything there is to survive."

My heart is truly with Lisa and Andrew. I think the world of Judy. And, when I look at you, I can't help but to think of her.

When I started having problems with mountaintop removal, I went to Boone County, then I went to the state, then I went to the federal, and then I went to Judy. And that's where Judy introduced me to the rest of the world. I spent a lot of time with Judy in the mountains. And that's the only place I can feel close to her right now. So when you feel, when you get that longing for Judy, when you need to feel Judy, go to the peaks. Go to the ones that's still there, and sit there. The sun coming through the trees, hitting you on the face—it's Judy. And when you slide and bust your rear-end, and you hear somebody laughin'—that's Judy!

I'm absolutely honored to have spent the time with Judy that I was able to spend. And it has literally laid the path for the rest of my life. And I think that each one of us can say that. Each one of us, because of the fact that we knew Judy, we can say that the direction of our lives have changed. The things that we thought were important wasn't really important, and Judy's the one that showed us that. We need clean water, we need clean air, and we need friends and love around us. And that's what Judy taught us.

Now, the outrage that you heard in Judy's voice when she was combating the lies of the industry, that same outrage is deep down inside of each one of the people in this room. And we have to take that outrage and anger and direct it, and focus it, and bring Judy's vision to pass—make it happen. It will happen, and we're going to be the ones to do it. That's why each one of us was blessed enough to know Judy Bonds.

Thank you.

"Fight Harder (What Would Judy Do?)"

ANDY MAHLER, Singer-Songwriter

When they're blowing up the mountains
When they're fillin' in the hollers, too
When they're building toxic sludge dams, ask yourself
What would Judy do?

She'd FIGHT HARDER! FIGHT HARDER!
For the mountains and the water
FIGHT HEART-ER! FIGHT SMARTER!
For the people and the planet, too.
FIGHT HARDER! FIGHT HARDER!
She never quit once she started
We could always count on her; can she count on you?
What would Judy do?

When the water's red with poison
And the air is toxic, too
When they're poisoning little children, ask yourself
What would Judy do?

She'd FIGHT HARDER! FIGHT HARDER!
For the mountains and the water
FIGHT HEART-ER! FIGHT SMARTER!
For the people and the planet, too.
FIGHT HARDER! FIGHT HARDER!
She never quit once she started
We could always count on her; can she count on you?
What would Judy do?

When you're faced with an injustice
Ecological destruction, too
When they're warming up the planet, ask yourself
What would Judy do?

She'd FIGHT HARDER! FIGHT HARDER!
For the mountains and the water
FIGHT HEART-ER! FIGHT SMARTER!
For the people and the planet, too.
FIGHT HARDER! FIGHT HARDER!
She never quit once she started
We could always count on her; can she count on you?
What would Judy do?

She would ask you to be more,
Because "You're the ones that you've been waiting for."

CHAPTER 12

Conclusion

> We're being sacrificed here for energy for the rest of the world.
> . . . Why should we give up everything we own for somebody
> else to have cheap energy? For a world of people that's already
> pampered to death. It's the injustice of it. Honey, this is discrimi-
> nation—and I don't use that word lightly, either.
> —PAULINE CANTERBERRY (pp. 38–39)

The twelve women whose stories fill this book have watched their communities, their mountains, their streams, their homes, their families, and their own
health be ravaged by destruction related directly to the coal industry. All of
these women have decided to take a stand against the injustices they have witnessed, despite the numerous barriers they have encountered to speaking out
against the coal industry. Like many other local, grassroots movements fighting
for environmental justice throughout the nation, working-class women have
been the ones to initiate and lead the struggle for justice in Central Appalachia.

Motivations for Action:
Motherhood and Beyond

Much of the research on women's grassroots activism has found that working-
class women often attribute their social-movement involvement to their roles
as mothers. Motherhood is called on both as a justification and as a resource
for environmental justice activism (Krauss 1993; Brown and Ferguson 1995;
Culley and Angelique 2003; Peeples and Deluca 2006). Parallel findings can
be seen among the women activists in this book. One of the most prevalent
themes throughout the narratives is that activism against the injustices of the
coal industry is an extension of these women's identities—and obligations—as
mothers and grandmothers. For instance, Patty Sebok explains her decision
to fight overweight, speeding coal trucks as being largely motivated by a fear
for her children's safety:

I didn't want [the coal trucks] driving through my community like they were doing. How would they feel if I came to their community in a big *tank* like that with their kids out playing or trying to learn how to drive and run down the road like that—how would they like it?

. . . I thought, "What have I got to lose?" They're going to kill me or my kids on the road, and it wasn't just in my hollow. Anytime I would do my errands it was just very, very dangerous. I was just, you know, a housewife and a mother doing my thing, taking care of my home and my kids (p. 97).

Similarly, when Lorelei Scarboro recounts how she explained to her son-in-law (a coal miner for Massey Energy) why she feels her activism is so important, she reveals justifying it through her desire to protect her granddaughter's access to clean drinking water:

. . . I said, "The reason I do what I do is, when I look at [my granddaughter], I try to think about the quality of water she's going to have to drink when she's of child-bearing age. What I do is about the water. It's not against mining, it's for the water. . . . You can't look at her and not think about the quality of water that she's going to have." That really, really helped him to understand—because we can live without electricity, but we've got three days without water. She's got three days without safe drinking water (p. 131).

Some women activists, like Maria Gunnoe, express a great deal of anger toward the coal companies for compromising their ability to adequately protect their children from harm. For these women, this anger becomes a motivating force, driving them to fight back. In her narrative, Maria vividly describes her daughter's birthday in June 2003, when her home was severely flooded because of runoff from a mountaintop-removal coal mine behind her house. Five acres of her land washed away that night, and the raging water nearly took her house as well. As Maria relates, "It was a night that I will never forget. If I live to be a hundred years old, I'll never forget that. . . . I literally thought we were gonna die in this house" (pp. 12–13). The psychological trauma the flood caused her children served as Maria's call to action:

There is tremendous fear when it rains . . . my daughter went through a, hey, I feel safe in calling it a posttraumatic stress disorder. She would set up at night—if it was raining or thundering, or any weather alerts or anything like that going on on the news, my daughter would not sleep. . . . I found out one morning at 3:00 in the morning, it was thundering and lightning, and I go in, and I find her sitting on the edge of her bed with her shoes and her coat and her pants [on]. [Pauses, deep breath, voice cracks.] And I found out then [pauses] what it was putting my daughter through. [Crying.] And that is what *pissed me off*. How *dare* they steal that from my child! The security of being able to sleep in her own bed. The coal companies now own that. They now own my child's security in her own bed. [Pauses.] And how can they expect me as a mother to look over that? . . . What if I created *terror* in their children's lives? And that is what it has done to my children.

. . . [A]ll I wanted to do was to be a mother. . . . [I]n order for me to be a mother, and in order for me to keep my children safe, . . . I've had—it's not an option—I've had to stand up and fight for our rights (pp. 13–14).

Maria's recounting of this terrifying event not only points to her extreme anger at the coal companies for the psychological damage they have caused to her children, but it also reveals her conviction that as a mother, it is *compulsory* for her to fight the injustices of the coal industry. Otherwise, she asserts, she would not be able to fulfill her obligation "to keep [her] children safe" (p. 14).

Confirming past research on working-class women's grassroots activism (Naples 1992, 1998; Collins 1990), many of the women in this book express that their motherhood duties extend beyond protecting their own children and grandchildren to fighting to protect *all* children. This identity of universal mother has been a driving force for Judy Bonds, who asserts, "Everyone's child has to have clean air, and everyone's child has to have clean water, and I want my great-great-grandchildren to be able to live on this earth. Why shouldn't they? Why *shouldn't* they be able to live on this earth? It's my duty to protect it for them. And that's what I'm doing" (p. 156). The idea of activism as duty is a strong theme throughout the interviews. For many women, the motherhood identity serves as both motivation for action and a resource for maintaining their involvement.

A number of interviewees expressed a belief that the reasons for women's leadership in the environmental justice movement run even deeper than an obligation or duty that women feel. Some, such as Debbie Jarrell, believe that a primordial "mothering instinct" drives women into environmental justice activism (p. 119). Maria Gunnoe also shares this conviction, further asserting,

As a mother, . . . part of seeing to it that your child grows up in a safe environment is seeing to it that the environment is tended to. . . . When you see your kids' water—future water—being polluted so that you can keep your lights on, it just becomes a no-brainer. All of a sudden, lights aren't that important anymore. . . . I really don't think that it's in a man's instincts to see that. I really believe that it's the mother's instincts that makes you realize how detrimental what's going on is to our children's future (pp. 21–22).

Maria maintains that the mothering "instinct" provides women with a heightened state of awareness about the effects of environmental issues on their children, an instinct she believes men simply do not have. The importance of the mothering "instinct" to activists' justifications for women's leadership in the environmental justice movement is in keeping with much of the literature on women's activism detailed in the introduction. Protest activities that mothers undertake on behalf of their children are often viewed apolitically and simply as extensions of a mother's role to protect, clothe, shelter, and feed her children. Framing women's activism as a result of mothering "instincts," rather than a conscious decision, affords women a level of cultural protection and legitimation for their protest activities.

The Protector Identity

While the motherhood identity is undoubtedly a significant motivating force among many of the narratives in this book, it is important to point out that this motherhood identity is discussed in ways that primarily emphasize a protector duty or role. For instance, in her reflection on why it tends to be women who populate the front lines of the environmental justice movement, Judy Bonds states, "[W]omen are the protectors, the mother figure. They protect their children, they want to protect their grandchildren, and they want to protect their communities" (p. 154). Similarly, Maria Lambert contends, "It's the need to protect, that need inside of most women, and I would say probably 99.9 percent of the women have that need to protect somebody, whether it's a husband, a child, a parent, a neighbor, an animal, whoever" (p. 79). Lorelei Scarboro further elaborates that what she and others perceive to be an inherent drive to protect is not limited to protecting people; it also includes the natural environment:

> I've always been a very fierce protector of my kids, and I'm still doing that. I'm still protecting what I have left. . . . Not only [my house and land], but the mountain behind it and the environment and the wildlife and the vegetation. I think I'm still a very fierce protector. I don't think that's something that I created. I think that's something that was handed down. . . . The majority of the Appalachian women that I know were born fighting and protecting (pp. 128–129).

As articulated by these three activists, they believe that the "drive to protect" is something inherent in most women, especially Appalachian women.

These interviews suggest that it is not simply a "motherhood identity" that motivates and legitimates the activism of many Central Appalachian women; rather, it is more accurate to describe their activism as stemming from a broader "protector identity." This protector identity both encompasses and extends the motherhood identity such that these women perceive that the moral authority for their activism emanates not only from a calling to protect their children and grandchildren from irresponsible mining practices, but also from an obligation to protect their communities, their mountains, their heritage, their family homeplaces, and their way of life.

Protecting Communities

Past research on working-class women activists has found that the drive to protect one's children from harm is often translated into efforts to defend the larger community (Collins 1990; Naples 1992, 1998; Seitz 1995). This link between family and community is also prevalent among the women in this book. In describing what drew her into activism, Teri Blanton recalls her motivation deriving from her anger at the destruction a coal company caused to her home community:

> I [grew up] in Harlan County in a little community called Dayhoit. It was like one of those communities that everybody took care of each other, and if somebody had too much of something, then you would share it. So it was a real caring community. Everybody watched out for everybody's kids. . . .
>
> I got a divorce, [and] I came back [to Dayhoit] with two kids. I moved [back] to my community, thinking, "I'm bringing them home to a safe place." [After] this coal company came [in], you would have to drive through coal muck to get in and out of my community. Sometimes it would flood so bad with the coal muck and the runoff from this processing plant that it would be up to your headlights. I was just really pissed off about it (pp. 85–86).

Teri's hopes to provide her children with a safe community to call home were wrecked by a coal company's negligent production practices. Thus, in Teri's eyes, in order to fight for her children's safety, she also had to fight for the protection of her community.

The way that Donetta Blankenship describes her motivation to protect her community is less directly tied to her children's health and safety and is more generally about her perception of social justice:

> Everybody has a right to live healthy. I'm going to go out and support and help my—I guess you call it—friends and neighbors and communities, because they need clean water, they need good health. I'm going to fight against what these people are doing so that [my friends and neighbors] can have homes and better health (p. 66).

Fighting for the protection of her neighbors' homes and drinking water is a major reason for Donetta's willingness to speak out publicly against problems related to the coal industry, despite her inherent shyness. As Donetta relates, "I just feel like I need to go and help other people that is in situations like this. It needs to get better for them" (p. 66).

In addition to being motivated to fight for the physical safety and health of members of their communities, a number of the women also describe feeling a drive to protect the social cohesiveness and relational aspects of their communities, which are also under threat of destruction. In her narrative, Maria Gunnoe describes the ruination of the town of Whitesville, a town just a few miles from where she lives that used to be the bustling center of life in the Coal River Valley:

> Whitesville is an example of what happens when you depopulate communities. The people that lived in Whitesville, say fifty years ago, made that community what it was. Those people were the people that had been there for generation on top of generation on top of generation. And they've left. The people that was there, the families that grew up there, they've left. There're still a few of them dotted here and there, but most of them's left. And there you take the community out of the community. When you take the people out that has been there for generation on top of generation, when you take them out, the sense of community is gone. You take the kinship out of the community. . . . And that's one reason I'm fighting so hard to save it (p. 17).

Maria describes watching the same depopulation taking place in her own neighborhood:

> I sit right here at my home every day and I see U-Hauls headed up and down the road with people moving out. And I see it happening right here, right now. I try my best to stop it. I talk to people and say, "Please don't sell out [to the coal company]. If you sell out, not only are you selling out your homeplace, but you're also selling out your neighbors. You're selling out your community." Yeah, it's hell to stay, but if we can stay, then we can eventually put them out. The coal companies are attacking the citizens here and making life so hard on them that they have to leave (pp. 16–17).

The loss of community, including the bonds, social networks, and kinship ties that are the building blocks of social capital, has very real consequences for those who remain behind. As I discuss elsewhere (Bell 2009), depopulation and the loss of social capital in coal-mining communities has devastating effects on the well-being of local citizens. Maria and others are fighting not only to safeguard the health and safety of the people who live in their communities, but also to protect the "community-ness" of their communities.

Protecting the Homeplace

Each of the women in this book has a deep connection to not only the people in her community, but also to the physical place that she calls home and the way of life that is connected to that place. Protecting "home" is a strong motive for activism described throughout these narratives.

The "Sylvester Dustbusters" Pauline Canterberry and Mary Miller became involved in the environmental justice movement in response to the massive quantity of coal dust emanating from a Massey Energy coal preparation plant adjacent to the town. A desire to protect their homes is what Pauline and Mary cite as their impetus for action. As Pauline relates,

> You know, it's not easy to sit and watch your home being destroyed, something you have worked for all your life. . . . [The coal dust] just took the value completely away from it. We found out through our lawsuit—because we all had our homes appraised—that our homes have lost 90 percent of their value. . . .
> I was mad. I worked hard for my home. I worked under a lot of hard conditions for my home, and I didn't think anybody had the right to destroy it (pp. 35–36).

Mary Miller echoes Pauline's feelings, stating, "I just think that's about the worst thing [that] could happen to somebody—when you see that you've worked all your life for this, and you're losing what you've loved and worked for" (p. 36). Rather than being motivated to join the environmental justice movement by a "motherhood identity," as many of the other activists describe, both Pauline and Mary began speaking out in order to protect their homes and their town from being destroyed by coal dust.

Donna Branham's entry into environmental justice activism was similarly prompted by the threat of destruction to her homeplace. In her narrative, she describes her desire to protect her farm and water supply from a mountaintop-removal mine that, according to the permit application, would operate directly behind her property:

> The creek and the holler they're talking about [are] right down the middle of my property. They're going to mine right down to my property line, and they say [there's] not going to be no impact, but I know there will be. I have animals here, we have fish ponds, gardens, all these things rely on the fresh water that flows through there. We've worked for years to get a stream coming down with the water hoses that I was describing yesterday at the hearing. I'm just real worried that it's going to affect that (p. 138).

Lorelei Scarboro also cites the threat to her home as one of the primary reasons she was spurred to action. As she relates, Massey Energy's Eagle 2 mine permit includes a portion of Coal River Mountain that is directly behind her house:

> I've got almost ten acres, which goes to the top of Coal River Mountain. It's a very peaceful place. I can sit in my living room and watch the deer with velvet

still on their antlers jump the fence next door. This morning, I was looking out my bathroom window, and I saw the groundhog that lives under the building out back that my granddaughter named "Rocky." Yesterday, on the way home, we had to stop twice on the way in Rock Creek for the turkey to cross the road. There's a freshwater stream that runs right by my driveway. It's a very quiet, peaceful, serene place that I don't believe *anybody* has the right to drive me out of.

My home's threatened. The family cemetery is threatened. The stream that runs by my house, the deer that I sit there and watch leap across the fence—everything, because of Eagle 2 [mine], is now threatened. So I really don't have a choice (p. 122).

Protecting "Appalachia"

A question commonly asked of Central Appalachian environmental justice activists is, "If things are so bad, why don't you just move?" To most people from outside the region, moving seems like a logical solution to the problems these residents face. However, as the activists in this book attest, many do not consider leaving to be an option. Their attachment to home and community is so strong that fighting back is the only acceptable solution they can see. Lorelei Scarboro expresses the intensity of this connection when remembering how she felt when, at a grassroots training session, the vice president of the company Patagonia said to her, "The easiest thing in the world to do would be to move":

> But it wouldn't. That would be the *hardest* thing to do, because that's the house I raised my kids in, that's the house my husband built. He's buried next door. The land that he loved has been in his family for generations, and I can't imagine driving out of the driveway for the last time and leaving him in the cemetery and everything else there. That would be the *hardest* thing to do. It's easier to fight and to try to, to try to save all that, because if I walk away from it, it's certainly destroyed. It's certainly blown apart and destroyed. So it's a whole lot easier to stay there and fight (p. 124).

These women feel a very deep connection to the physical place they call home; however, the land is important not only for its physical aspects, but also for the intangibles that it represents. As Lorelei further articulates, "It's difficult to explain the attachment, the sense of place that Appalachians have. It's a connectedness to the land, to your surroundings. It's not the value of the house, it's not the price of the ten acres. It's the memories. It's what you have there. It's the life you share with the people you love" (p. 124). According to Low and Altman (1992), "place attachment"—what Lorelei Scarboro is describing here—is the bond that connects individuals to their environment. This bond is not simply a relationship with the physical landscape; it is also composed of interpersonal, community, and social relationships. As Judy Bonds asserts, "It's my soul . . . it's not just these mountains—it's our culture and our heritage" (p. 156). Thus, just as important as the physical landscape (or perhaps more important) are the intangibles—culture, history, and community—that the land represents.

Protecting their culture and heritage is a calling so strong that some women activists, such as Maria Gunnoe, cling to their family homesteads even after floods, coal dust, or contaminated well water have destroyed their houses and land. Despite the continual threat of another flood and harassment by the coal company, Maria refuses to sell her homeplace: "My family was here long before they started mining coal. And why should we have to leave? Who in the hell are they to think they can put us out?" (p. 17) The land on which her family homeplace rests is more than just a place to live. According to Maria, selling out to the coal company would mean "allowing them to run me out of my ancestral home," and "allowing them to steal my children's culture and their heritage, and the upbringing that I had" (p. 15).

Social scientists have recognized the importance of place attachment to various forms of group and individual action, such as community revitalization, environmental protection, and planning efforts (Mesch and Manor 1998; Brown, Perkins, and Brown 2003; Vaske and Kobrin 2001; Manzo and Perkins 2006). As Mesch and Manor (1998) assert, place attachment "generates identification with place and fosters social and political involvement in the preservation of the physical and social features that characterize a neighborhood" (505). In other words, an attachment to place is an important component of community and political engagement. Furthermore, attachment to place also has implications for individual identity-formation processes (Proshansky, Fabian, and Kaminoff 1983; Twigger-Ross, Bonaiuto, and Breakwell 2003; Hague 2007; Walker 2007). Hague (2007) argues that as our attachment to certain places grows, "we start to identify ourselves with these places. . . . This results in self-concepts that are based in part on place" (44).

A number of the activists in this book express their place attachment and drive to protect the land through their identity as "Appalachians." As Debbie Jarrell relates, "We are Appalachian women, and . . . our roots run so deep, you can't distinguish us from the earth we live on. It's just a part of us" (p. 119). Maria Gunnoe further explains the connection she sees between being an "Appalachian woman" and fighting the injustices of the coal industry:

> The Appalachian women are the backbone behind the Appalachian family. And our Appalachian families are being put in danger. And it's our natural—it's our natural instinct to step up to the plate and say, "Excuse me, but you're killing something

I love." You know, and we will fight for it. That is our link to who we are. And it's a link to who our children are. And we can't allow it to be destroyed. As mothers of future generations of Appalachian boys and girls, we can't allow them to steal this from our children—it's too precious. And it can't be replaced (p. 21).

"Appalachian identity" is a notion that has been both celebrated and contested within the field of Appalachian Studies. Numerous scholars have argued that the geographic and cultural place of "Appalachia" is actually nothing more than an invention of travel writers, journalists, academics, and capitalists seeking to "other" the region. It has been depicted either as a romanticized, isolated mountain land populated by descendants of monolithically white,[1] Scots-Irish settlers who have maintained a connection to a simpler, purer time; or as a place filled with backward, violent, uneducated, "hillbilly" degenerates à la *Deliverance*. More than three decades of scholarship have contested these stereotypes, and many academics have theorized the purposes that these stereotypes have served (Shapiro 1978; Whisnant 1983; Batteau 1990; Anglin 1992; Wilson 1995; Billings, Norman, and Ledford 1999; Billings and Blee 2000; Eller 2008; Reid and Taylor 2010; Scott 2010). Many of these scholars have converged on similar conclusions: the rendering of the Appalachian region and people as "different" from mainstream America has functioned to lubricate the wheels of its exploitation. Scott (2010) notes that while the Appalachian region is (incorrectly) stereotyped as monolithically white, this whiteness is socially constructed to be a "problematic" whiteness, a marked whiteness. The unearned privileges that are typically bestowed on people with white skin do not translate to those who are Appalachian whites. As Cunningham (2010) argues, the material-historical reasons for stereotyping Appalachian people are parallel to the stereotyping of Native Americans. In order to justify the use (or theft) of the Appalachian region's land and resources, it was necessary for the nation to convince itself that these resources were not "possessed by full-fledged human beings" (75). As Reid and Taylor (2010) assert, the social construction of Appalachia as "premodern" or "savage" has allowed it to serve as a "sacrificial scapegoat" for the atrocities of capitalism, normalizing devastating practices like mountaintop-removal mining (45–46). Thus, we can trace Appalachia's treatment as an energy-sacrifice zone to its history as an "othered" locale.

Despite these origins, though, claiming the identity of "Appalachian" may, in fact, be a mobilizing and empowering act for some, as it reinforces place attachment. As scholar-activist Steve Fisher (2010) attests, "I've witnessed local social-justice struggles transformed as participants have come to see themselves as Appalachians" (59). Numerous scholars have observed the power of regional identity as a mobilizing force in various grassroots movements throughout Appalachia, from the activism of residents in Yellow Creek, Kentucky, against water pollution from a nearby tannery (Cable 1993) to the organizing efforts in Ashe County, North Carolina, to stop the building of a hydroelectric facility that would have flooded much of the land in the county (Foster 1993).

How can we reconcile the "invention" of Appalachia with the very real ways in which this identity (positively and negatively) affects the lives of many people living in this socially constructed region? Ann Kingsolver (1992) argues that we should conceive of Appalachian identity as an "activity of negotiation," rather than something that is "fixed" and immutable (101). In other words, Appalachian identity is not something that one automatically possesses by virtue of having grown up in the region. Rather, it is created through social interactions, and as such, it can both "grow out of and strengthen local resistance efforts" (Fisher 2010, 60). Indeed, the women in this book draw on their attachment to the place of "Appalachia" and their "Appalachian identity" as sources of strength and as a motivating force for their activism. They not only seek to protect their children, families, and communities, but they are also driven to protect those aspects of their lives and sense of self that are connected to their physical surroundings, family histories, and cultural traditions. Many of the women specifically designate these aspects of their lives as being "Appalachian."

Importantly, the protector discourse that these women use could potentially open up a wider space for Appalachian men to find a connection to the movement. While there are few local men involved in the environmental justice movement relative to women, those who are involved do, in fact, use similar language to the women activists when describing their motivations for environmental justice activism (Bell and Braun 2010). In particular, a number of the men I interviewed for Braun's and my study cite a desire to protect their communities as their impetus for action. For instance, Bill Price describes "a sense of responsibility to the community I grew up in," articulating feeling an obligation to draw on his professional skills and knowledge for the purpose of helping those who have suffered the effects of irresponsible coal-mining practices. Likewise, Ed Wiley links his decision to become an activist with the guilt he feels from working for the industry (and the very coal mine) that he asserts made his granddaughter sick. Thus, while the coal-related hegemonic masculinity of the Central Appalachian region may pose a barrier to local men's entry into the environmental justice movement, those men who *are* able to escape its influence may connect with identities that are closely aligned with the protector identities of local women activists (Bell and Braun 2010). Emphasizing this protector responsibility of Appalachian women *and* men may be a way to attract more local men into the movement.

Challenges to Activist Involvement

The twelve women activists in this book have become involved in the environmental justice movement in order to protect their families, communities, homes, land, and the Appalachian way of life from the destructive practices of the coal industry. After becoming involved in the fight for environmental justice, however, they continue to face numerous challenges to maintaining their participation, including family, friends, and/or neighbors with ties to the coal industry. Many have faced opposition and challenges to their activism in the form of relationships strains, gendered intimidation, or threats to their personal safety.

Relationship Strains

In communities where the coal industry has historically been a major source of employment, many residents remain loyal to coal, regardless of whether they are currently employed by the industry (Bell and York 2010). There are frequently social costs to speaking out against mining-related injustices, because taking such a stance is often perceived both as a threat and as a liability.

Many of the activists in this book have lost friends or have experienced strains to their relationships through their activist activities. Teri Blanton reveals, "You know, sometimes it's quite isolating [being an activist]" (p. 92). Maria Lambert further describes this isolation: "[I]t's like I'm unapproachable: 'You don't talk to her because she's one of them.' You know, 'You don't want to get into too much of a conversation with her because she has joined forces with them'—'them' being the environmental people" (p. 81). Similarly, Judy Bonds expresses that her activism "drew the line on some relationships . . . there are some people, you know, that won't talk to me now" (p. 155).

These relationship losses hit particularly hard in a region that has experienced large-scale outmigration over the past sixty years (Bell 2009). Especially for individuals living in communities already suffering from such disruptions to local social networks, further social loss is a significant sacrifice to endure.

Family relationships are also sometimes strained because of activist activities. One of the women in this book told me that she had experienced some problems with her husband since becoming involved in the movement.[2] She believes that a lot of men in the area feel threatened when their wives are active in the struggle for environmental justice, recalling a number of women she knows who wanted to become more involved in speaking up against coal-related problems in their community, but who were afraid to participate because of their husbands. I asked her whether she thought these women's reluctance was mainly because their husbands were employed by the coal industry or if it had to do with the men not wanting their wives engaged in community work. She responded, "Well, both," stating that she knew women whose husbands worked "nowhere near the mines" and were still opposed to their wives' involvement in the environmental justice movement.

Gendered Intimidation

Gendered social interactions with coal-industry workers, industry executives, regulatory agency officials, and politicians pose yet another challenge to these women's activist involvement. Through subtle and not-so-subtle means, men in positions of power have attempted to police these women's social activism, reinforcing the traditional ideology that a woman's place is in the home, not publicly protesting irresponsible coal-mining practices. For instance, when Donna Branham went to the West Virginia DEP office in Logan to complain about the deceptive manner in which a mining permit was advertised in the local newspaper, the official (a man) with whom she met attempted to make her feel guilty for not being home with her husband:

> He said, "I knew you'd be in here, Donna. I knew that you'd do this. Where's your husband?" I said, "He just had heart surgery." He said, "What are you doing over here?" I said, "I'm over here to protect my community." "Well, shouldn't you be with him?" I said, "I've *been* with him, and I'm going *back* to him. It's just Logan" (p. 139).

Patty Sebok describes being treated in a similar manner during a UMWA strike:

> [B]eing on the picket line, I've had a state trooper tell me, "You need to go home and do your dishes and [look after] your kids, where you should be" (p. 106).

As Culley and Angelique found was the case with the women environmental justice activists in their (2003) study, a number of the women in this book describe being belittled or dismissed by men in positions of power. When Donna Branham and her daughter Kelly attended a meeting with (all of whom were men) coal company executives and the same DEP official discussed above, they were talked down to, and their concerns about the impact of the mining permit were trivialized:

> This one guy from the mining company, it's like he was just trying to woo me, I thought. [Speaking in a soft voice], "Donna, I *promise* you, we will not harm you in any way . . . we're the best company there [is]. Our reputation speaks for itself. I promise you—your creek, your way of life, will *not* be impacted" (p. 140).

When Donna pushed the coal company executives to define what they meant when they said the mine would cause "minimal damage," they changed tactics from one of coddling to outright bullying:

We kept insisting with these same questions, because we wanted an answer that we could hold to. And that's whenever [one of them] got mad and said, "You're not going to have a creek for two-and-a-half years! It's going to be completely stopped up because we're going to be mining up there!" Kelly said, "You can't do that!" He said, "Yes we can" (p. 140).

Most of the women activists who describe being dismissed by officials and coal company executives feel that such dismissal is undoubtedly due to their gender. As Patty Sebok asserts, "[W]hen you're dealing with government agencies or coal companies and stuff, I don't think they take a woman as seriously as they do a man" (p. 105).

One way that women are often dismissed is by calling on common stereotypes of irrationality that have long been imposed on women. Patty Sebok recalls that during her protests of the overweight coal trucks, "They accused us of being 'emotional.' That was all it was—it was just emotion. It had nothin' to do with the law being broke, or anything—it was just emotion!" (p. 106). Teri Blanton describes similar experiences:

> I've been called passionate many times—I'm just being "emotional" and "passionate" because I'm a woman. That is dismissive of the actual—of what I'm saying. They [dismiss] my actions by saying I'm passionate: "Oh, you're, like, really passionate about this issue, aren't you?" (p. 92)

In addition to the ways that male supporters of the coal industry have mobilized the gender hierarchy in their attempts to silence, belittle, and dismiss women activists, some have also used gendered insults as a more blatant tactic of intimidation. Coal truck drivers referred to Patty Sebok as "the blonde bitch" (p. 104), and she and Judy Bonds were called "media whores" during the coal truck weight limit controversy (p. 105); Teri Blanton has been called a "hysterical housewi[fe]" (p. 92); Former Massey Energy CEO Don Blankenship called Pauline Canterberry and Mary Miller "the two bitches" (p. 40). Contemplating Blankenship's choice in insults, Mary conveys,

> I think that ["the two bitches"] is probably the worst thing [Don Blankenship] could think to call us. I really think he thinks that would make us mad. It doesn't make me mad. You know, he wants to call me a bitch? That's OK. I'll continue to fight, and he can continue to call me [a bitch]. They probably think a woman's place is not to go out and speak out, [but] to stay home and take care of things and not come out into the public with this (p. 40).

Maria Gunnoe reflects on the names she has been called, noting, "[I]t's always a gender attack. When I run into a strip miner and they have a problem with me, I'm always a 'bitch' or a 'whore,' you know, something to that effect. I've been called a 'loud-mouth woman'" (p. 18).

Brandishing gendered insults is a tactic of social control not at all uncommon when women are outspoken or involved in social movements. Maggard (1987) noted the same type of gendered policing of women activists in the Brookside Coal Strike in eastern Kentucky. The women who populated the picket lines drew "criticism and harassment framed in gender-specific terms" (19). Called "bitches" and "whores," these women were accused of engaging in behavior not fitting of "ladies." As one of Maggard's respondents amusedly recalled, "According to Eastover's lawyer we wasn't ladies. We were women. He kept saying any woman that would be on a picket line is not a lady. His *wife* is a lady" (Maggard 1987, 19).

Berdahl (2007) argues "the primary motive underlying all harassment is a desire to protect one's social status when it seems threatened." She further argues that gender-based insults, like those described above, are a form of sexual harassment wielded in order to protect one's social status in the gender hierarchy (641). Thus, calling these activist women "bitches" or "whores" is motivated by more than a desire to protect the power of the coal industry; it is also about protecting men's position of power in the social order—a position that has been threatened due to tremendous upheavals in the region's economy. There is a pervasive belief in the coal-mining region of Central Appalachia that masculinity is connected to employment in the coal industry (Yarrow 1991; Beckwith 2001); however, over the past sixty years, mechanization in the mines and, more recently, mountaintop removal, have caused a radical reduction in mining jobs throughout Central Appalachia (Burns 2007). Because of these reductions, service-sector jobs have replaced mining jobs as the leading sources of employment and earnings, and as a result, many women are now the primary breadwinners of their families (Maggard 1994; Miewald and McCann 2004). Miewald and McCann (2004) argue that while the strict gendered division of labor may have declined in the region, the related gender ideology "is still felt" (1054). This disconnect between ideology and economic reality has meant that the coal-related hegemonic masculine identity of the region is under threat (Bell and Braun 2010; Bell and York 2010). Thus, the fact that these activist women are publicly fighting coal-industry practices is not only a threat to the coal industry's impunity, but it may also be perceived as a threat to men's power within the already-vulnerable gender hierarchy.

Threatened Safety

In addition to the isolation, losses of relationships, and gender-based intimidation that a number of the activists have endured, some have also experienced threats to their safety and security. The threats affect all aspects of life. As Maria Gunnoe relates,

> [M]e and my husband haven't been out to dinner together in probably two years because of the fact we can't leave our home. You're afraid to leave your home because, I mean, there's so many people here that has been fighting the coal industry and they got put out of the fight because their house was burnt to the ground. That's a very common thing here—houses burning. There's always somebody here; my home is never left alone (p. 18).

Dealing with the threats is something that many activists have come to accept as a part of life. Judy Bonds explains,

> I'm aware, every time that I go to a store or that I'm out alone, I'm always aware of my surroundings . . .
>
> The last threat [against me] was a man that said there was rumors going around that they were gonna kill me and Bo [Webb] and throw us down a mine crack. We reported it to the police, but you know what? There's nothing I can do about that, other than be aware of where I'm at, you know? I carry pepper spray with me, I got a stick in the back trunk, but there's nothing I can do about that. If a coal truck wants to run me off the road—if they want to run over top of me, there's nothing I can do about it. You just have to be aware of what's going on, you have to raise your head up, look people in the eye, and know where you're at, know what your options are. Yeah, somebody could jump you, but you can't live your life afraid.
>
> The only thing I worry about is having my grandson in the car with me if that would happen. That's why [he] rarely travels with me; that's why I'm reluctant to be seen with my grandson. See, that's how it affects me—it doesn't really affect me by making me afraid that they're gonna hurt me. What else can they do to me? There's not much else they can do to me besides kill me. But, I am afraid for my family. You have to worry about your close relatives, you know, and that's why I don't really want to be seen with [them]. I really don't like for [my grandson] to be in the vehicle with me, or attend places where there's going to be functions (pp. 155–156).

In some cases, the intimidation has been more than scare tactics. For instance, while Patty Sebok was fighting overweight coal trucks, she learned that some coal-truck drivers had been plotting ways they could "accidentally" harm—or even kill—her:

> It was very, very dangerous before we started to fight them, but after we started to fight them, that's when they started to swerve at us on purpose. A few of the drivers knew me, and a lot of them went by my home. The ones that were haulin' by my house every day, they saw me. I had a Bronco that was one-of-a-kind. . . .

It's three to three-and-a-half miles up this hollow, and I couldn't go out that three-and-a-half miles without being run off the road a minimum of three times by a coal truck. At first it was just because they were speeding and overloaded and stuff like that. Then after I started to speak out, it got worse because they knew who I was and [that] I was speaking out. . . .

[My husband's] friend had a base CB, and he told him a year after the coal truck deal was passed that they had a hit out on me. They were going to catch me between two coal trucks and crush me to smithereens (p. 103).

Patty then describes an instance when she believes this plan was attempted. One day while going up Lens Creek Mountain behind a caravan of coal trucks, the coal truck drivers in front of her gave her the signal that she should pass them. Patty could see that it was not safe to attempt passing the trucks; there was a string of traffic coming in the opposite direction. Had she trusted their signal and started to pass the trucks, she surely would have been hit.

Maria Gunnoe has also experienced direct affronts to her personal safety:

I had a tire that was slashed completely across. . . . And then, in 2004—my truck was new so there was no reason for it to be running bad—and it was like it wouldn't take gas. I was like, "What in the world's going on with my truck?" So I took it to a mechanic, and . . . he said, "Somebody has attempted to vandalize your truck [by putting sand in the gas tank]." . . . [M]y mechanic also notice[d] that my brake line was collapsed to the point that, if enough pressure would build up behind it, I could hit my brake and my brake line would rupture, and I would have no brake. There were strikes on the rear end of the vehicle . . . where they had struck at it two or three times . . . thank God he found it, because . . . in this terrain you have a lot of mountain roads, no guardrails, and if you lose your brakes, you're going over a mountain. You're going over a mountain or into a mountain (p. 19).

Despite enduring threats to their own and their families' personal safety, these women continue to speak out against the coal-related injustices facing their communities. In the face of these challenges, what sustains their environmental justice work?

Sustaining Their Activism

Many of the women in this book express that their activism is a duty or calling that they feel compelled to answer, regardless of how difficult it becomes. As Lorelei Scarboro reveals, protecting her homeplace and community is "not just what I choose to do, it's also, I think, what I have to do" (p. 128). Donna Branham articulates the pressure that accompanies the calling she feels, stating, "[I]t needs to be done, and you're so afraid if you don't do it, it's not going to be done" (p. 146). Echoing the sense of responsibility that Donna describes, Maria Lambert states, "[I]f I quit, I'll feel like I've let down a lot of people, and most of all, let myself down for not doing what I've been called out to do" (p. 81). Judy Bonds feels that her activism is even more than a calling; she asserts that it is actually a necessary component of her life as a Christian: "I look at this, this creation—God loves His creation. Who am I to *not* protect what He gave us? And I would think, why would God or Jesus want anybody in heaven that destroyed His creation here on earth—why would they want somebody like that in heaven?" (p. 156)

The belief that they are on the side of justice is also a sustaining force. As Donna Branham relates, "I think the basis for [my strength] is because I *know* I'm right" (p. 147). Similarly, Judy Bonds states, "Knowing that what I'm doing is the right thing to do is also helpful to [my] fight . . . That's how I pay my rent for living on this planet—by being an activist and doing what I'm doing" (p. 155).

For some of the women, their activism has given them a sense of purpose that they did not feel before. Prior to becoming involved in the environmental justice movement, Maria Lambert remembers the longing she felt to have a cause in her life:

Last summer, 2007, my husband and I were driving somewhere, . . . and we were just riding along being quiet. I was looking out the window, and I started praying, "Lord, please, there's bound to be something out there. I know there's something out there that I can do. I want to make a difference in somebody's life so when I leave here, when I leave this earth, at my funeral I want them to be able to say, 'Maria done what she could.'" . . . it wasn't any time until all of this came about, and it's like, I knew that this is where I was supposed to be (p. 80).

Maria asserts that her activism has "brought out the best in me, or brought out what was there that needed bringing out" (p. 80) and has helped her find her "little niche in life . . . where I belong, that place of comfort" (p. 83).

One of the strongest themes throughout these narratives is the strength that these women gain from their activist community. Many describe the importance of the encouragement and support they have received from the new friends they have made in the environmental justice movement. Revealing the impact that other environmental justice activists have had on her self-esteem, Donetta Blankenship relates,

[Larry Gibson] used to tell me all the time that I'm *somebody*. Especially for people like me—a nobody—that's the way I would feel, you know? If I can go and be a part [of this movement]—like I'm starting to see that I'm doing now—being a part of making things better for everybody, then I'm gonna go do it. Trish calls me a community leader. I don't know—she [tells] me that all the time. I don't feel like I am, but she says I am, and other people does, too. [Laughs.]. People encouraging me—I think that's what, what makes me want to go [and be a part of this movement]. [Starts to tear up.] And I just have [pauses] so many wonderful, true friends. I, I can't express that enough (pp. 67–68).

Donna Branham also conveys the importance of the activist community to her ability to sustain her involvement:

I think just going to Kayford Mountain and meeting all the people involved, I've been able to draw from that strength. I hope that they understand what I was able to get from them, and I just hope I'm able to help other people, to radiate it or however you want to put it . . . "I'm going to let this light shine" (p. 145).

Again and again, the women in this book express the significance of the community they have gained through their involvement in the environmental justice movement. Social-movement scholars have revealed the importance of social networks for social-movement recruitment (Freeman 1973; Snow, Zurcher, and Ekland-Olson 1980; McAdam 1982, 1988; Friedman and Mc-Adam 1992; Gamson 1992; Passy 2002) and the role that the solidarity created within these activist networks plays in *maintaining* commitment to the social movement (Gamson 1992). As Doug McAdam (1988) found in his study of Freedom Summer volunteers, the community that was created among the activists he interviewed provided a sense of belonging and purpose so powerful and transformative that many sought to replicate that experience long after the summer of 1964 was over. As McAdam so eloquently states, "The volunteers had discovered a powerful sociological truth: the most satisfying selves we will ever know are those that attach to communities and purposes outside of our selves" (1988, 138). The sustaining power of the activist community to which these women have attached themselves is evident throughout their narratives. Maria Gunnoe explains, "I think the biggest benefit that people get from OVEC, and the other groups, I think the biggest benefit is a sense of community" (p. 24).

The importance of this sense of community may be even more powerful in Central Appalachia because of the widespread depopulation and losses in other community relationships discussed above. For many, the activist network has provided friendships and support that deeply enrich their lives. Teri Blanton reveals,

My "community" is my activist friends. I love them. I mean, I could go and climb on an airplane and go anywhere, and you walk in the room, whether it be twenty people or two hundred people, and you're at home. You could not know a soul there, [but] you know you're walking into *your community* because you know those people would not be there unless they had the same heart you did. So it's like you never feel like you walk into a room full of strangers. You know that you're walking into a room full of love, because those people love what they do or else they wouldn't be doing it. That's really the great part about it (pp. 92–93).

Drawing on the strength of the friends they have met through their activism, these women are able to sustain their fight in the face of threats, relationship strains, and community isolation. Both through the support that they receive from the activist community and through the empowerment they experience at being heard—many for the first time in their lives—these women are transformed. Their activist activities have become intertwined intimately with their lives, and many reach the point where they cannot *not* continue their activism—just as they cannot stop being mothers or stop being Appalachians. As Maria Lambert relates, "I feel that I'll always have this in my heart . . . [I]t's just that strong—it's just a part of who I am, where I came from" (p. 83).

"I am an Activist": Identity Transformation through Protest

Numerous scholars have identified the transformative power that social movement participation can have in women's lives (Krauss 1993; Maggard 1990; Cable 1992; Cable and Degutis 1997; Shriver, Chasteen, and Cable 2003; Culley and Angelique 2003). As Krauss (1993) found of the white, blue-collar women involved in environmental justice movements, theirs are "stories of transformations: transformations into more self-confident and assertive women; into political activists who challenge the existing system and feel powerful in that challenge; into wives and mothers who establish new relationships with their spouses (or get divorced) and new empowering relationships with their children, as they provide role models of women capable of fighting for what they believe in" (255). Culley and Angelique (2003) echo Krauss's findings: their interview respondents reported "a loss of naiveté, a new sense of strength, and confidence in oneself" (453).

Most of the grassroots women activists in this book had never spoken out publicly until becoming involved in the environmental justice movement. Pauline Canterberry describes feeling tremendous anxiety at her first experience testifying against Massey Energy, whose coal-preparation plant literally covered the town of Sylvester in coal dust: "I was a nervous wreck—they thought I was gonna have a stroke! I was shakin' from the top of my head to the bottom of my feet. I mean, I had never done anything like that—I'd never spoke out against anybody. I never had no reason to" (pp. 29–30).

Donna Branham expresses similar sentiments about her path to activism: "I thought really, really hard before I took a big, firm step here. I just feel like I'm standing here, and I'm not going to take a step back. I plan to go forward, and when I can't go forward, I'll just stand firm. And for me to do that is really hard because I'm not a really articulate person. I've never spoken out like this in my life" (p. 147).

Women like Pauline and Donna have found their voices through their involvement in social protest, transforming them from passive recipients of injustice into individuals who are taking a stand for themselves, their homes, and their communities. As Maria Lambert describes, "It was just an amazing transformation from being totally sedentary, doing nothing, to now I have a calling. Now I have a reason" (p. 74).

Of all the activists interviewed for this study, Donetta Blankenship from Rawl, West Virginia, may have been the most deeply affected by her involvement in the environmental justice movement. Like Pauline, Donna, and Maria, Donetta had never spoken out in her life, and it took numerous visits from environmental justice organizers to convince her that what she had to say was important. When I asked her if she believed her involvement in the environmental justice movement had changed her, she responded:

> [Voice shaking.] Me and my therapist talk about this all the time. It has changed me . . . [long pause] . . . in several different ways. One thing [pauses], like I've already said, I have more or less always felt like I'm a nobody. Now I feel like I'm somebody, I, I feel like I can [pauses, sobs softly] do something for somebody—do something for my kids (p. 68).

Donetta's experience with the environmental justice movement has been one in which she has, for the first time in her life, been made to feel that what she has to say matters. Her new identity as an activist has given her a sense of efficacy as a person who has something important to contribute and who can—and does—make a difference.

Through her community organizing work with OVEC, Maria Gunnoe has seen positive changes in the personal lives of numerous women activists:

> Working in this kind of work, it teaches you so much about getting along with other people and being able to resolve what seems to be the most serious problems. It teaches you how to be able to sit down and talk about these things and come to resolutions that works for everybody. It teaches you a lot . . . we have nonviolent trainings. We have media trainings. We have conflict resolution trainings. I mean, just everything you could imagine. It really teaches you how to better handle things in life . . . There've been women that's worked as volunteers [in the movement] that has been in bad situations at home that's come out of it

like warriors. [They have] literally taken themselves by the bootstraps and pulled themselves up out of the gutter and looked at their man and said, "We're not doing this anymore" and has taken her life in her own hands and changed things (pp. 22–23).

In addition to improving interpersonal communication and relationships, Maria Gunnoe also believes that involvement in the environmental justice movement has helped increase self-efficacy and self-esteem among some activist women:

It creates an internal power that makes you feel like you can literally take on the world, and no one can convince you that you can't take on the world. It creates an internal power that can't be stopped (p. 23).[3]

It is important to emphasize that these transformations have occurred in large part *because* of the supportive community that has been created through the environmental justice movement. In her reflections on meeting other activists at the Mountain Keepers' annual Fourth of July celebration on Kayford Mountain, Donna Branham expresses how much strength she drew from that supportive environment: "From that point on, I think I sort of changed a little bit. I mean, I think I was always sort of strong and stuff, but now I just feel I can do this. I can do this. I'm going to leave something behind, something good behind" (pp. 144–145). This activist community, made up of individuals from various towns, counties, and states, has provided the women in this book with emotional support and the motivation to continue speaking out against the coal industry, despite the many obstacles they face.

Appalachian women are the leaders of the environmental justice movement to protect mountain communities. Their power, perseverance, and passion have helped push this movement forward, drawing the attention of people from all over the country and world. The narratives of the women in this book are stories of empowerment and transformation, women who, through challenging the coal industry's exploitation of Central Appalachia, simultaneously challenge stereotypes about Appalachian women's agency and strength. These women—whose roots in the Appalachian mountains "run deep as ironweed"—deserve to be recognized and celebrated as the driving force behind the movement to save their Appalachian families, communities, culture, and land.

NOTES

INTRODUCTION

1. Composed of southern West Virginia, eastern Kentucky, southwest Virginia, and eastern Tennessee, Central Appalachia is one of the primary coal-producing areas in the United States.

2. More than 1 million acres of land and over 500 mountains have been destroyed by mountaintop-removal coal mining in this region (Geredien 2009), and residents must contend with devastating floods, well-water contamination, coal slurry impoundment breaches, unsafe road conditions, air pollution, ecosystem destruction, and elevated rates of cancer, chronic illnesses, birth defects, and mortality due to coal industry practices (Flood Advisory Technical Taskforce 2002; Orem 2006; United States Environmental Protection Agency 2005; Erikson 1976; Scott et al. 2005; Bell 2010; Bell and York 2010; Bell and Braun 2010; Palmer et al. 2010; Hendryx, Ahern and Nurkiewicz 2007; Hendryx 2008; Hendryx and Ahern 2008; Ahern and Hendryx 2008).

3. Environmental justice movements differ from mainstream environmental movements in their attention to issues of social justice. Rather than focusing only on the preservation of nature in itself, environmental justice movements seek social justice for people who live, work, play, and learn in the most polluted environments in the world (Cole and Foster 2001).

4. Judy Bonds passed away from cancer on January 3, 2011.

5. However, do see Bell and Braun (2010) and Barry (2012).

6. While the anti-mountaintop-removal mining movement has scaled up tremendously, there is still quite a ways to go before reaching the goals of these grassroots organizations. As Betsy Taylor has reminded me, the scaling-up process has been unpredictable and could easily collapse, given the history of national disinterest and

"othering" of Appalachia. See Reid (1996) for a discussion of the cycles of national disinterest and rediscovering of Appalachia, and see Anglin (1992); Billings, Norman, and Ledford (1999); Reid and Taylor (2010); and Scott (2010) for thorough discussions of Appalachian "othering." Furthermore, there are entrenched power structures within Appalachia that pose tremendous barriers to the movement. For more exploration of these, see Gaventa (1980), Eller (2008), Reid (1996), and Bell (2010).

7. These interviews are also part of the dataset used in Bell and Braun 2010 (described below).

8. Bell, Shannon Elizabeth (Ed). *Through Their Eyes, In Their Words: Forty Women Telling the Story of Their Home: The Southern West Virginia Photovoice Project.* Charleston, West Virginia: Photographic Production Services.

9. However, see Cable 1992 for an important exception to this trend.

10. These are the same twelve women in this book.

CHAPTER 2. "WE BECAME TWO DETERMINED WOMEN"

1. The reader may notice occasionally throughout these narratives the use of the singular "a" with the plural "mines" ("a mines" or "an underground mines"). This is a common speechway throughout parts of Central Appalachia, so when it was said in this way, I did not change it. (Although, it's also worth noting that the same person sometimes switches back and forth between saying "a mines" and "a mine" during the same interview.)

2. West Virginia Department of Environmental Protection.

CHAPTER 4. "YOU GOTTA GO AND DO EVERYTHING YOU CAN—*FIGHT* FOR YOUR KIDS"

1. Larry Gibson was a well-known activist in West Virginia who fought tirelessly against mountaintop-removal mining. He lived on Kayford Mountain, which has belonged to his family for many generations. The mountain is surrounded on all sides by mountaintop-removal mining operations. Larry started the Keepers of the Mountains Foundation and turned Kayford Mountain into an educational site, inviting visitors to witness for themselves the ravages of the coal industry. Sadly, Larry passed away from a heart attack on September 9, 2012.

CHAPTER 5. "IT'S JUST A PART OF WHO I AM"

1. Drawing on research by Loo et al. (2003), which found evidence that manganese in drinking water attracts the cavity-causing bacteria *Streptococcus gordonii*, Walker and Payne (2012) suggest that the high concentrations of manganese in coal slurry (Stout and Paipillo 2004) may contribute to the high rates of tooth decay in the

coal-mining region of Central Appalachia. Thus, coal-slurry contamination in Prenter could explain the tooth decay problems that Maria describes.

CHAPTER 7. "I'M NOT GOING TO BE RUN OUT, I'M NOT GOING TO BE RUN OVER, I'M NOT GOING OUT WITHOUT A FIGHT"

1. Patty describes this incident below. An adult brother and sister were killed in Hernshaw when a coal truck hauling more than twice the legal limit rear-ended them and pushed them into the path of an oncoming coal truck.

CHAPTER 8. "OUR ROOTS RUN SO DEEP, YOU CAN'T DISTINGUISH US FROM THE EARTH WE LIVE ON"

1. On October 11, 2000, a coal slurry impoundment in Martin County, Kentucky, collapsed, spilling 250 million gallons of coal waste and polluting more than seventy miles of West Virginia and Kentucky waterways. See Scott et al. (2005) for more about the aftereffects of this disaster.

2. Buffalo Creek Hollow, West Virginia, is the site of a tragic coal-waste accident. On the morning of February 26, 1972, a coal-sludge impoundment that held 132 million gallons of coal waste collapsed, sending a torrent of black coal water through the community. One hundred twenty-five people died that day, and thousands were left homeless and forever scarred by the devastation they witnessed (Erikson 1976).

3. Dr. Simonton's initial report is available at http://sludgesafety.org/research -library/initial-expert-report-fugitive-and-respirable-coal-dust-marsh-fork-elementary (accessed February 27, 2013).

4. See Bell and Braun (2010) for a description of the barriers that prevent many local coalfield men from speaking out against the coal industry and an analysis of the social circumstances that have facilitated the activism of certain local men like Ed and Bo, who have been able to overcome these barriers.

CHAPTER 9. "IT'S NOT JUST WHAT I CHOOSE TO DO, IT'S ALSO, I THINK, WHAT I *HAVE* TO DO"

1. Kayford Mountain, close to Cabin Creek, West Virginia, is owned by the Stanley Family Heirs, one of whom was the late activist Larry Gibson, who, along with his family, turned the jointly owned mountain and family cemetery into a fifty-acre private land trust in order to protect the mountain from mountaintop-removal mining. Kayford Mountain is one of the best locations to view the devastation of mountaintop removal, as it is completely surrounded by over seventy-five hundred acres of MTR sites. The "Keeper of the Mountains Foundation," which was founded by

Larry in 2004, hosts festivals and provides tours for individuals, groups, classes, and organizations throughout the year in order to educate people about the impacts of mountaintop-removal mining.

2. "I don't care to" is a colloquialism of the region that actually means "I don't mind."

CHAPTER 11. "I WANT MY GREAT-GREAT-GRANDCHILDREN TO BE ABLE TO LIVE ON THIS EARTH!"

1. Judy is referencing the coal-slurry water contamination that residents of Rawl, West Virginia, experienced.

CHAPTER 12. CONCLUSION

1. There is, in fact, a long history of racial and ethnic diversity in Appalachia, particularly in certain areas. For instance, see Turner and Cabbell (1985), Lewis (1987), and Lewis (1999) for the history of African-Americans in Appalachia.

2. This individual asked me to remove her discussion of marital difficulties from her chapter, but she gave me permission to discuss her experience generally and without her name attached to it.

3. While a number of scholars (for example, McAdam 1988, Ferree and Hess 1985, Evans 1979) have found that social justice activism leads to an increase in feminist attitudes and behaviors among women activists, the women in my study seem to fall more in line with the working-class women activists in Sherry Cable's (1992) study, who, despite expressing that their activism brought about increased confidence, self-esteem, and important changes in the domestic sphere, did not always identify as feminists.

REFERENCES

Ahern, Melissa M., and Michael Hendryx. 2008. "Health Disparities and Environmental Competence: A Case Study of Appalachian Coal Mining." *Environmental Justice* 1 (2): 81–86.

Anglin, Mary K. 1992. "A Question of Loyalty: National and Regional Identity in Narratives of Appalachia." *Anthropological Quarterly* 65 (3): 105–16.

———. 2002. *Women, Power, and Dissent in the Hills of Carolina*. Urbana: University of Illinois Press.

Appalachian Voices. 2007. "What Are the Economic Consequences of Mountaintop Removal in Appalachia?" Available at http://www.appvoices.org/index.php?/mtr/economics (accessed August 21, 2007).

Ballard, Sandra L., and Patricia L. Hudson. 2003. *Listen Here: Women Writing in Appalachia*. Lexington: University Press of Kentucky.

Batteau, Allen W. 1990. *The Invention of Appalachia*. Tucson: University of Arizona Press.

Beckwith, Karen. 2001. "Gender Frames and Collective Action: Configurations of Masculinity in the Pittston Coal Strike." *Politics & Society* 29:297–330.

Bell, Shannon Elizabeth. 2010. "Fighting King Coal: The Barriers to Grassroots Environmental Justice Movement Participation in Central Appalachia." PhD diss., Department of Sociology, University of Oregon.

———. 2011. "The Southern West Virginia Photovoice Project: Community Action through Sociological Research." In *Sociologists in Action*, edited by Kathleen Odell Korgen and Jonathan M. White, 178–83. Thousand Oaks, Calif.: Sage.

———. Forthcoming. "'Sacrificed So Others Can Live Conveniently': Social Inequality, Environmental Injustice, and the Energy Sacrifice Zone of Central Appalachia." In *Understanding Diversity: Celebrating Difference, Challenging Inequality*, edited by Claire M. Renzetti and Raquel Kennedy Bergen. Boston: Allyn and Bacon.

Bell, Shannon Elizabeth, and Yvonne A. Braun. 2010. "Coal, Identity, and the Gendering of Environmental Justice Activism in Central Appalachia." *Gender & Society* 24 (6): 794–813.

Bell, Shannon Elizabeth, and Richard York. 2010. "Community Economic Identity: The Coal Industry and Ideology Construction in West Virginia." *Rural Sociology* 75 (1): 111–43.

Berdahl, Jennifer L. 2007. "Harassment Based on Sex: Protecting Social Status in the Context of Gender Hierarchy." *Academy of Management Review* 32 (2): 641–58.

Billings, Dwight B., and Kathleen M. Blee. 2000. *The Road to Poverty: The Making of Wealth and Hardship in Appalachia.* New York: Cambridge University Press.

Billings, Dwight B., Gurney Norman, and Katherine Ledford, eds. 1999. *Back Talk from Appalachia: Confronting Stereotypes.* Lexington: University Press of Kentucky.

Braun, Yvonne A. 2008. "'How Can I Stay Silent?': One Woman's Struggles for Environmental Justice in Lesotho." *Journal of International Women's Studies* 10 (1 [October]): 5–20.

Brown, Barbara B., Douglas Perkins, and Graham Brown. 2003. "Place Attachment in a Revitalizing Neighborhood: Individual and Block Levels of Analysis." *Journal of Environmental Psychology* 23:259–71.

Brown, Phil, and Faith I. T. Ferguson. 1995. "'Making a Big Stink': Women's Work, Women's Relationships, and Toxic Waste Activism." *Gender & Society* 9 (2): 145–72.

Bullard, Robert D. 1990. *Dumping in Dixie: Race, Class, and Environmental Quality.* Boulder, Colo.: Westview.

Bullard, Robert D., Paul Mohai, Robin Saha, and Beverly Wright. 2007. "Toxic Wastes and Race at Twenty: 1987–2007. A Report Prepared for the United Church of Christ Justice & Witness Ministries." Cleveland: United Church of Christ.

Burns, Shirley Stewart. 2007. *Bringing Down the Mountains: The Impact of Mountaintop Removal on Southern West Virginia Communities.* Morgantown: West Virginia University Press.

Cable, Sherry. 1992. "Women's Social Movement Involvement: The Role of Structural Availability in Recruitment and Participation Processes." *Sociological Quarterly* 33 (1): 35–50.

———. 1993. "From Fussin' to Organizing: Individual and Collective Resistance at Yellow Creek." In *Fighting Back in Appalachia: Traditions of Resistance and Change,* edited by Stephen L. Fisher, 69–83. Philadelphia: Temple University Press.

Cable, Sherry, and Beth Degutis. 1997. "Movement Outcomes and Dimensions of Social Change: The Multiple Effects of Local Mobilizations." *Current Sociology* 45:121–35.

Čapek, Stella. 1993. "The 'Environmental Justice' Frame: A Conceptual Discussion and an Application." *Social Problems* 40 (1): 5–24.

Carawan, Guy, and Candie Carawan. 1996 [1975]. *Voices from the Mountains: The People of Appalachia—Their Faces, Their Words, Their Songs.* Athens: Brown Thrasher / University of Georgia Press.

Cole, Luke W., and Sheila R. Foster. 2001. *From the Ground Up: Environmental Racism and the Rise of the Environmental Justice Movement*. New York: New York University Press.

Collins, Patricia Hill. 1990. *Black Feminist Thought: Knowledge, Consciousness, and the Politics of Empowerment*. New York: Routledge.

Culley, Marci R., and Holly L. Angelique. 2003. "Women's Gendered Experiences as Long-Term Three Mile Island Activists." *Gender & Society* 17 (3): 445–61.

Cunningham, Rodger. 2010. "Reflections on Identity and the Roots of Prejudice." Appalachian Identity: A Roundtable Discussion. *Appalachian Journal* 38 (1): 74–76.

Eller, Ronald D. 2008. *Uneven Ground: Appalachia Since 1945*. Lexington: University Press of Kentucky.

Epstein, Barbara. 1995. "Grassroots Environmentalism and Strategies for Change." *New Political Science* 32: 1–24.

Erikson, Kai T. 1976. *Everything in Its Path: Destruction of Community in the Buffalo Creek Flood*. New York: Simon and Schuster.

Evans, Sara. 1979. *Personal Politics: The Roots of Women's Liberation in the Civil Rights Movement and the New Left*. New York: Vintage.

Faber, Daniel. 2008. *Capitalizing on Environmental Injustice: The Polluter-Industrial Complex in the Age of Globalization*. New York: Rowman & Littlefield.

———. 2009. "The Unfair Trade-off: Globalization and the Export of Ecological Hazards." In *Environmental Sociology: From Analysis to Action*, edited by Leslie King and Deborah McCarthy, 181–99. New York: Rowman & Littlefield.

Ferree, Myra Marx, and Beth B. Hess. 1985. *Controversy and Coalition: The New Feminist Movement*. Boston: Twayne.

Fisher, Steve. 2010. "Claiming Appalachia—and the Questions That Go with It." Appalachian Identity: A Roundtable Discussion. *Appalachian Journal* 38 (1): 58–61.

Flood Advisory Technical Taskforce. 2002. "Runoff Analyses of Seng, Scrabble, and Sycamore Creeks, Part I." Division of Mining and Reclamation, Department of Environmental Protection. Available at http://www.wvdep.org/Docs/1593_Part%20I .pdf (accessed October 8, 2007).

Foster, Stephen William. 1993. "Politics, Expressive Form, and Historical Knowledge in a Blue Ridge Resistance Movement." In *Fighting Back in Appalachia: Traditions of Resistance and Change*, edited by Stephen L. Fisher, 303–15. Philadelphia: Temple University Press.

Fox, Julia. 1999. "Mountaintop Removal in West Virginia: An Environmental Sacrifice Zone." *Organization & Environment* 12 (2): 163–83.

Freeman, Jo. 1973. "The Origins of the Womens's Liberation Movement." *American Journal of Sociology* 78: 792–811.

Friedman, Debra, and Doug McAdam. 1992. "Collective Identity and Activism: Networks, Choices, and the Life of a Social Movement." In *Frontiers in Social Movement Theory*, edited by Aldon D. Morris and Carol McClurg Mueller, 156–73. New Haven, Conn.: Yale University Press.

Gamson, William A. 1992. "The Social Psychology of Collective Action." In *Frontiers in Social Movement Theory*, edited by Aldon D. Morris and Carol McClurg Mueller, 53–76. New Haven, Conn.: Yale University Press.

Gaventa, John. 1980. *Power and Powerlessness: Quiescence and Rebellion in an Appalachian Valley*. Urbana: University of Illinois Press.

Geredien, Ross. 2009. "Assessing the Extent of Mountaintop Removal in Appalachia: An Analysis using Vector Data." Technical Report for Appalachian Voices, Boone, N.C. Available at http://ilovemountains.org (accessed May 20, 2010).

Giesen, Carol A. B. 1995. *Coal Miners' Wives: Portraits of Endurance*. Lexington: University Press of Kentucky.

Goodell, Jeff. 2012. "Big Coal's Sleazy War." *Rolling Stone*, June 7. Available at http://www.rollingstone.com/politics/blogs/national-affairs/big-coal-s-sleazy -war-20120607 (accessed August 29, 2012).

Hague, Ashild Lappegard. 2007. "Identity and Place: A Critical Comparison of Three Identity Theories." *Architectural Science Review* 50 (1): 44–52.

Hall, Jacquelyn Dowd. 1986. "Disorderly Women: Gender and Labor Militancy in the Appalachian South." *Journal of American History* 73 (2): 354–82.

Hendryx, Michael. 2008. "Mortality Rates in Appalachian Coal Mining Counties: 24 Years Behind the Nation." *Environmental Justice* 1 (1): 5–11.

Hendryx, Michael, and Melissa M. Ahern. 2008. "Relations between Health Indicators and Residential Proximity to Coal Mining in West Virginia." *American Journal of Public Health* 98: 669–71.

Hendryx, Michael, Melissa M. Ahern, and Timothy R. Nurkiewicz. 2007. "Hospitalization Patterns Associated with Appalachian Coal Mining." *Journal of Toxicology and Environmental Health* 70:2064–70.

Hufford, Mary. 2004. "Knowing Ginseng: The Social Life of an Appalachian Root." *Cahiers de Littérature Orale*. 53–54:265–92.

Kaplan, Temma. 1997. *Crazy for Democracy: Women in Grassroots Movements*. New York: Routledge.

Kingsolver, Ann E. 1992. "Five Women Negotiating the Meaning of Negotiation: Introduction to the Special Issue on Negotiating Identity in Southeastern U.S. Uplands." *Anthropological Quarterly* 65 (3): 101–4.

Krauss, Celene. 1993. "Women and Toxic Waste Protest: Race, Class, and Gender as Resources of Resistance." *Qualitative Sociology* 16 (3): 247–62.

Lewis, Ronald L. 1987. *Black Coal Miners in America: Race, Class, and Community Conflict, 1780–1980*. Lexington: University Press of Kentucky.

———. 1999. "Beyond Isolation and Homogeneity: Diversity and the History of Appalachia." In *Back Talk from Appalachia: Confronting Stereotypes*, edited by Dwight Billings, Gurney Norman, and Katherine Ledford, 21–43. Lexington: University Press of Kentucky.

Loo, C. Y., K. Mitrakul, I. B. Voss, C. V. Hughes, and N. Ganeshkumar. 2003. "Involvement of the adc Operon and Manganese Homeostasis in *Streptococcus gordonii* Biofilm Formation." *Journal of Bacteriology* 185:2887–900.

Low, Setha, and Irwin Altman. 1992. "Place Attachment: A Conceptual Inquiry." In *Place Attachment*, edited by Irwin Altman and Setha Low, 1–12. New York: Plenum.

Maggard, Sally Ward. 1987. "Women's Participation in the Brookside Coal Strike: Militance, Class, and Gender in Appalachia." *Frontiers* 9 (3): 16–21.

———. 1990. "Gender Contested: Women's Participation in the Brookside Coal Strike." In *Women and Social Protest*, edited by Guida West and Rhoda Lois Blumberg, 75–98. New York: Oxford University Press.

———. 1994. "From Farm to Coal Camp to Back Office and McDonald's: Living in the Midst of Appalachia's Latest Transformation." *Journal of the Appalachian Studies Association* 6 (1): 14–38.

———. 1999. "Coalfield Women Making History." In *Back Talk from Appalachia: Confronting Stereotypes*, edited by Dwight B. Billings, Gurney Norman, and Katherine Ledford, 228–50. Lexington: University Press of Kentucky.

Manzo, Lynne C., and Douglas D. Perkins. 2006. "Finding Common Ground: The Importance of Place Attachment to Community Participation and Planning." *Journal of Planning Literature*, 20 (4): 335–50.

Masterson-Allen S., and P. Brown. 1990. "Public Reaction to Toxic Waste Contamination: Analysis of a Social Movement." *International Journal of Health Services* 20 (3): 485–500.

McAdam, Doug. 1982. *Political Process and the Development of Black Insurgency, 1930–1970*. Chicago: University of Chicago Press.

———. 1988. *Freedom Summer*. New York: Oxford University Press.

McDonnell, Tim. 2012. "GOP Ally of Big Coal Smears Environmental Activist with Kiddie Porn Accusation." *Mother Jones*, June 5. Available at http://www.motherjones.com/blue-marble/2012/06/coal-activist-kiddie-porn-accusation (accessed August 29, 2012).

McNeil, Bryan T. 2005. "Searching for Home Where Mountains Move: The Collision of Economy, Environment, and an American Community." PhD diss., Department of Anthropology, University of North Carolina–Chapel Hill.

Mesch, Gustavo S., and Orit Manor. 1998. "Social Ties, Environmental Perception, and Local Attachment." *Environment and Behavior* 30 (4): 504–19.

Miewald, Christina E., and Eugene J. McCann. 2004. "Gender Struggle, Scale, and the Production of Place in the Appalachian Coalfields." *Environment and Planning A* 36 (6): 1045–64.

Mohai, Paul. 1992. "Men, Women and the Environment: An Examination of the Gender Gap in Environmental Concern and Activism." *Society and Natural Resources* 5:1–9.

Naples, Nancy A. 1992. "Activist Mothering: Cross-Generational Continuity in the Community Work of Women from Low-Income Urban Neighborhoods." *Gender & Society* 6:441–63.

———. 1998. *Grassroots Warriors: Activist Mothering, Community Work, and the War on Poverty*. New York: Routledge.

Newman, Joanie. August 27, 2009. "Prenter Community Celebrates Groundbreaking on Waterline." *Coal Valley News*. Available at http://www.coalvalleynews.com

/pages/full_story/push?article-Prenter+community+celebrates+groundbreaking+on
+waterline%20&id=3274157-Prenter+community+celebrates+groundbreaking
+on+waterline&instance=home_news_lead (accessed September 30, 2012).

Norris, Randall, and Jean-Philippe Cyprès. 1996. *Women of Coal*. Lexington: University Press of Kentucky.

Nyden, Paul J. 2002. "Heaviest Trucks Carrying Coal; Most Stopped Trucks above Limit Sought by Industry, Group Says." *Charleston Gazette*, February 25.

Ohio Valley Environmental Coalition. 2003. "Coalfield Residents Speak." Available at http://www.ohvec.org/issues/mountaintop_removal/articles/2003_12_07 _EIS_speakanon.pdf (accessed October 27, 2008).

Orem, W. H. 2006. "Coal Slurry: Geochemistry and Impacts on Human Health and Environmental Quality." U.S. Geological Survey, Eastern Energy Resources Team. Presentation to the Coal Slurry Legislative Subcommittee, West Virginia Senate Judiciary Committee, November 15, 2006.

Palmer, M. A., E. S. Bernhardt, W. H. Schlesinger, K. N. Eshleman, E. Foufoula-Georgiou, M. S. Hendryx, A. D. Lemly, G. E. Likens, O. L. Loucks, M. E. Power, P. S. White, and P. R. Wilcock. 2010. "Mountaintop Mining Consequences." *Science* 327 (5962): 148–49.

Passy, Florence. 2002. "Social Networks Matter—But How?" In *Social Movements and Networks: Relational Approaches to Collective Action*, edited by Mario Diani and Doug McAdam, 21–48. New York: Oxford University Press.

Peeples, Jennifer A., and Kevin M. DeLuca. 2006. "The Truth of the Matter: Motherhood, Community, and Environmental Justice." *Women's Studies in Communication* 29 (1): 59–87.

Pellow, David Naguib. 2004. *Garbage Wars: The Struggle for Environmental Justice in Chicago*. Cambridge, Mass.: MIT Press.

———. 2007. *Resisting Global Toxics: Transnational Movements for Environmental Justice*. Cambridge, Mass.: MIT Press.

Proshansky, Harold M., Abbe K. Fabian, and Robert Kaminoff. 1983. "Place-Identity: Physical World Socialization of the Self." *Journal of Environmental Psychology* 3:57–83.

Reid, Herbert G. 1996. "Global Adjustments, Throwaway Regions, Appalachian Studies: Resituating the Kentucky Cycle on the Postmodern Frontier." *Journal of Appalachian Studies* 2 (2): 235–62.

Reid, Herbert, and Betsy Taylor. 2010. *Recovering the Commons: Democracy, Place, and Global Justice*. Urbana: University of Illinois Press.

Scott, Rebecca R. 2010. *Removing Mountains: Extracting Nature and Identity in the Appalachian Coalfields*. Minneapolis: University of Minnesota Press.

Scott, Shaunna L. 1995. *Two Sides to Everything: The Cultural Construction of Class Consciousness in Harlan County, Kentucky*. Albany, N.Y.: State University of New York Press.

Scott, Shaunna L., Stephanie McSpirit, Sharon Hardesty, and Robert Welch. 2005.

"Post-Disaster Interviews with Martin County Citizens: 'Gray Clouds' of Blame and Distrust." *Journal of Appalachian Studies* 11 (1–2): 7–28.

Seitz, Virginia Rinaldo. 1995. *Women, Development, and Communities for Empowerment in Appalachia.* Albany, N.Y.: State University of New York.

———. 1998. "Class, Gender, and Resistance in the Appalachian Coalfields." In *Community Activism and Feminist Politics: Organizing Across Race, Class, and Gender,* edited by Nancy A. Naples. New York: Routledge.

Shapiro, Henry D. 1978. *Appalachia on Our Mind: The Southern Mountains and Mountaineers in the American Consciousness, 1870–1920.* Chapel Hill, N.C.: University of North Carolina Press.

Shogan, Robert. 2004. *The Battle of Blair Mountain: The Story of America's Largest Labor Uprising.* Boulder, Colo.: Westview.

Shriver, Thomas E., Amy L. Chasteen, and Sherry Cable. 2003. "Women's Work: Women's Involvement in the Gulf War Illness Movement." *Sociological Quarterly* 44 (3): 639–58.

Snow, David A., Louis A. Zurcher, and Sheldo Ekland-Olson 1980. "Social Networks and Social Movements: A Microstructural Approach to Differential Recruitment." *American Sociological Review* 45: 787–801.

Stout, Ben M. and Jomana Papillo. 2004. "Well Water Quality in the Vicinity of a Coal Slurry Impoundment near Williamson, West Virginia." Prepared in response to January 15, 2004, training session of the Coal Impoundment Location and Warning System, Delbarton, West Virginia. Wheeling Jesuit University.

Taylor, Elizabeth M. 1992. "The Taxidermy of Bioluminescence: Tracking 'Neighboring' Practices in the Coal-Camps of West Virginia." Special Issue on Negotiating Identity in Southeastern U.S. Uplands. *Anthropological Quarterly* 65 (3): 117–27.

Turner, William H., and Edward J. Cabbell, eds. 1985. *Blacks in Appalachia.* Lexington: University Press of Kentucky.

Twigger-Ross, Clare, Marino Bonaiuto, and Glynis Breakwell. 2003. "Identity Theories and Environmental Psychology." In *Psychological Theories for Environmental Issues,* edited by Mirilia Bonnes, Terence Lee, and Marino Bonaiuto, 203–33. Aldershot, England: Ashgate.

U.S. Census Bureau. 2010. Table 1: 2009 Poverty and Median Income Estimates—Counties. Small Area Estimates Branch. Available at http://www.census.gov/did/www/saipe/data/statecounty/data/2009.html (accessed July 27, 2011).

U.S. Energy Information Administration. 2011. Figure ES 1. U.S. Electric Power Industry Net Generation, 2009. *Electric Power Annual 2009.* Available at http://www.eia.gov/cneaf/electricity/epa/epa_sum.html (accessed June 30, 2011).

U.S. Environmental Protection Agency. 2005. *Mountaintop Mining/Valley Fills in Appalachia—Final Programmatic Environmental Impact Statement.* Available at http://www.epa.gov (accessed September 28, 2007).

Vaske, Jerry J., and Katherine C. Kobrin. 2001. "Place Attachment and Environmentally Friendly Behavior." *Journal of Environmental Education* 32 (4): 16–21.

Walker, Elizabeth and Deborah Payne. 2012. "Health Impact Assessment of Coal and Clean Energy Options in Kentucky." Kentucky Environmental Foundation.

Walker, Robyn C. 2007. "An Alternative Construction of Identity: A Study of Place-Based Identity and Its Implications." *American Communication Journal* 9 (3).

Ward, Ken. 2011. "Alpha Natural Resources to Buy Massey $8.5B Deal: Must Be OK'd by Federal Regulators." *Charleston Gazette*, January 29. Available at http://wvgazette.com/News/201101291042?page=1 (accessed October 6, 2012).

Weiss, Chris. 1993. "Appalachian Women Fight Back: Organizational Approaches to Nontraditional Job Advocacy." In *Fighting Back in Appalachia: Traditions of Resistance and Change*, edited by Stephen L. Fisher, 151–64. Philadelphia: Temple University Press.

Wells, Leigh Ann. August 13, 2006. "Lawsuits Muddy Water Project." *Appalachian News-Express*. Available at http://www.newsexpresssky.com/articles/2006/07/30/top_story/01water.txt (accessed August 13, 2006).

Whisnant, David E. 1983. *All That Is Native and Fine: The Politics of Culture in an American Region*. Chapel Hill: University of North Carolina Press.

Wilson, Darlene. 1995. "The Felicitous Convergence of Mythmaking and Capital Accumulation: John Fox Jr. and the Formation of An(Other) Almost-White American Underclass." *Journal of Appalachian Studies* 1 (1): 5–44.

Yarrow, Michael. 1991. "The Gender-Specific Class Consciousness of Appalachian Coal Miners: Structure and Change." In *Bringing Class Back In: Contemporary and Historical Perspectives*, edited by S. G. McNall, R. F. Levine, and R. Fantasia, 285–310. Boulder, Colo.: Westview.

INDEX

Note: Page numbers in *italics* represent illustrations.

activism sustainment, 184–187. See also *specific women*
air pollution. *See* coal dust; coal trucks; "Sylvester Dustbusters"
Alliance for Appalachia, 85
Alpha Natural Resources, 43. *See also* Massey Energy
Americans Who Tell the Truth (Shetterly), 85
Angelique, Holly L., 8, 180
Annenberg Foundation, 119
anti-activist retaliation. *See* coal industry actions and reactions
Appalachia, 2–3, 194n1
Appalachian cultural silence, 89–90
"Appalachian identity," 177–179, 194n1
Appalachian Voices, 3, 42, 67
"Appalachia" protection, 175–178
Appalachia Rising, 93
Arch Coal, 54

Bailey and Glasser, 31, 33–34
Balancing the Scales, 88
Ballard, Sandra L., 4
Bell, Shannon Elizabeth: gendering of environmental justice activism, 8–9; interviews with activist men, 178; motivations for writing the book, 4; Photovoice project, 6; social capital losses, 173
Birch Hollow, 149, 159
black lung disease, 36, 92, 123–124, 128, 136, 160
Blair Mountain march, 150–151
Blankenship, Don, 37–38, 181
Blankenship, Donetta, *60*; activism as transformative force, 65, 68–69; activism sustainment, 185–186; Appalachian Voices, 67; community protection, 172; hope, 68–69; illness from water toxicity, 61–63, 65; Massey Energy lawsuit, 64; personal transformation through activism, 188; sense of community and friendships, 66–68; state legislator conversations, 64; United Nations address, 64; women's "protector identity," 65
Blanton, Teri, *84*; activism and gender, 91–92; activism sustainment, 186–187; anger, 85, 86–87; arrests for activism, 93; cancer, 91; challenges to activism, 89–90; civil disobedience, 92–93; community protection, 172; Environmental Protection Agency (EPA), 87–88; gendered intimidation, 181; heritage, 85; landslides, 86; life expectancy, 91; lobbying efforts, 85; maternal inspiration and example, 91; motivations for activism, 85, 89–91; "pro-

tector identity," 85, 86–87; relationship strains, 179; retaliation efforts suffered due to environmental justice activism, 86–87; solidarity, 93; speaking at conferences and panels, 85; toxic pollution of water, 87–88

"blighted" area, 23–24

Bonds, Judy, *148*; "Appalachia" protection, 176; award, 149; biographical information, 149; coal dust, 149; Coal River Mountain Watch, 150–151; contributions to Appalachian environmental protection, 157–159; courage, 154–156, 161–162, 166–167; cultural constraints against activism, 153–154; death from cancer, 149, 154; emotional suppression when dealing with power-holders, 132, 133; eulogies, 157–167; gendered intimidation, 181; homeplace loss, 151–153; illnesses and deaths, 149; ironweed, 1, 9; Lambert collaboration, 74; legacy, 157–167; memorial service, 156–167; mono-economy, 154; motivations for activism, 154–156; personal costs of activism, 154–156, 161; "protector identity," 171; relationship strains, 161, 179; school closures in local communities, 126; sludge dams, 152; threatened safety, 183; women's predominance in environmental justice activism, 154–155

Bonds, Julia. *See* Bonds, Judy

book methodology and overview, 4–6

Boone County: as "blighted," 17; Boone-Raleigh Community Group, 107, 134; coal dust, 28; Gunnoe, 165; hillbilly identity, 23, 24; ironweed, *10*; Lambert, 71; Public Service District, 77, 165; Sebok, 95; Stollings, 83

Boone-Raleigh Community Group, 107, 134

Boytek, Haskell, 138–139

Branham, Charlie, 136, 140, 143, 145

Branham, Donna, *135*; activism sustainment, 184, 185, 186; biographical information, 136; coal mining v. mountaintop removal, 136; fear and mistrust in local inhabitants, 142–144; gendered intimidation, 180–181; homeplace loss, 138–142; homeplace protection, 174; leadership, 144–145; personal transformation through activism, 187–188, 189; "protector identity," 138–142, 145–147; strengths of Appala-

chian women, 144–145; transformations through activism, 147

Braun, Yvonne A., 8–9

Brown, Phil, 8

Burrell, Benji, 67

Cable, Sherry, 192n9, 194n3

Canary Leadership Network, 85, 88

Canary Project, 88

Canterberry, Pauline, *27*; Bonds collaboration, 154; gendered intimidation, 181; homeplace protection, 174; injustice, 168; personal transformation through activism, 187. *See also* "Sylvester Dustbusters"

Caputo, Mike, 99–100, 102

Cazy, 52

Central Appalachia, 2–3, 191n1

Central Appalachian Women's Tribunal on Climate Justice, 120, 135

Challenge West Virginia, 126–128, 132

Citizens for Coal, 3

Citizens Preserving Marsh Fork and Clear Fork Community, 126–127

Civil Society Caucus, 64

Clear Fork, 118, 126,

Clear Fork High School, 126–127

climate change, 89

"Coal, Identity, and the Gendering of Environmental Justice Activism in Central Appalachia" (Bell and Braun), 8

Coal Association, 121. *See also* West Virginia Coal Association

coal dust, 28–43, 95–96, *111*, 149. *See also* illnesses and deaths

coal industry actions and reactions: anti-activist backlash encouragement, 18–20; arrogance and defiance, 113–114; environmental terrorism, 92–93; gendered intimidation, 92–93, 104–106, 181; insults to Appalachian population and culture, 34, 101–102, 152–153; retaliation against activists, 18–20, 86–87, 96–97, 103–104, 130–131, 150–151; unsafe working conditions, 78–79; violence against activists, 150–151, 155

Coal River Mountain Watch: Bonds, Judy, 125, 150–151, 163; Lambert, Maria, 74, 83; Linville, Joan V., 49, 58; Marsh Fork Elementary School, 119; media contact efforts, 3; Nease, Janice, 163; office, 163; Scarboro, Lorelei, 122, 125–134; Sebok, Patty, 98–99, 163; "Sylvester Dustbusters," 42; toxic pollution of water, 107

coal sludge. *See* sludge

coal slurry. *See* slurry

Coal Truck Protest of 1989, 95

coal trucks, *51*, *55*; coal dust, 95–96; legislative failures, 99–100; Linville, Joan, 52, 54; public complaint hotline, 104; Sebok, Patty, 95–104; traffic accidents and deaths, 97–98, 193n1

coal waste. *See* sludge; slurry

Collins, Patricia Hill, 7

Combs, Ollie "Widow," 9

Commission on Sustainable Development, 64

community destruction. *See* "protector identity"; *specific issues; specific women*

Concerned Citizens of Prenter Road, 74

connection to place. *See* "protector identity"; *specific women*

Consol Coal Company, 140

Cooper, Ruth, 95–96

Coordinating Committee for the Alliance for Appalachia, 85

CSX coal-hauling train, 51, *51*

Culley, Marci R., 8, 180

cultural constraints against activism, 89–90, 142–144, 153–154

Dayhoit, 85–86, 172

Delbarton Mining Company, 136–137. *See also* Massey Energy

DeLuca, Kevin M., 8

dental disease, 192–193n1. *See also* illnesses and deaths; Lambert, Maria; toxic pollution of water

Department of Environmental Protection. *See* West Virginia Department of Environmental Protection (DEP)

Department of Health and Human Resources (DHHR), 76

Department of Transportation (DOT), 102–103, 104

depopulation, 17, 37–39

destruction of communities. *See* "protector identity"; *specific issues; specific women*

destructive plant locations, 28–29

devaluation of people of Central Appalachia, 34, 152–153. *See also* "blighted" area; depopulation; "sacrifice zone"

disease. *See* illnesses and deaths

Dorothy, 163

Duncan, Jimmy, 93

Elk Run Coal Company, *27*, 32–33, 35. *See also* Massey Energy

environmental hazards overview, 1–2

environmental justice activism: coal industry retaliation efforts, 3–4; as gendered experience, 104–106; male involvement in Central Appalachia, 8–9; national figures, 4; as practical and political, 4; women, 2–3, 4, 6–7. *See also specific organizations; specific women*

environmental justice movement, 2–4, 8–9, 191n3. *See also specific organizations; specific women*

Environmental Protection Agency (EPA), 87–88

environmental terrorism analogy, 92–93

Epstein, Barbara, 8

eyesores for the community, *55*

FACES of Coal, 3

fear and mistrust in local inhabitants, 142–144. *See also* cultural constraints against activism

Feeney, Tricia, 63, 143, 185

Ferguson, Faith I. T., 8

Fisher, Steve, 177

Flood Advisory Task Force, 115

Flood of 2003, 12–14, 45, 115

floods: Blanton, Teri, 86, 172; described, 1, 4, 15, 25, 45, 193n2; Gunnoe, Maria, 12–14, 48–49, 154, 169, 176; Jarrell, Debbie, 115; Linville, Joan, 45, 48–49; property devaluation, 15, 48; Sebok, Patty, 99. *See also* landslides

Freeman, Jordan, 143

Friends of Coal, 3

gender dynamic in environmental justice activism, 129–130, 179–180. *See also* women's predominance in environmental justice activism

gendered intimidation, 92–93, 104–106, 180–182

Gibson, Larry: Coal Mountain River Watch; environmental justice activism, 119, 151; Kayford Mountain, 67, 163, 193–194n1; Keepers of the Mountain Foundation, 192 ch4 n1; as protector, 129

Glen Daniel, 118,

Global Earth Summit, 64

global warming, 89

Goals Coal Company, 112, 113–114

Goldman Environmental Prize, 12, 149

Griffith, Morgan, 93

Gunnoe, Maria, *11*; activism as transformative force, 22–23; Appalachian family-centered culture, 21–22; "Appalachia" protection, 176–177; awards and honors, 12; Bonds memorial service, 165–166; coal industry actions and reactions, 18–20, 24–25, 183–184; community backlash, 18–20; community destruction, 16–17; community protection, 173; depopulation history, 17; devaluation of people of Central Appalachia, 22–25; Flood of 2003, 12–14; gendered intimidation, 181; Goldman Environmental Prize, 12; habitat destruction, 15–16; heritage, 12; homeplace loss, 16–17; honors and awards, 12; landslides, 12–14; Linville collaboration, 48–49, 58; motherhood, 169–171; motivation for activism, 24–25; mountain destruction, 14–15; personal transformation through activism, 22–23, 188–189; private property destruction and devaluation, 15; psychological trauma, 13–14, 15; as public activist, 24–25; Scarboro collaboration, 129; strengths of Appalachian women, 21–22; threatened safety, 183, 184; Whitesville, 17

habitat destruction, 15–16, *108*, 122, 138, 149

Haltom, Sarah, 132

Haltom, Vernon, 125, 157–159

Hannah, Darryl, 4

Hansen, James, 4

Harlan County, 7, 85, 172

Heckler, Ken, 151

Hernshaw, 97, 98, 99, 150, 151, 193n1

hillbilly: Blanton, Teri, 85; Bonds memorial service, 157, 165; Gunno, Maria, 23, 24–25; negative stereotype, 177. *See also* "Appalachian identity"

homeplace protection: Bonds, Judy, 151–153; Branham, Donna, 136, 138–142, 174; Gunnoe, Maria, 16–17; Miller, Mary, 174; overview, 173–175; Scarboro, Lorelei, 123–125, 174–175. *See also* "protector identity"

Hudson, Patricia L., 4

Hunter, Jon Blair, 134

illnesses and deaths: Blankenship, Donetta, 61–63, 65; Blanton, Teri, 87–88, 90, 91; Bonds, Judy, 149; Branham, Donna, 136, 137, 174; Jarrell, Debbie, 117; life expectancy reduction, 91; lung disease, 36, 53, 123–124; Scarboro, Lorelei, 123–124; Sebok, Patty, 107; toxic water connection, 61–63, 65, 72, 74. *See also* black lung disease

"I Love Mountains Day," *84*

interview methodology, 5–6

intimidation. *See* coal industry actions and reactions

ironweed, 1, 9, *10*, 154–155, 189

Jarrell, Debbie, *112*; "Appalachia" protection, 176; commitment of women activists, 119; forced depopulation, 118; illness, 117; men and environmental justice activism, 113–119, 119; slurry impoundment flood of 2000, 113–114; slurry impoundment location dangers, 113–119

Kaplan, Temma, 7

Kayford Mountain educational site, 133, 186, 189, 192 ch4 n1, 193–194n1

Keepers of the Mountains Foundation, 192 ch4 n1, 193–194n1

Kennedy, Bobby Jr., 4

Kentuckians For The Commonwealth, 3, 85, 88

Kentucky Beyond Coal, 88

Kentucky Fair Tax Coalition, 88. *See also* Kentuckians For The Commonwealth

Kercheval, Hoppy, 100

Kingsolver, Ann, 178

Krauss, Celene, 8

Lambert, Maria, *70*; activism sustainment, 184–185, 187; Bonds collaboration, 74;

commitment to activism, 81, 83; family history and activism overview, 71; letter writing campaign, 74; personal transformation through activism, 188; photographs, *73, 75, 77, 82*; "protector identity," 79–80, 129, 171; relationship strains, 179; Sebok collaboration, 74, 107; sustaining activism and involvement, 80–83

landslides, 12–14, 45–48, *47*, 86, 122. *See also* floods; stream headwater manipulation and destruction

Laurel Creek Coal Company, 140

law enforcement failures, 95–96, 100–101, 102–103, 105, 106

Linville, Janie, *59*

Linville, Joan V., *44*; Appalachian women's strength and skills, 49; biographical information, 45; Coal River Mountain Watch, 49; coal trucks, 51–54; destruction of quality of life, 49–54; Flood of 2003, 45; Gunnoe collaboration, 48–49, 58; ironweed articulation, 9; landslides, 45, 45–48, *47*; photographs, *47, 51, 53, 55, 56, 59*; refusal to relocate, 54, 57–58; slurry impoundment location dangers, 50, 52; soil contamination, 47; stream headwater manipulation and destruction, 50, 52; toxic pollution of water, 45; West Virginia political corruption, 50

Listen Here: Women Writing in Appalachia (Ballard and Hudson, editors), 4

Logan County, 23, 24, 125, 127, 151

Logan County Commissioners, 151

logging, 17

lung disease, 53. *See also* black lung disease; illnesses and deaths

Maggard, Sally Ward, 182

Mahler, Andy, 166–167

Marfork Coal Company, 113, 149. *See also* Massey Energy

Marfork Hollow, 37, 149, 151–153, 164

Marsh Fork Elementary School, 113–119

Marsh Fork High School, 126–127

Martin, Julian, 129

Massey Energy: corporate behavior and attitudes, 37–38, 64; destructive plant location, 28–29; devaluation of people of Central Appalachia, 34; environmental impact overview, 160–161; failure to act on promises, 30–33; forced depopulation, 37–39; habitat destruction, 149; lawsuit against, 31, 33–34, 64, 65; Marsh Fork Elementary School donations, 119; mountaintop removal coal mining permits, 122; ongoing air pollution production, 34–39; school closures in local communities, 127–128; slurry impoundment location dangers, 36; token air pollution reduction efforts, 30, 33; toxic pollution of water, 131. *See also* coal industry actions and reactions

Mattea, Kathy, 67, 157

McAdam, Doug, 186

McDowell County, 23, 24

McGraw, Darrell, 105

men and environmental justice activism, 116

methodology, 4–6

Miller, Mary, *27*, 154, 174, 181. *See also* "Sylvester Dustbusters"

Mingo County, 24, 63–64, 106, 136–137, 150

mono-economy, 102, 125–126, 130, 131, 154

motherhood and environmental activism, 168–171. *See also* "protector identity"; women's predominance in environmental justice activism

mountain destruction, 14–15, *59*. *See also* floods; habitat destruction; landslides; recreation area destruction

Mountain Justice, 3, 143. *See also* Mountain Justice Summer

Mountain Justice Summer, 164

Mountainkeepers, 144

mountaintop removal coal mining, 89; acreage destroyed, 191n2; climate change relationship, 89; coal dust, 28–43, 95–96, 149; coal trucks, *51*, 52, 54, *55*, 97–98; community destruction, 16–17; corporate encouragement of anti-activist backlash, 18–20; depopulation, 17; destruction of quality of life, 49–54; destructive impact overview, 191n2; devaluation of property and economic hardship, 152–153; devastation of mountains, *59*; disrespect and devaluation of local population, 117; environmental impact, 3, 160–161, 191n2; eyesores, *55*; floods, 12–14, 86, 113–114, 193 n1; forced depopulation, 16–17, 37–

39, 117, 118, 122, 151–153; fragility of environmental movement against, 191–192n6;
global warming relationship, 89; habitat
destruction, 16–17, *108*, 122, 138, 149;
homeplace destruction, 15–16, 123–125,
136–142, 173–175; homeplace loss, 16–17,
151–153; landslides, 12–14, 45–48, *47*, 86,
122; lung disease, 53; mountain destruction, 14–15; PCBs, 87–88; political
corruption, 81, 102–103, 128; private
property destruction and devaluation, 15,
35–36; psychological trauma, 13–14, 15;
recreation area destruction, 16–17, *109–110*;
regulatory agency failures, 138–142;
school closures in local communities,
126–127; secret underground mines, 52;
slurry impoundment location dangers,
36, 50, 52, 113–119; soil contamination,
47; statistics, 191n2; stream headwater
manipulation and destruction, 15–16,
50, 52; surface mine location dangers,
114–115; as terrorism against Appalachian
population, 92–93; toxic pollution of
water, 14, 45, *60*, 87–88, 131, 136–137;
West Virginia political corruption, 50;
wildlife habitat and vegetation destruction, 138. *See also* coal industry actions
and reactions; illnesses and deaths; *specific
coal and energy corporation names; specific
environmental destruction types*
Mountain Watch. *See* Coal River Mountain
Watch
Mwara, Abe, 63

Naples, Nancy, 7
National Environmental Justice Advisory
Council (NEJAC), 85
National Mining Association, 92–93
Native Americans, 177
Nease, Janice, 125, 150, 154, 163

Office of Surface Mining, 29–30
Ohio Valley Environmental Coalition
(OVEC): Blankenship, Donetta, 62,
63–64; Gunnoe, Maria, 24, 48–49,
165–166; Lambert, Maria, 74, 83; Linville,
Joan V., 58; purpose, 3; "Sylvester Dust-
busters," 42–43
Old Detroit Mines, *53*

Packsville, 149, 160,
PCBs, 87–88. *See also* toxic pollution of
water
Peeples, Jennifer A., 8
Pennies of Promise Campaign, 118
personal transformation through activism,
187–189. See also *specific women*
Photovoice project, 6, 95, 192n8; photostories *9, 47, 51, 53, 55, 56, 59, 73, 75, 77, 82, 108–111*
Pittston Coal Strike (1989–1990), 7, 95
"place attachment," 175–178. *See also* "Appalachian identity"; homeplace protection
plants. *See* habitat destruction
Pocahontas Land Company, 47
political corruption, 50, 102–103, 128, 130,
131, 132, 151. *See also* regulatory agency
failures
pollution. *See* coal dust; slurry impoundment
location dangers; toxic pollution of water
Prenter, 70–83, 95, 106–107, *108–111*, 128
Prenter Water Fund, 83
Price, Bill, 163–164, 178
private property destruction and devaluation, 15, 35–36, 152–153
"protector identity": "Appalachia" protection, 175–178; Blankenship, Donetta, 65;
Blanton, Teri, 85, 86–87; Bonds, Judy,
129, 154–155, 171; Branham, Donna,
138–142, 145–147; Canterberry, Pauline,
36; community protection, 172–173;
gender dynamic in environmental justice
activism, 9; Gibson, Larry, 129; Gunnoe,
Maria, 21–22, 173, 176–177; homeplace
protection, 173–175; as impetus for
men's activism, 178; Jarrell, Debbie, 119;
Lambert, Maria, 79–80, 129, 171; Linville,
Joan, 49, 54, 57–58; Martin, Julian, 129;
Miller, Mary, 36; overview, 171–172;
Scarboro, Lorelei, 128–130; Sebok, Patty,
104–106, 168–169; Sylvester Dustbusters,
36. *See also* women's predominance in
environmental justice activism
Public Service Commission, 104

Rahall, Nick, 93, 128, 132–134
Raleigh County: Bonds, 149; Boone-Raleigh
Community Group, 107, 134; Scarboro,
123; schools, 117–119, 126; Sylvester Dustbusters, 40

Raleigh County School Board, 119
Raney, Bill, 100, 105
Rawl, 61, 63–64, 71, 106, 144, 188
recreation area destruction, 109–110
regional identity, 177–179, 194n1
regulatory agency failures, 138–142, 152, 180, 187–188. *See also* political corruption
renewable energy alternatives, 125–126
retaliation against activists. *See* coal industry actions and reactions; cultural constraints against activism; *specific women*
Rock Creek, 17, 113, 119, 149, 153
Rockefeller, Jay, 133, 162
Rogers, Hal, 93
Roland Land Company, 118, 129

"sacrifice zone," 1, 54, 56–58, 177. *See also* "blighted" area
Sammons, B. I., 63
Scarboro, Lorelei, *120*; activism sustainment, 184; "Appalachia" protection, 175–176; biographical information, 121, 123–124; Bonds collaboration, 124, 128, 129, 132; Boone-Raleigh Community Group, 134; coal mining v. mountaintop removal, 121–122; connection to place, 123–125; Gunnoe collaboration, 129; homeplace protection, 174–175; intimidation, 131; ironweed, 1; Lambert collaboration, 129; mono-economy, 130, 131; motherhood, 169; motivations for activism, 127–128; renewable energy job creation, 125–126, 134; school closures in local communities, 126–127; Sebok collaboration, 107; suppressing emotion for power-holders, 132–134; wind farm alternative, 126; women's predominance in environmental justice activism, 129–130
School Building Authority, 119
school closures, 126, 126–127
Sebok, Butch, 95, 107
Sebok, Patty, *94*; Bonds collaboration, 99, 100–101, 102, 105, 120; Coal River Mountain Watch, 163; Coal Truck Protest of 1989, 95; courage, 97–98, 103–104; gendered intimidation, 180, 181; illnesses and deaths, 128; Lambert collaboration, 74, 107; lessons of activism, 107; lobbying efforts, 99–100, 104; media contact

efforts, 105; motherhood, 168–169; photographs, *108–111*; Scarboro collaboration, 107; threatened safety, 183–184; toxic pollution of water, 106–107; women and activism, 104–106
secret underground mines, 52
Shetterly, Robert, 85
Sierra Club, 58, 163–164
Simonton, Scott C., 114–115, 193n3
sludge, 61–62, 71, *73*, 76–77, 83, 106–107, 113. *See also* slurry impoundment locations; slurry injection sites
sludge dams. *See* slurry impoundment locations; slurry injection sites
Sludge Safety Project, 83. *See also* Coal River Mountain Watch
slurry, 61–62, 71, *73*, 76–77, 83, 106–107, 113. *See also* slurry impoundment locations; slurry injection sites
slurry impoundment locations: Blankenship, Donetta, 66; Brushy Fork impoundment, 113, 152; Jarrell, Debbie, 113–119; Lambert, Maria, 76, 78, 83; Linville, Joan, 50, 52; Marsh Fork Elementary School, 113–119; Massey Energy, 36; school closures in local communities, 113–119; toxic pollution of water, 61–63
slurry injection sites, 60–69, 83, 106–107. *See also* slurry impoundment locations; toxic pollution of water
Snodgrass, Lisa Henderson, 159–160
social capital losses, 17, 24, 37–39, 54, 57–58, 151–152, 173
soil contamination, 47, 52, 60–69, 83, 106–107
Southwings, 14
Sprouse, Randy, 150
Stollings, Ron, 83
stream headwater manipulation and destruction, 15–16, 50, 52. *See also* floods; habitat destruction; landslides; recreation area destruction
strip mining. *See* mountaintop removal coal mining
Supreme Court of the United States, 127
Surface Mining and Reclamation Act laws, 114
sustaining activism and involvement. *See* activism sustainment
Sylvester, 187. *See also* Sylvester Dustbusters

"Sylvester Dustbusters," *27*; Appalachian Voices, 42; coal dust impact, 28–29; courage, 29–30; determination of women, 1; evidence collection efforts, 30–33; humor, 37; lawsuit against Massey Energy, 31, 33–34; ongoing commitment and methods, 40–42; ongoing monitoring of Massey Energy coal dust production and disposal, 30–33, 34–39; optimism, 43; as protectors of their homes, 36, 174; responsible coal mining, 36; support, 42–43; West Virginia Department of Environmental Protection (DEP), 29–30

Tar Sands Action, 93
Taylor, Betsy, 5, 191–192n6
terrorism analogy, 92–93
threatened safety, 182–184. *See also* coal industry actions and reactions; cultural constraints against activism
toxic pollution of water, *60*; Blankenship, Donetta, 61–69; Blanton, Teri, 87–88; Bonds, Judy, 149, 152; Branham, Donna, 136–137; Gunnoe, Maria, 14; Lambert, Maria, 71–83; Lambert photographs, *73, 75, 77, 82*; Linville, Joan, 45; Snodgrass, Lisa Henderson, 161; overview, 61. *See also* illnesses and deaths
traffic accidents and deaths, 97–98, 193n1. *See also* coal trucks
trains, 51, *51*
transformation. *See* personal transformation through activism
trucks. *See* coal trucks

underground mine fires, *53*
Underwood, Cecil H., 103
United Mine Workers of America (UMWA), 7, 151, 180

United Nations' Commission on Sustainable Development, 64

Van, 45, 46, 50, *55*
vegetation. *See* habitat destruction

water pollution. *See* toxic pollution of water
Webb, Bo, 116–117, 119, 155, 183
Weikle, Kathy, 72, 74. *See* Coal River Mountain Watch
West Virginia Coal Association, 100–101. *See also* Coal Association
West Virginia Department of Environmental Protection (DEP): Bonds, Judy, 152; Branham, Donna, 137–142; Lambert, Maria, 74, 76, 83; Massey Energy, 33; Scarboro, Lorelei, 132–134; slurry impoundment location dangers, 114–115; "Sylvester Dustbusters," 28, 29–30, 35. *See also* regulatory agency failures
West Virginia Senate Bill 583, 104
Whitesville, 17, 28, 34, 99, 161, 173
wildlife. *See* habitat destruction
Wiley, Ed, 113, 118–119, 178
wind farm alternative, 134
women's predominance in environmental justice activism: activism sustainment, 184–187; Bonds, Judy, 154–155; challenges, 179–184; gendered intimidation, 179; leadership, 6–7; motherhood element, 7–8, 168–171; motherhood politicization, 7–8; overviews, 2–3, 6–7; personal transformation through activism, 187–189; relationship strains, 179–180; Scarboro, Lorelei, 129–130. *See also* "protector identity"; *specific women*

"Y&O," *53*

SHANNON ELIZABETH BELL is an assistant professor
of sociology at the University of Kentucky.

The University of Illinois Press
is a founding member of the
Association of American University Presses.

University of Illinois Press
1325 South Oak Street
Champaign, IL 61820-6903
www.press.uillinois.edu